David W...
Plays...

The Gingerbread Man, The See-Saw Tree, The Ideal Gnome Expedition, Mother Goose's Golden Christmas

The Gingerbread Man: '. . . is told not only with the lightest and most stylish of touches, but is frequently very funny indeed.' *Observer*
'David Wood's strength has always been that he does not talk down to children: he gets down on his knees and looks at the world with their eyes instead.' *Times Educational Supplement.*

The See-Saw Tree: 'David Wood – as the most successful children's playwright of this century – is trying through entertainment to teach the younger generation to preserve the world they live in and opt for conservation rather than commercial gain.' *The Stage*

The Ideal Gnome Expedition: 'The young ones' cries of delight fill the theatre; they all seem to get the message, leaving us with a warm glow.' *The Stage*

Mother Goose's Golden Christmas: 'The perfect family Christmas entertainment with all the traditions of panto. A really strong storyline which at the same time includes a host of fairytale characters . . . some marvellously inventive twists.' *Thurrock Gazette*

David Wood began writing as a student at Oxford University in the sixties. He wrote his first play for children in 1967 and has since written about forty more. They are performed all over the world and include *The Gingerbread Man* (nine London seasons), *The Owl and the Pussycat Went to See . . .* (six London seasons, co-written with Sheila Ruskin), *The Selfish Shellfish*, *The See-Saw Tree*, *Save the Human* (from the story he wrote with cartoonist Tony Husband), *The Ideal Gnome Expedition* and *The Plotters of Cabbage Patch Corner*. His stage adaptations of well-known books include Dick King-Smith's *Babe, the Sheep Pig*, Roald Dahl's *The BFG* and *The Witches*, both of which played long tours and two West End seasons, HRH The Prince of Wales' *The Old Man of Lochnagar*, Michael Foreman's *Dinosaurs and all that Rubbish*, Helen Nicoll and Jan Pieńkowski's *Meg and Mog Show* (five London seasons for Unicorn Theatre). He was dubbed 'the national children's dramatist' by Irving Wardle in *The Times*. He has directed many of his plays for his own company, Whirligig Theatre (founded with John Gould in 1979), which tours to major theatres nationwide including Sadler's Wells in London. Film screenplays include *Swallows and Amazons* and *Back Home*, which won a gold award at the New York Film and TV Festival in 1991. Writing for television includes the series *Chips' Comic*, *Chish 'n' Fips* and *The Gingerbread Man*; and *Tide Race*, his filmed drama for Central Television and the European Broadcasting Union, has won several international awards. He also writes children's books and has followed a parallel career as an actor, being remembered as Johnny in L............ .... to Jacqueline Stanbury; they .... Rebecca.

The Operats of Rodent Garden (Illustrated by Geoffrey Beitz)*
The Discorats (Illustrated by Geoffrey Beitz)*
The Gingerbread Man (Illustrated by Sally Ann Lambert)
Playstage (Two Robin Hood plays, co-written with Dave and Toni Arthur, in an anthology)*
Chish 'n' Fips (Illustrated by Don Seed)
Playtheatres: Jack and the Beanstalk, The Nativity (created with and illustrated by Richard Fowler)
Sidney the Monster (Illustrated by Clive Scruton)
Happy Birthday Mouse! (Created with and illustrated by Richard Fowler)
Save the Human (Created with and illustrated by Tony Husband)
Baby Bear's Buggy Ride (Created with and illustrated by Richard Fowler)
The BFG: Plays for Children (Adapted from the book by Roald Dahl)
Meg and Mog: Four Plays for Children (Adapted from the books by Helen Nicoll and Jan Pieńkowski)
Pop-Up Theatre: Cinderella (Created with and illustrated by Richard Fowler)
Bedtime Story (Created with and illustrated by Richard Fowler)
The Magic Show (Created with and illustrated by Richard Fowler)
The Christmas Story (A nativity play)
Mole's Summer Story (Created with and illustrated by Richard Fowler)
Mole's Winter Story (Created with and illustrated by Richard Fowler)
Silly Spider (Created with and illustrated by Richard Fowler)
Theatre for Children: Guide to Writing, Adapting, Directing and Acting (With Janet Grant)
Rock Nativity (A musical play)
Dinosaurs and all that Rubbish (play text)
The Old Man of Lochnagar (play text)
The See-Saw Tree (play text)
Kingfisher Book of Comic Verse (anthology, Ed. Roger McGough)
The Much Better Story Book (anthology)

*published by Methuen

DAVID WOOD

Plays: 1

The Gingerbread Man
The See-Saw Tree
The Ideal Gnome Expedition
Mother Goose's Golden Christmas

introduced by the author

Methuen Drama

Published by Methuen in 1999

1 3 5 7 9 10 8 6 4 2

First published in the United Kingdom in 1999 by
Methuen Publishing Limited
20 Vauxhall Bridge Road, London SW1V 2SA

Random House Australia (Pty) Limited
20 Alfred Street, Milsons Point, Sydney, New South Wales 2061, Australia
Random House New Zealand Limited
18 Poland Road, Glenfield, Auckland 10, New Zealand
Random House South Africa (Pty) Limited
Endulini, 5A Jubilee Road, Parktown 2193, South Africa

The Gingerbread Man was first published by Samuel French in 1997
Copyright © 1997 by David Wood
The See-Saw Tree was first published by Amber Lane Press in 1987
Copyright © 1987 by David Wood
The Ideal Gnome Expedition was first published by Samuel French in 1982
Copyright © 1982 by David Wood
Mother Goose's Golden Christmas was first published by Samuel French in 1978
Copyright © 1978 by David Wood

Collection and Introduction Copyright © 1999 by David Wood

Methuen Publishing Limited Reg. No. 3543167

A CIP catalogue record for this book is available from the British Library

ISBN 0 413 73700 4

Typeset by SX Composing DTP, Rayleigh, Essex
Printed and bound in Great Britain by
Cox & Wyman Ltd, Reading, Berkshire

Caution

Contents

David Wood
A Chronology

Children's plays and musicals

1967   *The Tinderbox*, book, music and lyrics. Based on the story by Hans Andersen. Swan Theatre, Worcester. Unpublished.

1968   *The Owl and the Pussycat Went to See* . . . , co-written with Sheila Ruskin, based on the verses and stories of Edward Lear. Swan Theatre, Worcester, subsequently WSG Productions Ltd produced at Jeannetta Cochrane Theatre, London (1969) and many more Christmas seasons.*

1969   *Larry the Lamb in Toytown*, co-written with Sheila Ruskin, adapted from the stories of SG Hulme-Beaman. Swan Theatre, Worcester, subsequently WSG Productions Ltd, produced at the Shaw Theatre London, 1973.*

1970   *The Plotters of Cabbage Patch Corner*, book, music and lyrics. Swan Theatre, Worcester, subsequently Knightsbridge Theatrical Productions Ltd/WSG Productions Ltd at the Shaw Theatre, 1971 and 1972, and Whirligig Theatre Tour including Sadler's Wells Theatre, London, 1979.

1971   *Flibberty and the Penguin*, book, music and lyrics. Swan Theatre, Worcester, subsequently Whirligig pilot tour, 1978.*

1972   *Tickle*, one-act, book, music and lyrics. The Dance Drama Theatre tour, subsequently Wakefield Tricycle Company production at Arts Theatre, London, 1977.
          The Papertown Paperchase, book, music and lyrics. Swan Theatre, Worcester, subsequently Whirligig Theatre tour, including Sadler's Wells, 1984.*

1973   *Hijack over Hygenia*, book, music and lyrics. Swan Theatre, Worcester.

1975   *Old Mother Hubbard*, book, music and lyrics. Queen's Theatre, Hornchurch.

1976   *The Gingerbread Man*, book, music and lyrics.

Towngate Theatre, Basildon, subsequently
Cameron Mackintosh/David Wood production,
The Old Vic (1977 and 1978) and many other
London seasons.*
Old Father Time, book, music and lyrics. Queen's
Theatre, Hornchurch.

1977   *Nutcracker Sweet*, book, music and lyrics. Redgrave
Theatre, Farnham, subsequently Whirligig Theatre
tour including Sadler's Wells, 1980.*
Mother Goose's Golden Christmas, book, music and
lyrics. Queen's Theatre, Hornchurch.

1978   *Babes in the Magic Wood*, book, music and lyrics.
Queen's Theatre, Hornchurch.

1979   *There Was an Old Woman . . .* , book, music and
lyrics. Haymarket Theatre, Leicester.
Cinderella, book, music and lyrics. Queen's Theatre,
Hornchurch.

1980   *The Ideal Gnome Expedition*, (originally called *Chish 'n'
Fips*), book, music and lyrics. Liverpool Playhouse,
subsequently Whirligig tour, including Sadler's
Wells, 1981.*
Aladdin, book, music and lyrics. Queen's Theatre,
Hornchurch.

1981   *Robin Hood* (co-written with Dave and Toni Arthur).
Nottingham Playhouse, subsequently Young Vic,
London, 1982.
Meg and Mog Show (from books by Helen Nicoll and
Jan Pieńkowski), book, music and lyrics. Unicorn
Theatre, London.*
Dick Whittington and Wondercat, book, music and
lyrics. Queen's Theatre, Hornchurch.

1982   *Jack and the Giant*, book, music and lyrics. Queen's
Theatre, Hornchurch.

1983   *The Selfish Shellfish*, book, music and lyrics. Redgrave
Theatre, Farnham, subsequently Whirligig Theatre
tour, including Sadler's Wells, 1983.*

1984   *Jack the Lad* (co-written with Dave and Toni
Arthur). Library Theatre, Manchester.

1986   *The See-Saw Tree*, book, music and lyrics. Redgrave

Theatre, Farnham, subsequently Whirligig Theatre
tour including Sadler's Wells, 1987.*
The Old Man of Lochnagar (based on the book by
HRH The Prince of Wales), book, music and lyrics.
Whirligig Theatre tour including Sadler's Wells and
Christmas season at the Albery Theatre, London.*
Dinosaurs and all that Rubbish (adapted from the book
by Michael Foreman), music by Peter Pontzen.
Howells School, Denbigh, subsequently Whirligig
Theatre production, Sadler's Wells and tour, 1988.*

1988   *The Pied Piper* (co-written with Dave and Toni
Arthur, adapted from Robert Browning's poem).
Orchard Theatre, Barnstable and tour.

1990   *Save the Human* (based on a story by Tony Husband
and David Wood). Cambridge Theatre Company
at the Arts Theatre, Cambridge and on tour.
Subsequently Whirligig Theatre tour including
Sadler's Wells, 1990.*

1991   *The BFG* (based on the book by Roald Dahl).
Clarion Productions, tours and West End seasons at
the Aldwych and Albery Theatres.*

1992   *The Witches* (based on the book by Roald Dahl).
Clarion Productions, tours and West End seasons at
the Duke of York's and Vaudeville Theatres.*

1993   *Rupert and the Green Dragon* (based on the Rupert
stories and characters by Mary Tourtel and Alfred
Bestall), book, music and lyrics. Layston
Productions tour.*
Noddy (based on the stories by Enid Blyton), book,
music and lyrics. Clarion Productions tour,
including Lyric Theatre, Hammersmith.*

1995   *More Adventures of Noddy* (based on the stories of Enid
Blyton), book, music and lyrics. Clarion Promotions
tour.*

1997   *Babe, the Sheep Pig* (based on the book by Dick King-
Smith). Whirligig Theatre tour and Manchester
Library Theatre Christmas season.*

1998   *The Forest Child*, libretto for children's opera (based
on the book by Richard Edwards), music by Derek

Clark, commissioned by Welsh National Opera.

1999   *The Twits* (based on the book by Roald Dahl).
Belgrade Theatre, Coventry.

*also directed the production.
(All the above plays, except *Forest Child*, are published as
acting editions by Samuel French Ltd.)

Other Writing (Theatre, Film and TV)

1964   Songs for *Hang Down Your Head and Die*. Oxford
University Experimental Theatre Club, Oxford
Playhouse and Comedy Theatre, London.

1965   Lyrics for *The Oxford Line*, revue (music by John
Gould). Oxford Theatre Group, Edinburgh Festival
and tour.
Lyrics for *And Was Jerusalem* (music by John Gould,
book by Mick Sadler). Oxford University
Experimental Theatre Club, subsequently as *A
Present from the Corporation*, Swan Theatre, Worcester
and (showcase) Fortune Theatre, London.

1967   Music and lyrics for *A Life in Bedrooms* (book by
David Wright). Traverse Theatre, Edinburgh,
subsequently as *The Stiffkey Scandals of 1932*, on
BBC2 TV and at the Queen's Theatre, London,
1969. Subsequently revived as *The Prostitutes' Padre*,
Norwich Playhouse, 1997.

1968   Lyrics for *Three to One On*, revue (music by John
Gould). Tour, Edinburgh Festival and BBC2 TV.

1969   Lyrics for *Postscripts*, revue (music by John Gould).
King's Head, London.
Songs for *Have You Seen Manchester?* 69 Theatre
Company, Manchester.

1970   Lyrics for *Dead Centre of the Midlands*, revue (music by
John Gould). Swan Theatre, Worcester.
Lyrics for *Cinderella* (book by Sid Colin, music by
John Gould). Citizens Theatre, Glasgow.

1971   Lyrics for *Down Upper Street*, revue (music by John
Gould). King's Head, London.

1972   Lyrics for *Turn Your Own Sod*, revue (music by John

Gould). Swan Theatre, Worcester.

1973   Lyrics for *Just the Ticket*, revue (music by John
Gould). Thorndike Theatre, Leatherhead.

1974   *Maudie* (co-written with Iwan Williams), a musical
diary of Maudie Littlehampton. Thorndike
Theatre, Leatherhead.
Rock Nativity, book and lyrics (music by Tony Hatch
and Jackie Trent). Playhouse, Newcastle.
Subsequently on tour, 1975. TV productions STV
and RTE.
Swallows and Amazons (film screenplay based on the
book by Arthur Ransome). Anglo-EMI.

1975   Lyrics and sketches for *Chi-Chestnuts*, revue.
Assembly Rooms, Chichester.
Lyrics for *Think of a Number*, revue (music by John
Gould). Key Theatre, Peterborough.

1977   Lyrics for *Bars of Gould*, revue (music by John
Gould). Northcott Theatre, Exeter and tour.
Emu's Christmas Adventure LWT.

1978   *Writer's Workshop*. Thames Schools' TV.
The Luck of the Bodkins (based on the book by PG
Wodehouse, co-written with John Gould). Theatre
Royal, Windsor.

1984   *Abbacadabra*, book, with lyrics by Don Black and
music by Abba. Lyric Theatre, Hammersmith.
Chips' Comic (Early Learning TV series).
Verronmead/Channel 4.
Chish 'n' Fips (children's TV series based on play by
David Wood). Holmes Associates/Central.

1986   *Seeing and Doing* Thames Schools' TV series.
The Gingerbread Man. Channel 4 production of David
Wood play.

1987   *The Old Man of Lochnagar* (adaptation for TV from
David Wood's play based on the book by HRH
The Prince of Wales). Channel 4.

1989   *Back Home* (film screenplay based on the book by
Michelle Magorian). Verronmead/TVS/Disney
Channel. Daytime Emmy Nomination for best
screenplay.

1990   *Tide Race*. TV film for Central TV/European
       Broadcasting Union.
1992   *Watch*. Schools' TV series. Spelthorne/BBC.
       The Gingerbread Man (animated children's TV series).
       FilmFair/Central.

Acting (stage and film)

1963–6 Oxford University, including *Hang Down Your Head
       and Die* (Oxford Playhouse and Comedy Theatre,
       London) – nomination for Best New Actor (Variety
       Critics). The Fool in *King Lear*, Algernon in *The
       Importance of Being Earnest*, Wagner in Richard
       Burton/Elizabeth Taylor *Doctor Faustus*, all at
       Oxford Playhouse; Puck in *A Midsummer Night's
       Dream* (Stratford Open Air); *A Spring Song*,
       Edinburgh Festival and Mermaid Theatre, London;
       The Oxford Line, Edinburgh Festival; *Four Degrees
       Over*, Edinburgh Festival, tour and Fortune Theatre,
       London.
1967–9 Repertory at Worcester, Watford, Edinburgh,
       Windsor and Salisbury. Directing at Worcester.
1968   Johnny in *If . . .*, film (Memorial Enterprises)
       directed by Lindsay Anderson.
1969   *Three to One On*, revue, tour and Edinburgh Festival.
1970   Roger in *After Haggerty* (David Mercer), RSC at the
       Aldwych and Criterion Theatres, London.
       The Son in *Voyage Round My Father* (John Mortimer),
       Greenwich Theatre, London. Nomination for Best
       New Actor (*Plays and Players*). Subsequently,
       opposite Sir Michael Redgrave, Royal Alexandra
       Theatre, Toronto, 1972.
1971   James in *Me Times Me Times Me* (Alan Ayckbourn),
       tour.
1972   *Husbands and Lovers* (Molnár), Soho Poly, London.
       Frank in *Mrs Warren's Profession* (Shaw), Thorndike
       Theatre, Leatherhead.
1973   *Just the Ticket*, revue, Thorndike Theatre,
       Leatherhead.
       The Provok'd Wife (Vanburgh), Greenwich Theatre,

London.

1974 *Pig of the Month* (Jonathan Lynn), Prince of Wales,
Wimbledon.

1975 *Think of a Number*, revue, Key Theatre,
Peterborough.
Bingo Little in *Jeeves* (Wodehouse, Ayckbourn,
Lloyd Webber), Her Majesty's Theatre, London.

1976 Thompson in *Aces High*, film (Benjamin Fisz
Productions, director Jack Gold).
The Flight of the Bumble B. (William Fairchild),
Haymarket, Leicester.

1980 Bowers in *Terra Nova* (Ted Tally), Chichester
Festival Theatre.
Sweet William film (Don Boyd Productions, director
Claude Whatham).
North Sea Hijack, film Cinema Seven Productions,
director Andrew V. McClaglen.

1982 and continuing
The David Wood Magic and Music Show in UK
theatres, featuring Peter Pontzen at the piano.
David Wood is an Associate Member of the Inner
Magic Circle (with Silver Star).

Acting (TV)

Many TV appearances since 1968 include: Wednesday Play
Mad Jack, (dir. Jack Gold), BBC; classic serials *Fathers and
Sons*, *Cheri*, BBC; *Disraeli*, ATV; children's programmes
Playaway, *Jackanory*, *Tricky Business*, BBC; he also co-starred
opposite Shelley Winters in *The Vamp*, LWT.

Introduction

I am delighted that Methuen Drama is publishing collected
editions of my plays. It reflects a growing general awareness
of the importance of theatre for children. Those of us who
specialize in this exciting, if unglamorous, genre constantly
struggle against low budgets, low funding, low media
coverage and low status; yet ironically, perhaps as a result of
these constraints, our work is regularly praised for its
imagination and invention, its vitality and theatricality and
its ability to encourage our young audiences towards a long-
term appreciation of theatre. Not that we do it simply as an
investment for the future; our aim is to excite and inspire
children *today*. But the theatre establishment is short-sighted
if it ignores the importance of our special contribution to the
ongoing health of the nation's theatre in general. And the
future certainly looks more positive than when I began
creating plays for children more than three decades ago. In
schools, even though drama is largely ignored by the
National Curriculum, there is now much more awareness of
its value both as something to witness and as something to
participate in. Teachers appreciate its power to trigger the
imagination, to improve communications skills, to
encourage tolerance of other points of view and, above all,
for most children, to provide enjoyment.

Theatre for children can now boast a wide range of
product ranging from pure fantasy entertainment to issue-
based educational drama. Hopefully, if we practitioners
bang our drums hard enough, our work will develop and
grow, not only in specialist companies, but in the national
and regional companies too. More and more writers,
directors, designers and actors, in spite of a lack of training
opportunities, are showing a desire to focus on work for
young audiences. It is up to the funding bodies and theatre
managements to embrace their skills and to offer them a
theatrical landscape in which children's theatre becomes a
priority rather than an optional extra. Maybe one day,
nationwide, children's theatre buildings will present round-

the-year productions. Maybe one day we will have a
National Children's Theatre.

The Gingerbread Man

I shall always remember Ronnie Stevens, the original and
archetypal Herr von Cuckoo, saying in the dressing room
after the first performance that the enthusiastic audience
reaction suggested that *The Gingerbread Man* looked set to
have a successful future. But neither of us could have
imagined that it would end up becoming my most-
performed play, not only in Great Britain but all over the
world. The simple story, set on a giant-scale Welsh dresser,
seemed, and still seems to me, so parochial in its
Englishness, that I could never have believed it would
become so popular in, for example, Germany or even
Japan, where it toured on and off for a decade. I was lucky
enough to see the Japanese production, and, knowing I was
in a country where gingerbread men and Welsh dressers
were unheard of, had to pinch myself to confirm I wasn't
dreaming. It was also somewhat alarming when, before
curtain up, three children carrying banners with Japanese
writing on, accompanied by a rather stern lady, walked on
stage. The Japanese director explained, through an
interpreter, that the audience were being taught the three
rules of theatre. They had to promise not to wander round
during the performance, not to eat anything, and finally, not
to talk during the show. The first two rules seemed quite
sensible, but the third worried me, because *The Gingerbread
Man* depends upon the audience's vocal participation to
further the plot; without it, the play would grind to an early
conclusion. But I needn't have worried. Just like their British
counterparts, the Japanese children immediately entered
into the spirit of the performance and were yelling out
advice and helping catch Sleek the Mouse as though to the
manner born. It was heart-warmingly reassuring to witness
such positive confirmation of my long-held belief that
children everywhere share a basic willingness to suspend

disbelief, to enjoy (unlike most adults) openly displaying their emotional involvement with the characters, and to react vehemently to any infringement against natural justice.

The play was commissioned by Malcolm Jones, then manager of the Towngate Theatre, Basildon. The theatre had a small, nicely-raked auditorium, ideal for children, but the stage had very little space in the wings and no flying facilities. My brief was to write a play for six actors on one basic set. I started thinking of ideas, but nothing immediately sprang to mind, let alone a title. After a few weeks, Malcolm rang to say that he wanted to organize a float in the local carnival to publicize the show. He needed a title. I offered to ring him back within a week, but he was adamant that he needed an instant answer to relay to his planning committee the next day. In desperation I closed my eyes, frantically searching for inspiration, then blurted out 'The Gingerbread Man'. Where on earth the idea came from I'll never know, but Malcolm seemed satisfied and hung up. Now I was lumbered with finding a play to match a title. I knew I didn't want to recreate the nursery tale about the Gingerbread Man who eventually gets eaten by the fox, so started to think of a more contemporary situation, in which a freshly-baked gingerbread man might affect the day-to-day lives of other characters living in the kitchen where he had been baked. A Welsh dresser, complete with giant plates, a teapot, a radio and other domestic clutter, eventually suggested itself as the ideal location. To this basic set nothing needed be added or taken away, which satisfied the practical problems of the Basildon stage. Salt and Pepper were fairly obvious characters. The idea of a teabag was appealing, particularly if she was a crotchety, lonely 'old bag', who could pose a threat to the new arrival, who, it gradually dawned on me, should be the equivalent of a child, forced to learn the well-established lores of dresser life. I added to the character list a hungry mouse, who lived behind the dresser, an outsider, an intruder, who could provide another kind of threat – he wanted to eat our hero. Another idea was to have a cuckoo clock next to the dresser, in which an elderly cuckoo could live. In fact he became the mainspring of the plot by losing his voice; unable to perform his job, he is in danger of being thrown into the dreaded dustbin by the Big Ones, the human beings in whose kitchen the play is set. The Big Ones, unseen but often heard, had first appeared in my earlier play, *The Plotters of Cabbage Patch Corner*. Many years later, incidentally, while researching a play about Rupert Bear, I discoverered a story in which a cuckoo-clock cuckoo also lost his voice. I can't help wondering whether I had read the story as a child and retained it in my subconscious.

The play was designed by my regular team-member, Susie Caulcutt, who cleverly incorporated the cuckoo-clock into the dresser, allowing the dresser to fill the stage. This idea produced a dresser unlike any dresser I have ever seen in my life, yet it worked superbly and became the prototype of dozens of subsequent productions. Nobody has ever questioned its authenticity!

We managed to secure an excellent cast and a talented director – Jonathan Lynn, who went on to write *Yes, Minister* and direct Hollywood movies. Jonathan made sure that the story was played 'for real', and the production worked a treat. Cameron Mackintosh came to see it and immediately offered to co-produce it with me in London the following year, at the Old Vic, no less. This led to many subsequent Christmas seasons in London, four national tours, a television production and an animated television series.

Over the years I have directed *The Gingerbread Man* many times, often making small, and sometimes not so small, changes, most of which are incorporated in this edition. For instance, the first Old Bag scene included a section where she petulantly proved that nobody liked her by directly challenging the audience; she asked them how many didn't like tea, how many preferred rubbishy drinks like orange squash, coca cola or even coffee! For many years she always managed to get the required answer – very few children actually liked tea. Today's children, however, seem to actually enjoy drinking tea! Furthermore, the scene regularly descended into rabble rousing and needed re-working. Also, the yodelling songsheet towards the end of Act Two, originally inserted as an enjoyable Christmas pantomime-style bit of fun, seemed unnecessary at other times of the year. It has been included in this edition as an optional extra. The song 'The Dresser Hop', has also been included, mainly because I rather like it. But several years ago, reluctantly, though wisely, I think, I decided to cut it. It doesn't progress the plot and holds up the introduction of the Gingerbread Man, the character the audience are eagerly waiting to meet.

The Ideal Gnome Expedition

When William Gaunt, then Director of the Liverpool Playhouse, asked me to write a play, I came up with the title *Chish'n'Fips*, which he liked and immediately advertised in his seasonal brochure. The play I eventually delivered bore no relation whatsoever to the title, but luckily nobody seemed to mind. Searching for an idea for the play, I saw in the window of a second-hand book shop an intriguing Scandinavian book all about gnomes. It proved to be an imaginative spoof anthropological treatise, describing in detail the daily life and living conditions of a gnome community. This led me to think about the quaint British tradition of displaying garden gnomes on the lawn or by the pond. Their lives, I felt, must be rather boring. What if they were given the opportunity to go off on adventures beyond the narrow confines of their garden existence? I imagined Mr Wheeler, with his wheelbarrow, and Mr Fisher, with his fishing rod, climbing over the garden wall, once their owners (the Big Ones again) had gone on holiday.

But whom might they meet and what dangers might they face? Clearly there were opportunities for large-scale props as the gnomes travelled through a human landscape. Furthermore the idea gave me the possibility of combining a fantasy situation with the depiction of a real contemporary cityscape, familiar to today's children. A street lamp, an adventure playground, roadworks, a traffic island, would seem like a concrete jungle to the unworldly gnomes, who could be guided through its potential dangers by the audience. This offered an opportunity to introduce the basic principles of road safety, not in a didactic, 'listen boys and girls, this is how you must cross roads' way, rather asking the experienced children to instruct the naïve gnomes. This felt much less patronising. As the idea grew, characters emerged like a streetwise alley cat and a manic pneumatic machine used to flatten newly-laid tar. I gave the cat the name Chips, in a modest attempt to link at least one character with the title of the play. Searching for a name for the pneumatic machine, I rang the local council roads department and asked what the machines were called in the trade. It was quite a thrill to discover they were called 'wackers'; to have a character called Wacker in a play to be produced in Liverpool seemed like a favourable omen.

The play was well received and it was decided that Whirligig Theatre, my touring children's theatre company, should subsequently produce it in large and middle-scale theatres all over Great Britain. It seemed right to take this opportunity to change the title, to describe more accurately the content of the play. I wrestled with this problem for ages, far longer than it had taken to write the play, and it was only on the day of the printer's publicity deadline that I happened to read a newspaper article about the Ideal Home Exhibition. Suddenly I'd got it! – *The Ideal Gnome Expedition*.

The play became one of Whirligig's most popular, mainly, perhaps, because teachers liked the road safety aspect. But also I realized that the structure of the play was really a quest, always a good basis for a children's play.

Later I was invited to adapt the play into a television series, and eventually a second series involving a new storyline was also screened. The television producer somewhat confounded me by saying he preferred the title *Chish 'n' Fips* to *The Ideal Gnome Expedition*, as a result of which I located the gnomes in the backyard of a fish and chip shop called, you've guessed it, 'Chish 'n' Fips'. So the wheel came full circle.

For the television series I wrote a new song in which the

gnomes railed against the Big Ones for leaving so much litter in the street. When Whirligig revived the stage play, we decided to insert this song, to encourage teachers and children to discuss awareness of the litter problem. It has been included in this edition of the play.

The See-Saw Tree

During the sixties and seventies a polarity, even antagonism, developed between children's theatre and Theatre-In-Education. While some practitioners preferred to present entertainment-based plays in traditional theatre buildings, others opted to work in schools, offering issue-based educational theatre. The T.I.E. lobby decried theatres as the promulgators of middle-class values and saw drama as a teaching tool. Children's theatre was more theatrically stimulating, but tended towards the cosy and unchallenging. I had a foot in each camp. My first professional job was with the Watford T.I.E. Company, working as an actor and writer; I loved it and appreciated the value of the work, but my heart really remained in the theatre. I believed, and still do, that children's imaginations are most effectively triggered by offering them something special, away from the familiarity of the school hall. Why should they be denied the theatrical magic that so excited me in my childhood? At the same time I knew how effectively the techniques of T.I.E. could broaden young minds and illustrate abstract concepts such as tolerance, justice or collective responsibility. Both disciplines were highly valuable. I believed they complimented each other and should collaborate rather than compete.

In the eighties attitudes mellowed. T.I.E. began to embrace more entertainment to promote its messages, and children's theatre took on more challenging ideas. I certainly saw *The See-Saw Tree* as a synthesis of the two disciplines. The play uses fantasy to illustrate a very real contemporary problem. Should a beautiful, ancient oak tree be chopped down to make way for a supermarket car-park?

Should the greed of the property developer be allowed to destroy the environment?

Stephen Barry, then artistic director of the Redgrave Theatre, Farnham, invited me to write a play to be produced not as a festive Christmas production, rather as a spring-term offering aimed directly at school parties. The commission coincided with a request from Sue Clifford and Angela King of Common Ground, an organization that promotes awareness of the environment through the arts. A special year focussing on the importance of trees in people's lives was planned. Could I write a play about trees? *The See-Saw Tree* was the result.

Children love animals. In the theatre the quickest way to gain their emotional involvement is to introduce a mute animal character who needs help. It was somehow inevitable that, when thinking about a play, I should consider the dilemma of a condemned tree from the point of view of the creatures who inhabit it. I found a splendid book called *Oakwatch*, in which the naturalist Jim Flegg describes the oak tree as a community of interdependent creatures, complete with its own hierarchy and daily routine. I subsequently met Jim, who kindly allowed me to pick his brains. I was delighted to encounter a scientist who was willing to think anthropomorphically. He described various creatures' characteristics in human terms. The owl was the boss, the mistlethrush was untidy, the dunnock was a drudge, the cuckoo was an opportunistic visitor. Jim's contribution was invaluable. A shape began to emerge wherein a bickering tree community would be forced to forget their domestic problems and unite to try to save their home.

But I also wanted to give the audience a feeling of real responsibility. The decision as to whether or not the tree should be doomed or saved should be in their hands. So I decided to begin the play with the house lights up, at a parish open meeting at which various options would be put to the local community – the audience. Naturally I didn't want them simply to vote in favour of saving the tree right from the outset. There needed to be a conflict of interest.

The solution was somewhat manipulative, but I think justified. At the parish meeting it would be explained that the tree would be felled to make way for a children's playground, to enable parents to shop while leaving their children safely at play. A vote would be taken. An audience of children would, I felt sure, vote in favour of the playground. But then an environmental activist would interrupt the proceedings to defend the tree, pointing out its historical significance in the locals' lives. Furthermore he would point out the devastating effect the removal of the tree would have on the creatures that dwelt among its branches. This would take us into a play-within-a-play, in which we would see the story develop from the creatures' point of view. At the end, another vote would be taken, by which time I hoped the audience would have changed its mind and want to save the tree. Happily this notion worked and the final celebration when the tree was saved never failed to bring a lump to my throat.

I decided to make the human beings at the parish meeting mirrored counterparts of the tree creatures. So Mrs Wise, the Chairperson of the council, 'became' Owl, Mr Storer, the Treasurer, became Squirrel, the hoarder of nuts, Mr Jay, the property developer, became an opportunistic Jay bird. This meant that the actors could double up, which was interesting for them and necessary for the budget! I don't think the children all took on board the shared characteristics of human and animal, but to me it added a satisfying unity to the play.

After Farnham, the play toured for Whirligig and was seen in several foreign countries. But never in Germany. I had thought that such a green, environmentally-conscious country would have warmly welcomed it. But my German agent turned it down because Rabbit dies a heroic death towards the end; attempting to stop the chainsaw doing its worst, he bites through the cable and is electrocuted. In the production the death is pretty frightening, but not staged realistically; it is performed in stylized slow motion and the actor very quickly revives and assumes his other role of Mr Bunn, the environmental activist. None of that was relevant, said the agent; in Germany they simply could not tolerate a death in a children's play. I have never believed that the idea of death should be taboo for children, who surely understand it as much or as little as adults. As Bettelheim demonstrates in *The Uses of Enchantment*, we cannot hide from children the nasty things of life. A story or a play enables us to present them in a form that permits children to integrate them without trauma. My German agent offered to take *The See-Saw Tree* if I would re-write the scene, allowing Rabbit to live. But I said no.

Mother Goose's Golden Christmas

Mother Goose's Golden Christmas is one of what I call the 'pantomime substitutes' I wrote for John Hole when he ran the Queen's Theatre, Hornchurch. At first I was unsure of whether I really wanted to write what would be billed as a Christmas pantomime. I had always considered that this most English of traditions was something of a mixed blessing. As a child I had always enjoyed panto, but undoubtedly preferred *Peter Pan*. As an adult, now immersed in children's theatre, I saw pantomime as a hybrid entertainment, a hotchpotch of songs and sketches, presented with scant regard for storyline. It tried to appeal to everybody, yet ultimately satisfied nobody. The employment of star pop singers, comedians and even television and sports personalities led to a style of acting which bent over backwards to be tongue-in-cheek. There was a constant refusal to delve below sea level, to explore the dramatic life-and-death situations most of the classic pantomime subjects offered. When Aladdin was locked in the cave by Abanazar, the audience was never really concerned that he might never see the light of day again. A superficial jollity pervaded the proceedings. And much of the humur, based on innuendo, went straight over the children's heads. Indeed the children in the audience were often bored because the story was so unclear and underplayed. The moment a lovey-dovey song struck up, they trotted off to the lavatory. Furthermore, the weird tradition of cross-dressing and inviting pointless music-hall participation – 'Oh, yes I am!' 'Oh, no you're not!' – didn't seem to connect with children at all. On the other hand, I had to admit that pantomimes often had an endearing sentimentality which made them arguably the most popular form of British entertainment, achieving huge success at the box office and playing to vast numbers of people who probably never entered a theatre to see any other kind of show. Pantomime was traditionally the means by which many children were introduced to live theatre, children who probably would not have had the opportunity otherwise. Maybe, I thought, if the entertainment could be geared more directly towards children, the experience would be more valid. For it is wrong to assume that, when pantomimes began, they were presented as shows for children. The spectacular Drury Lane pantomimes were very much intended for adults. Classic fairy tales like *Cinderella* or *Jack and the Beanstalk* were used as fantasy vehicles for the music-hall stars of the day to strut their stuff at the festive season. Children may have been taken as part of the family, but they were not seen as the priority target. I also realised that the classic pantomime titles were, in fact, based on very strong stories which could, if treated more like a through-line musical play, be genuinely involving and exciting, not just for children but adults too.

One remembered incident also made me decide that I would like to have a go at this genre. When I was at university, I went to see a big commercial pantomime. No fellow student wanted to come with me, because, I suppose, they felt a pantomime would be a waste of time. But I had always had an interest in light entertainment. By the age of eleven I was a rather precocious cabaret artiste, performing magic and singing songs with a local dance band. I was particularly interested in the way entertainers could 'work' an audience. So along I went. It was a matinee. The theatre was packed, mainly with children. Most of them became restless as the story became less and less involving. Towards the end of the second half, as was customary at the time, the star comedian came on to do a longish cabaret-style spot. At one point he cracked an off-colour joke. It went straight over the children's heads, but some of the adults in the audience cackled appreciatively, whereupon the comedian leaned over the footlights and said, 'Come on, let's get the children out of here, then we can get started!' I remember feeling my hackles rising. I even blushed in the darkened auditorium. I felt incensed that this man, who was being paid a lot of money to entertain these children, should so disregard them. He had made it quite clear he would rather be doing his late-night adult routine. Surely, I thought, as I left the theatre, we shouldn't be short-changing the children like this. But then I realised how little entertainment purely for children was on offer. *Peter Pan* in London, but not in the provinces, *Toad of Toad Hall*, again in London, but sometimes seen in repertory theatres, the occasional adaptation of *Alice in Wonderland* or *The Wizard of Oz*, but precious little else. In a way, that visit to the pantomime sealed my fate. It was almost inevitable that I should become a children's playwright, although it took several years for the idea to really set in.

So for Hornchurch I tried to write family musicals which, while retaining certain traditional elements of pantomime, would also have a strong through plot, with no irrelevant speciality acts. I attempted to include slapstick humour and a broader style of dialogue than I had hitherto written. I retained the Dame character, though decided not to have a female principle boy. The songs were all original, not rehashes of current pop chart successes, and the characters would hopefully be strong enough to withstand interference from television sit-com actors who wanted to present a stage version of their television character, complete with familiar catch phrases. There was nothing specially new about my approach. Many repertory theatres had for years written and produced their own in-house pantomimes with more integrity than the more commercial shows in larger theatres. But even they appeared to me to often end up as a glorified romp, an end-of-season treat for the actors, who often seemed to have more fun on stage, trying to make each other laugh, than the audience. I suppose my attitude was rather puritanical. I wanted the pantomime played seriously, 'for real'. That did not mean it would not be funny or entertaining, rather it would present the audience with a more rounded, magical, exciting theatrical experience, giving full value to the strength of the story. At Hornchurch I was able to re-tell traditional stories like *Cinderella*, *Aladdin* or *Dick Whittington*, but also create original stories within a pantomime framework. Thus *Mother Goose's Golden Christmas* is not based on the traditional Mother Goose tale. Hopefully audiences are not disappointed by this. Hopefully they find it refreshing not knowing what comes next. Finally, it is only fair to note that many of today's commercial pantomimes are, in my opinion, much better than the one I saw as a student. Producers are now far more insistent on telling the story well and, although I still can't accept the tongue-in-cheek approach of much of the acting, I concede that children are given a much better deal.

David Wood
London, 1999

The Gingerbread Man

The Gingerbread Man was originally commissioned by the Towngate Theatre, Basildon, and produced there by the Theatre Royal, Norwich (Trust) Ltd, on the 7 December 1976, with the following cast:

Herr Von Cuckoo	Ronnie Stevens
Salt	Tim Barker
Pepper	Pearly Gates
The Gingerbread Man	Jack Chissick
The Old Bag	Veronica Clifford
Sleek the Mouse	Keith Varnier

Directed by Jonathan Lynn
Designed by Susie Caulcutt
Musical direction by Peter Pontzen
Lighting by Martyn Wills

The play was subsequently presented at The Old Vic, London, by Cameron Mackintosh and David Wood, by arrangement with the Cambridge Theatre Company, for a Christmas season opening on 13 December 1977, with the following cast:

Herr Von Cuckoo	Ronnie Stevens
Salt	Tim Barker
Pepper	Cheryl Branker
The Gingerbread Man	Andrew Secombe
The Old Bag	Vivienne Martin
Sleek the Mouse	Keith Varnier

Directed by Jonathan Lynn
Designed by Susie Caulcutt
Musical direction by Peter Pontzen
Lighting design by Mick Hughes

Characters

Herr Von Cuckoo, *the Swiss-made cuckoo in the cuckoo clock. He wears leder-hosen.*

Salt, *a salt cellar, based in design on the blue-and-white horizontal striped variety, thus making him look like a sailor, and indeed that's how he sees himself.*

Pepper, *a well-groomed, svelte, elegant female pepper-mill.*

The Gingerbread Man, *who looks like what he is!*

The Old Bag, *an elderly, short-tempered, tea bag, who lives on the shelf, inside a cottage-style teapot.*

Sleek the Mouse, *an American gangster-style villain. Not as smooth as he'd like to appear.*

The Voices of the Big Ones, *these can either be pre-recorded or doubled by other members of the cast. They are the voices of the family who own the house in whose kitchen and on whose dresser the action takes place.*

Author's Note

As this is a musical play, not a pantomime, it helps if all the cast play their lines and situations for truth and reality (even though their characters may seem to belong in the realm of fantasy!), rather than adopt a superficial, 'knowing' style of performance often associated, sadly, with panto. The original production of this play proved that audience participation and involvement works best when it is motivated by genuine concern for the characters and their problems; and this concern is created by the *cast's* genuine concern for them.

The action of the play takes place on a kitchen dresser.

Act One   At Night
Act Two   Immediately following

Act One

The action of the play takes place on a kitchen dresser. The characters are all but inches high; therefore the set is magnified. It is one structure, which remains throughout the play.

The stage surface is the 'top' of the dresser, in other words the working surface. The edge of the stage can therefore be the edge of the dresser. Positioned, say, 12 or 15 feet upstage is the back of the dresser, incorporating one practical shelf, and hopefully the beginnings of another (non-practical) shelf. Naturally at stage surface level there is a 'shelf-like area', under the practical shelf above. On the 'lower' shelf are two plates standing upright, one of which is practical in that it slides to one side to reveal a hole in the wooden back of the dresser, through which **Sleek the Mouse** *enters; the other is practical in that it is used in the action to put things on. There is also a practical mug. There are several hooks along the edge of the shelf. There is also a length of string, which could be in a tin, or just the remains of an opened parcel; also a sugar bowl, with several practical lumps of sugar; and an egg cup. A gaily-coloured pocket transistor radio can be either suspended from another hook, or horizontal on the top surface. On the 'upper' (practical) shelf is a cottage-style teapot. It has a practical front door. Next to it are various herb jars, which never move, but could have lids. There is a pot of honey. Other larger jars could be visible (probably painted, or simply the front façades). Beside or in the middle of the shelved part of the dresser, is a cuckoo clock, with a practical door.* **Herr Von Cuckoo** *should be able to reach from his cuckooing position to the dresser working surface, perhaps by swinging on the short end of the pendulum or by having a pendulum with rungs, like a ladder. But as two characters have to make the return journey – i.e. from dresser to clock, it may be more feasible to make the 'podium' a sort of balcony, reachable by stepping up from the working surface. On the working surface itself sits a rolling pin. A tea-cloth is somewhere handy. Other dresser clutter could be visible – non-practical fixed 'dresser dressing'. This could extend up to a non-practical top shelf, which could extend into the flies; or the very top of the dresser could be visible.*

The set is backed by black tabs, and hopefully a floor cloth, with the dresser surface painted on; this should have black surrounds extending from the surface edges to the wings, thus truly defining the working area. If possible, a front cloth could be used instead of tabs. This would have the show's title and possibly a gingerbread man motif, plus a design of the dresser (on its own or as part of a kitchen scene.) This could help the establishing of the large-scale set.

If an overture is required, it is suggested that a verse and chorus of 'Toad in the Throat' be played.

As the curtain rises we hear the ticking of the cuckoo clock, the hands of which point to twelve o'clock. The dresser is revealed in lighting which suggests moonlight, though it must obviously be bright enough to see everything clearly, as this will be the basic lighting for most of the play. **Salt** *and* **Pepper** *stand, respectively back and front to the audience, under the practical shelf. An envelope stands between them, leaning against* **Pepper**. **Salt** *and* **Pepper** *are in frozen positions. Suddenly the door of the cuckoo clock opens, and* **Herr Von Cuckoo** *enters. Rather ostentatiously he clears his throat.*

Herr Von Cuckoo (*warming up*)   Mi, mi, mi, mi. (*He looks up at the clock face to check the time, and launches into his rhythmic twelve-cuckoo call.*) Cuckoo! Cuckoo! Cuckoo! Cuckoo! (*The first four are confident and perky. Between each one he nods or turns his head in a clockwork manner. He keeps count on his fingers. Under his breath.*) Vier. Four. (*He carries on.*) Cuckoo! Cuckoo! Cuckoo! Cuckoo! (*During the second four, it becomes a bit of an effort, breathing-wise and counting-wise. Under his breath.*) Er – acht. Eight. (*He carries on.*) Cuckoo! Cuck-oo! (*Breath.*) Cuck-oo! Cu–ck–ooooh. (*The sound changes into one of disgust. During the last four he has developed a husky frog in the throat, and it is a real strain to get the sound out. He tries clearing his throat. A very husky note.*) Aaaah. What a noise horrible, nicht war? Hoppla! Ich ze toad in ze throat have. (*He tries a scale, but it cracks up nastily.*) Doh, ray, me, fah, so – (*Repeating.*) – fah – so – fah so . . . (*Speaking.*) So far so no good! (*Singing.*) La – (*Straining.*) – te . . . (*He tries 'doh', but nothing comes out; he has to go back down the octave to the lower 'doh'.*) DOH! (*He sighs.*) Oh . . .

SONG: **Toad in the Throat**

Herr Von Cuckoo

I was made in the mountains of
    Switzerland
(*Yodel.*)
From a fine piece of pine I was
    carved by hand
(*Yodel.*)
With all
My power
I call
The hour
On a clear and unwavering note
But I
Declare
To my
Despair
Today I've a toad in my throat.

(*Yodelling chorus.*)

'Cross the valleys of Switzerland you
    can hear
(*Yodel.*)
It's the sound of a yodelling
    mountaineer
(*Yodel.*)
He's all
Alone
Can't call
By 'phone
On a mountainside high and remote
When in
Distress
He's in
A mess
If he gets a toad in his throat.

(*Half chorus of yodelling.*)

Oh dear, oh dear

What can I do
I'm a cuckoo clock cuckoo who
    can't cuckoo.

So before people notice there's
    something wrong
(*Husky yodel.*)
I must try to recover my cuckoo
    song
(*Husky yodel.*)
A Swiss
You'll find
Is dis-
Inclined
To let a thing get on his goat
So I
Won't rest
I'll try
My best
To banish this toad from my throat.

After the song, **Herr Von Cuckoo** *shakes his head, checks to see that all is clear, then locks his door and, pocketing the key, makes his way on to the dresser. He arrives near* **Salt** *and* **Pepper**. **Salt** *is nearest him. Both are asleep.*

Herr Von Cuckoo (*in a husky whisper*)   Herr Salt. (*He tries to speak louder but cannot.*) Herr Salt. (*Giving up, he goes round to* **Pepper**. *He stands three paces from her.*) Fräulein Pepper. (*He moves in to her.*)

Pepper *wakes and starts to sneeze.*

Pepper   A – A – A . . .

Herr Von Cuckoo   Bitte . . .

Pepper   Tishoo!

Pepper'*s sneeze sends him reeling back. He tries again.*

A – A – A . . .

Herr Von Cuckoo   Entschuldigen Sie . . .

Pepper   Tishoo!

Again **Herr Von Cuckoo** *reels back. He tries again.*

A– A– A . . .

Herr Von Cuckoo   Fräulein . . .

Deftly he pulls out a handkerchief and puts it to her nose in the nick of time. This successfully stops the 'Tishoo'. **Pepper** *holds in her breath.* **Herr Von Cuckoo** *waits a moment, checks to see he has stopped it, removes the handkerchief and meticulously starts to fold it and put it in his pocket.*

Pepper (*just when* **Herr Von Cuckoo** *least expects it*) Tishoo!

Herr Von Cuckoo *jumps.* **Pepper** *wakes up.*

What's going on? Oh, Herr Von Cuckoo, it's you.

Herr Von Cuckoo (*huskily*)   Ja. Guten Tag.

Herr Von Cuckoo *shakes her hand and kisses her on both cheeks.*

Pepper   Cuckoo, please! You'll knock me over. (*She becomes aware of the envelope leaning against her.*) Oh no, the Big Ones have done it again. (*Calling.*) Mr Salt. Mr Salt.

The envelope is now leaning on **Salt**. *He wakes up.*

Salt   Shiver me timbers! Storm to starboard! Ready about! Man the lifeboats! We're running aground! S.O.S.! (*He keeps the envelope from falling on him as he turns to face the audience.*)

Pepper   All right! It's all right, Mr Salt. Wake up. We're not running aground. You were having one of your nautical nightmares.

Salt   Sorry, Miss Pepper. I dreamed the windblown sails were enveloping us.

Pepper   No, Mr Salt, we are being enveloped by an envelope. Kindly remove it.

Salt   Ah. Aye, aye, ma'am. (*He salutes and starts to struggle with it.*)

Pepper   I refuse to be used as a letter rack.

Herr Von Cuckoo *helps with the envelope.*

Salt   We'll anchor it here. Thank you, shipmate. Couldn't have heave-hoed it on my own. Might have spliced my mainbrace. Ha, ha. Good morrow to you! (*He salutes.*)

Herr Von Cuckoo (*huskily*)   Guten Tag.

Herr Von Cuckoo *shakes* **Salt**'s *hands and kisses him on both cheeks.*

Salt   Aye, aye. (*Rather embarrassed.*) Aye, aye! What can we do for you, shipmate?

Sadly, **Herr Von Cuckoo** *points to his mouth and opens and shuts it.*

Speak up. Don't be shy. (*To* **Pepper**.) What's he doing? Looks fishy to me! (*He opens and shuts his mouth.*)

Pepper   Maybe he's hungry.

Salt (*to* **Herr Von Cuckoo**)   Are you hungry?

Herr Von Cuckoo (*whispering*)   Nein. Ich need your 'elp.

Salt (*whispering*)   What?

Herr Von Cuckoo (*whispering*)   Ich need your 'elp.

Pepper (*to* **Salt**)   What?

Salt (*to* **Pepper**, *whispering*)   Ich need your 'elp.

Pepper (*in normal voice*)   Why?

Salt (*whispering*)   I don't know.

Pepper   No. I mean ask *him* why.

Salt (*to* **Herr Von Cuckoo** *whispering*)   Why?

Herr Von Cuckoo (*whispering*)   Ich have ein difficulty.

Salt (*to* **Pepper**, *whispering*)   Ich have ein difficulty.

Pepper   What are you whispering for?

Salt (*to* **Herr Von Cuckoo**, *whispering*)   What are you whispering . . .

Pepper   No, no, I'm asking *you*. What are *you* whispering for?

Salt   I don't know.

Pepper   Then don't.

Salt   I won't.

Pepper   Now, what is your difficulty?

Salt   Well, I keep whispering.

Pepper   No, no. Ask *him*. 'What is your difficulty?' My, you're stupid.

Salt (*to* **Herr Von Cuckoo**)   What is you difficulty? My, you're stupid.

Pepper   No!

Salt   No!

Pepper   Out of the way.

Salt   I'm sorry, ma'am.

Pepper *and* **Salt** *swap places.*

Pepper (*to* **Herr Von Cuckoo**)   What is your difficulty?

Herr Von Cuckoo (*whispering*)   Ich have my voice lost.

Salt (*to* **Pepper**)   What?

Pepper (*to* **Salt**)   Ich have my voice lost.

Salt (*to* **Pepper**)   Well, that's very careless of you, Miss Pepper. When did you last see it?

Pepper   Not *me*. Him!

Salt   Ha, ha. I know. Only pulling your peppercorns! (*To* **Herr Von Cuckoo**.) Now then, shipmate, you have lost your voice, right?

Herr Von Cuckoo   Ja.

Salt   Why? I will hazard a guess you have lost it on account of all that 'cuckoo, cuckoo' palaver all day long. Take my advice, have a rest. Stop 'cuckoo, cuckooing' for a few days.

Herr Von Cuckoo   Impossible. Is my job.

Salt   What?

Pepper   Is his job. He means that a cuckoo clock that cannot 'cuckoo' is nothing short of useless. Correct?

Herr Von Cuckoo   Ja.

Pepper   I tend to agree. If you ask me, Mr Salt, Cuckoo could be a likely candidate for the Dustbin.

Dramatic chord.

Herr Von Cuckoo   Ach, nein. Nein. (*In panic, he flaps his wings.*)

Salt   Miss Pepper! What a cruel thing to say. Calm down, Cuckoo, calm.

Pepper   I'm only being realistic. What do the Big Ones do if they've finished with something or if something doesn't work? Throw it in the Dustbin.

Herr Von Cuckoo *trembles again.*

Bang. The end. Never seen again.

This is true. A gloomy pause.

Salt   He must go on leave. (*He has an idea.*) To the seaside. Get some salty sea-air in your lungs and your voice'll come back loud as a fog-horn.

Pepper   How do you know? You've never seen the sea. The nearest the sea you've ever got was that willow-pattern sauce-boat on the top shelf. And what happened to that? One day the Big Ones found it was cracked and – bang –

Salt   – the Dustbin. All the more reason for Cuckoo to see the real sea. I've had salt in me all my life and I've never lost my voice. Go on, shipmate. Weigh anchor and fly away.

Herr Von Cuckoo *shakes his head.*

Why not?

Herr Von Cuckoo   You forget. Ich cannot fly. My wings are wooden. (*He begins to weep with despair.*)

Salt   You shouldn't have mentioned the Dustbin.

Pepper *thinks, then goes to comfort* **Herr Von Cuckoo***.*

Pepper   Herr Von Cuckoo. I was very unkind. But standing on the shelf all day I get so bored and bad-tempered. When night-time comes I take it out on my friends. I'm sorry. Forgive me.

After a pause, **Herr Von Cuckoo** *accepts the apology, by kissing her on both cheeks.*

Salt   Now, come on. Show a leg. All hands on deck for a party. Eh? It's after twelve-hundred hours midnight, so we're safe. We can dance and sing.

Herr Von Cuckoo *points to his throat.*

Sorry, shipmate. You dance. We'll do the singing.

Pepper   Herr Von Cuckoo, may I have the pleasure of the next waltz?

Herr Von Cuckoo *cannot resist the invitation. He bows politely.*

SONG: **The Dresser Hop**

This may be danced by all three, but it would be effective if **Salt** *could play a squeeze-box to accompany the dancing of* **Pepper** *and* **Herr**

Von Cuckoo. *If considered preferable the verses may be sung in unison.*

Dramatic licence suggests that **Herr Von Cuckoo** *could join in the chorus work!*

Pepper	In approximately eighteen-fifty
	When the dresser was new
	Come midnight
	The dresser-folk
	Had nothing much to do
Pepper	So one night they put their heads together
Herr Von Cuckoo	Came up with the answer
All	And ever since ev'rybody on
	The dresser's been a dancer.
	So kindly take your partners
	The dresser dance has begun
	Come skip and hop
	Round the working top
	With a one, two, three, one.
Pepper	As we gaily trip the light fantastic
	All our cares we forget
Cuckoo	Avoiding
	The rolling pin
	We waltz and minuet
Pepper	Palais glide or military two-step
Salt	Quadrille or the Lancers
All	We sing and sway till the break of day
	The dresser ballroom dancers.
	So kindly take your partners
	The dresser dance has begun
	Come skip and hop
	Round the working top
	With a one, two, three, one.

Salt ⎫	Herr Von Cuckoo
Pepper ⎭	Dashing as a white sergeant
	Jives to a gentle gavotte
Pepper	No-one can fault
	Mister Salt
	As he saunters
Salt	And at the foxtrot
	Miss Pepper is hot.
All	So kindly take your partners
	The dresser dance has begun
	Come skip and hop
	Round the working top
	With a one, two, three one
	Come skip and hop
	Round the working top
	With a one, two, three,
	One, two, three,
	One, two, three,
	One.

Salt   Bravo!

Herr Von Cuckoo (*with a bow*)   Danke schön.

Pepper   Thank you.

Herr Von Cuckoo *starts towards his clock.* **Pepper** *sighs.*

Salt   Well, that was fun.

Pepper   Old-fashioned.

Salt   I enjoyed it.

Pepper   Only did it to cheer up Cuckoo. Oh, if only
something exciting, out of the ordinary, would happen.

Suddenly **Herr Von Cuckoo**, *who has just passed the rolling pin,
flaps his wings excitedly.*

Herr Von Cuckoo (*croaking*)   Herr Salt, Fräulein Pepper.
Schnell, schnell!

Salt   Smell, what smell? What's he croaking about?

Pepper   Schnell. Quick.

Salt *and* **Pepper** *go to the rolling pin. All look behind it.*

Herr Von Cuckoo   Was ist das? What is zat?

Salt   Let's heave-ho it over here and have a good look.

Salt *and* **Herr Von Cuckoo** *pick 'it' up and carry 'it' over the rolling pin, standing 'it' up, facing away from the audience.*

Funny, it's warm. (*To the audience.*) Anyone seen one of these before? What is it?

The audience should shout out 'a Gingerbread Man'.

A what?

The audience shout again.

Pepper   Of course! A Gingerbread Man. The Big Ones must have baked him.

Herr Von Cuckoo   Guten Tag.

He goes to shake hands, but as this point, the **Gingerbread Man** *bends at the stomach.*

Salt   They didn't bake him very well. He's all rubbery. Hey up.

They lift the **Gingerbread Man**, *but he collapses again. Business repeated a couple of times. His arms flail wildly. Eventually, he is still.*

Phew! I hope you're finished! You're heavy!

Pepper   That's it! He's not!

Salt   He *is*! He's very heavy.

Pepper   No. Finished. He's not finished. Look. No eyes, no mouth, no nose . . .

Salt   No nose?

Pepper   No, no nose.

Salt   No no nose?

Pepper   Yes!

Herr Von Cuckoo (*an idea*)   Ich knows.

Salt   *Your* nose?

Herr Von Cuckoo   Nein. Ich *knows*. Ich idea have. Let us him finish.

Pepper   How?

Herr Von Cuckoo   Give him eyes und mouth und nose . . .

Pepper   Good idea, Cuckoo; now what could we use? (*To the audience.*) What could we use for the Gingerbread Man's eyes?

Audience   Currants.

Pepper   Yes! Currants. And we'll use another currant for his nose as well.

Cuckoo   Yes, but what can we use for the Gingerbread Man's mouth? Something red.

Audience   A cherry.

Cuckoo   A cherry. Danke! Danke! Good idea. A cherry.

Salt   So we want currants and a cherry. Let's find some. And while we're looking (*To the audience.*) would you look after the Gingerbread Man for us please?

Audience   Yes.

Salt   You would?

Audience   Yes.

Salt   Thankee.

They all rush to the back, in search. Slowly, the **Gingerbread Man** *begins to topple sideways. The audience may call out. In any case,* **Salt** *suddenly sees and rushes back to catch him in time.*

Salt   Hey! Hup!

Salt *rebalances the* **Gingerbread Man** *and returns to work.*

(*To the audience.*) Thankee.

After a moment, the **Gingerbread Man** *topples the other way. Herr Von Cuckoo has to rush in and stop him falling.*

Herr Von Cuckoo   Ach! Ach! Ach! Hup! (*He rebalances him. To the audience.*) Danke!

Meanwhile various currants and peel have been collected behind the rolling pin. The **Gingerbread Man** *begins to topple once more – towards* **Salt**'*s side.*

Salt (*rushing back*)   Hey! (*He catches the* **Gingerbread Man**.)

Pepper (*holding up the currants and cherry*)   Got some!

Salt   Well done, Miss Pepper. (*To* **Herr von Cuckoo**.) Let's heave-ho him on to the rolling pin.

He and **Herr Von Cuckoo** *lift him and sit him, back to the audience, on the rolling pin. Tension music is heard as they 'finish' the* **Gingerbread Man**'*s face. This can be mimed or cheated as he is sitting back to the audience.*

Herr Von Cuckoo   One eye.

Salt   Aye.

Herr Von Cuckoo   Two eyes.

Salt   Aye, aye.

Herr Von Cuckoo   Three eyes.

Salt
Pepper   } No!

Herr Von Cuckoo   One nose, one mouth.

Salt   Right. Reception party – assemble. I'll pipe him aboard.

Pepper *and* **Herr Von Cuckoo** *stand formally.* **Salt** *blows his whistle.*

Salt (*to the* **Gingerbread Man**)   Welcome aboard this dresser, shipmate.

They stand back. **Salt** *salutes. Tension music builds – but nothing happens.*

Herr Von Cuckoo   Is he all right?

Salt   No, he's all wrong. Why won't he wake up? He's got all his tackle.

Pepper   I know. Make him sneeze.

Salt   How, Miss Pepper?

Pepper   Me. Herr Von Cuckoo, kindly twist my grinder a touch.

Herr Von Cuckoo *obeys. Percussion accompaniment.*

Thank you.

Pepper *bends and picks up the pepper (this can be imaginary), then gingerly holds it under the* **Gingerbread Man***'s nose. Tension music. The* **Gingerbread Man** *builds to an enormous sneeze, which blows everyone back a little.*

Gingerbread Man   A – a – a – tishoo!

The **Gingerbread Man** *slowly starts to move, one limb at a time, until he is standing. A sudden jump turns him to face the audience for the first time. He looks excitedly about – he can see for the first time. The others come forward to watch. Suddenly he sees them and does not know how to react.* **Salt** *comes forward to shake hands.*

Salt   Welcome aboard, shipmate. I'm Salt.

Pepper   How do you do? I'm Pepper.

Herr Von Cuckoo   Hallo! Herr Von Cuckoo at your service. (*He bows politely.*)

With an effort, the **Gingerbread Man** *opens his mouth and tries to speak.*

Gingerbread Man   H – ha – hall – o. Ha –– llo. (*He laughs with pleasure at being able to speak.*) Hallo! Salt, Pepper, Herr Von Cuckoo, hallo! (*Leaping and shouting with excitement, he jumps about, nearly knocking people over.*) Hallo! Hallo! Hallo! Hallo!

Pepper   Maybe I made his mouth a little large.

Salt   No, no. Only the excitement of his first voyage.

The **Gingerbread Man** *comes bounding back. He talks very loudly.*

Gingerbread Man   I say, where am I?

Salt   In the kitchen.

Pepper   On the dresser.

Herr Von Cuckoo   You are baked freshly.

Gingerbread Man   Baked freshly?

Salt   By the Big Ones.

Gingerbread Man   The Big Ones?

Pepper   The human people who live here.

Salt   Talking of whom, I wonder, shipmate – could you turn down the volume a little? If they should wake up . . .

Gingerbread Man (*just as loudly*)   Certainly, Salty! Ha, ha. (*He slaps* **Salt** *on the back heartily.*) Say no more.

Herr Von Cuckoo *attempts to 'Shhhh' the* **Gingerbread Man** *but in vain. He leaps off to explore, moving behind a plate.*

Hallo! Hallo!

Herr Von Cuckoo   Shhhh!

Salt (*trying to be broadminded*)   Just high spirits . . .

Salt *turns to see the* **Gingerbread Man** *peering behind the plate.*

Hey, mind that plate! Oh my.

Herr Von Cuckoo   What have we done?

Pepper *starts laughing.*

Pepper   I think it's splendid.

Salt   It won't be if he disturbs the Big Ones on the upper deck.

Pepper   Why not? A spicy whiff of excitement. Danger. Exactly what we need. Just what I wanted.

The **Gingerbread Man** *finds the transistor radio.*

Gingerbread Man (*loudly*)   I say! Salty, what's this?

Salt   Shhh! What?

Herr Von Cuckoo (*concerned*)   Aah! Ze radio.

Salt (*to* **Herr Von Cuckoo**)   On no. (*To the* **Gingerbread Man**, *trying to be calm.*) That, shipmate? Nothing special. I wouldn't touch it if I . . .

Too late. The **Gingerbread Man** *finds the switch and turns it on. Rock music blares out.*

Oh no!

The **Gingerbread Man** *starts gyrating to the rhythm.*

(*Loudly.*) Miss Pepper, what are we to do?

Pepper *smiles at* **Salt** *gleefully and goes over to the* **Gingerbread Man**, *and starts happily gyrating with him.*

Mutiny! That's all we need!

Gingerbread Man (*loudly*)   Hey, Pepper!

Pepper (*loudly*)   Yes?

Gingerbread Man   One thing nobody told me.

Pepper   What?

Gingerbread Man   Who *I* am?

Pepper   You? You're the Gingerbread Man!

During the song, **Salt** *and* **Herr Von Cuckoo** *eventually relent and join in.*

SONG: **The Gingerbread Man**

Gingerbread Man	Newly baked this morning
	Take a look at my tan
	Hey hey
	I'm the Gingerbread Man
	Like a magic spell I
	Just appeared with a bang
	Hey hey
	I'm the ginger, ginger
	Ginger, ginger, ginger
	Ginger, ginger
	Gingerbread Man.
All	Ginger, ginger
	Ginger, ginger, ginger
	Ginger, ginger
	Gingerbread Man.
Gingerbread Man	Suddenly you found me
	Like a flash in the pan
	Hey hey
	I'm the Gingerbread Man
	Bold and brown and bouncy
	As an orang-utan
	Hey hey
	I'm the ginger, ginger
	Ginger, ginger, ginger
	Ginger, ginger
	Gingerbread Man.
All	Ginger, ginger
	Ginger, ginger, ginger
	Ginger, ginger
	Gingerbread Man.

Gingerbread Man	From the tips of my toes To the top of my head I'm guaranteed genuine Gingerbread
All	Gingerbread, gingerbread.
Salt, Pepper **Herr Von Cuckoo**	Soon as you arrived the Dresser party began Hey hey You're the Gingerbread Man
Pepper	Ginger you're the greatest I'm your number one fan
All	Hey hey You're the ginger, ginger Ginger, ginger, ginger Ginger, ginger, Gingerbread Man.
	Ginger, ginger Ginger, ginger, ginger Ginger, ginger, Gingerbread Man.
Gingerbread Man	One more time
All	Ginger, ginger Ginger, ginger, ginger Ginger, ginger, Gingerbread Man.

At the end of the song they all applaud happily.

Pepper   That's more like it!

Herr Von Cuckoo   Encore! Encore!

Salt   I must say that was invigorating.

Gingerbread Man (*turning up the volume*)   Go on then!

Salt   What?

Gingerbread Man   Say it!

Salt   That was invigorating!

All laugh as the music starts again. They all start dancing once more.

Suddenly – we hear, loudly, the noise of a door opening. Then a violent lighting change – all up to a blinding full – tells us someone has come into the kitchen.

All react with horror to this. **Herr Von Cuckoo** *scurries back to his clock, and goes insides.* **Pepper** *dashes to her original position, maybe even trying to replace the envelope.* **Salt** *has finished up near the radio, which is still blaring out. He starts to dash back to join* **Pepper***, but suddenly remembers to turn the radio off. Then he freezes, but can see the* **Gingerbread Man***, who has never experienced the blinding light before. He is standing transfixed.*

(*Whispering through clenched teeth.*) Hey, Gingerbread Man. Down! Lie down!

In the nick of time, the **Gingerbread Man** *lies down, virtually in the position he had been left. Now, as the voices of the* **Big Ones** *are heard, perhaps we see their shadows looming threateningly over the set.*

Mrs Big One   There you are, dear, nothing.

Mr Big One   Extraordinary, darling. I could have sworn I heard the radio blaring out.

Mrs Big One   Well, you were wrong, dear, weren't you?

Mr Big One   Must have been, I suppose.

Mrs Big One   Anyway, it couldn't have just switched itself on, could it?

Mr Big One   Ah, but – it might have been left on.

Mrs Big One   What do you mean?

Mr Big One   Well, darling, you er – might – not have switched it off.

Mrs Big One   Of course I never switched it off –

Mr Big One   Aaaah!

Mrs Big One   – because *I* never switched it on in the first place. *You* did. For the football results. If anyone left it on, you did.

Mr Big One   I didn't.

Mrs Big One   What?

Mr Big One   Leave it on.

Mrs Big One   Then what are we arguing for?

Mr Big One   I'm not arguing. I thought I heard music, that's all.

Mrs Big One   Well, it must have come from next door. Come on, dear, I'm getting cold.

Mr Big One   All right, darling. But I could have sworn I heard music.

During the last speech, the clock door opens and **Herr Von Cuckoo** *emerges and clears his throat (with difficulty).*

Herr Von Cuckoo (*huskily*)   Mi, mi, mi, mi. (*He looks up to check the time – one o'clock. Very huskily.*) Cuckoo! (*He shrugs his shoulders, shakes his head and goes back inside, curled up with embarrassment.*)

Mrs Big One   What a weedy little noise.

Mr Big One   Needs a bit of oil, maybe.

Mrs Big One   Past it, more like. Have to get rid of it if it can't do better than that.

The lights return to 'normal' and we hear the door slam. The shadows have gone. Pause. First to emerge is **Herr Von Cuckoo**. *He comes out of his door, and locks it, in a terrible state.*

Herr Von Cuckoo   Ach! Ach! Ach! Ach! 'Have to get rid of it', she said. Herr Salt!

He goes towards **Salt** *and* **Pepper** *and meets the* **Gingerbread Man**, *who is nervously shaking.*

Gingerbread Man   Hey! What was all that about?

Herr Von Cuckoo (*avoiding the* **Gingerbread Man**)
Bitte, Herr Salt.

Salt *and* **Pepper** *move.* **Salt** *ignores* **Herr Von Cuckoo**.

Pepper (*recovering*)   A-a-tishoo!

Salt (*angrily*)   Gingerbread Man!

Gingerbread Man   What happened?

Salt   You woke up the Big Ones, that's what happened.
Now listen. You're very young, the youngest member of the
crew; you were only baked today. But this ship will sink if
you behave . . .

Pepper (*intervening*)   Please, Mr Salt. Let me. Gingerbread
Man. You're very welcome here; you've given us more
excitement tonight than we've had for years, *but* we dresser
folk, for our own good, should never cross with the Big
Ones.

Herr Von Cuckoo *reacts to this remark.*

Gingerbread Man   I'm sorry.

Pepper   They can be very cruel.

Herr Von Cuckoo *starts sobbing.*

Salt   Cheer up, Cuckoo.

Herr Von Cuckoo   Did not you hear? Zey will throw me
in the Dustbin.

Gingerbread Man   What's the Dustbin?

Pepper   Anything they don't want, the Big Ones throw in
the Dustbin and it's never seen again.

Herr Von Cuckoo *sobs even more.*

Sorry, Cuckoo, but he must be told.

Gingerbread Man   Why should they want to throw Cuckoo away?

Herr Von Cuckoo *sobs even more.*

Herr Von Cuckoo   Because ich have a toad in ze throat.

Salt   I think you mean 'frog', shipmate.

Herr Von Cuckoo   Frog, toad, what is ze difference?

Salt   Well, a toad is larger with fatter cheeks . . .

Herr Von Cuckoo *sobs again.*

I'm sorry, shipmate. Most unfeeling.

Pepper   The point is, he can't sing his cuckoos; he's a cuckoo-less cuckoo clock cuckoo.

Herr Von Cuckoo *sobs harder.*

Gingerbread Man   Listen. Let me help. To make up for waking the Big Ones.

Herr Von Cuckoo   What could you do?

Gingerbread Man   Find something to make you better.

Pepper   Something to soothe a sore throat.

Salt   What have we got on board that's soothing? Silky smooth, full of goodness?

Hopefully the audience will help by shouting out 'honey'. This will work if the pot (on the shelf) is marked clearly enough to have been established.

Pepper   Of course, honey!

Gingerbread Man   Honey. Right, where is it?

Salt   It means a voyage of exploration to the High Shelf.

Dramatic chord. All look up at the honey.

Gingerbread Man   Simple! Back in a jiffy.

The **Gingerbread Man** *walks towards the back. The others look at each other.*

Salt   Wait!

The **Gingerbread Man** *turns.*

Before you set sail . . .

Pepper   Beware.

Gingerbread Man   Beware?

Herr Von Cuckoo   Of ze Old Bag.

Gingerbread Man   Of what?

All Three   The Old Bag.

Pepper   The most horrible, dangerous, ruthless – tea-bag.

Salt   The terror of the High Shelf.

SONG: **Beware of the Old Bag**

If considered preferable the verses may be sung in unison.

Pepper	She lives in the teapot up there
Salt	But to visit her – don't you dare.
Herr Von Cuckoo	She keeps herself
	To her shelf
Salt	And her shelf
	To herself
All	And trespassers had better . . .
	Beware
	Of the Old Bag
	She's not fond of company
	Take care
	She's an old hag
	She's nobody's cup of tea.
Pepper	She's the terror of the teapot
	And her temper's quick to brew
Salt	From the gloom she will loom

Like a ghost to frighten you

Salt   So look out,
Pepper   Look out,
Herr Von Cuckoo Look out,
All   She's lying in wait
                    Ev'ry perforation oozing hate.

Beware
Of the Old Bag
She's not fond of company
Take care
She's an old hag
She's nobody's cup of tea.

Salt   And she hides behind the herb jars
                    Looking out for passing spies
Pepper   If you peep, out she'll creep
Herr Von Cuckoo And you'll get a big surprise
All   So look out, look out, look out
                    For Gingerbread Man
                    She will surely catch you if she can.

Beware
Of the Old Bag
She's not fond of company
Take care
She's an old hag
She's nobody's cup of tea

Herr Von Cuckoo So look out,
Pepper   Look out,
Salt   Look out,
All   Take care
                    Beware.

Towards the end of the song, the **Gingerbread Man** *has been 'frightened' by the others to hide behind the rolling pin. Now, at the end of the song, as the others freeze in their final positions, arms outstretched for the big finish, we hear a ghostly noise.*

Gingerbread Man (*behind the rolling pin*)   Woooooh,
Woooooooooh!

*Dramatic rumble. The others face front and react frightened, as a
ghostly figure looms from behind the rolling pin. It is the*
Gingerbread Man *with a tea cloth over his head.*

Salt
Pepper   } (*in a frightened whisper*)   It's the Old
Herr Von Cuckoo   Bag

The **Gingerbread Man** *creeps to one side, making his ghostly
noise. The others tremble with fear. All together they turn their eyes to
the noise, see the apparition, react, turn, bump into each other, and
then, all together, run screaming to the side edge of the dresser. The*
Gingerbread Man *pursues. They, having apparently nearly
fallen off the dresser, run in their group to the other side. He pursues
them to the edge. They nearly 'fall off', then in their huddle escape to
the centre. The* **Gingerbread Man** *throws the tea cloth over them.
They punch around inside it, and then emerge from it. The*
Gingerbread Man *is laughing.*

Pepper   It was him all the time. (*She sneezes to recover.*)

Gingerbread Man (*laughing*)   Sorry, Pepper. Just a little
joke.

Salt   Just a little joke? We nearly fell overboard, didn't we
Cuckoo?

Herr Von Cuckoo *opens his mouth to reply, but nothing comes
out.*

Eh?

Herr Von Cuckoo *tries again. Now all take notice. Not a sound
comes out. He shakes his head.*

(*To the others.*) Listen.

Gingerbread Man   I can't hear anything.

Salt   Exactly. There's nothing to hear. Cuckoo's got no
voice at all. Come on, shipmate, I'll take you home.

Music, as the sad **Herr Von Cuckoo** *is led by* **Salt** *to his door. As they go in,* **Pepper** *and the* **Gingerbread Man**, *who have watched in a sort of worried reverie, snap out of it.*

Pepper The honey. Please. You'll have to hurry. It's an emergency now.

Gingerbread Man Certainly, certainly, quick as I can. You can rely on the Gingerbread Man!

Music as he flexes himself in preparation. **Pepper** *watches as he advances to the shelf. He jumps to reach it, but cannot (or reaches it but cannot pull himself up). He tries this a couple of times, unsuccessfully, then looks at* **Pepper** *in consternation. She looks around.*

Pepper Sugar lumps! Use them as steps!

Pepper *runs to the sugar bowl. She and the* **Gingerbread Man** *take out three or four lumps and make a pile, leaving a 'step' on each one. Gingerly the* **Gingerbread Man** *climbs the pile, but at the last minute he topples over and the pile collapses. He lands on the 'floor'. At this moment,* **Salt** *emerges from the cuckoo clock.*

Salt Ahoy there! What's up?

Gingerbread Man I'm down! (*Setting up the sugar lumps again.*) Just on my way.

Salt You'll never get up there like that.

Pepper Think of a better way.

Salt Well ... Well ... Well ...

As **Salt** *thinks, the* **Gingerbread Man** *again climbs the sugar lumps, topples and falls again. He makes an angry frustrated noise.*

Pepper Well?

Salt Well ...

Pepper Come on. Here's a chance to show off your nautical know-how.

Salt I'm thinking, I'm thinking. What would a real old salt of the sea do? Got it! A capstan.

Gingerbread Man   Of course! A capstan! (*Pause.*) What's a capstan?

Salt   I'll show you, shipmate. Miss Pepper, be good enough to heave-ho that piece of string that came on the Big Ones' parcel yesterday.

Pepper   String. (*She goes to find it, stops and turns, and smiles.*) Aye, aye, Captain! (*She salutes and carries on. She is thoroughly enjoying the excitement.*)

Salt   Gingerbread Man. Give us a hand rolling the rolling pin.

Gingerbread Man   Aye, aye, Captain.

Salt *and the* **Gingerbread Man** *push the rolling pin to beneath the shelf, under a vacant cup hook on the shelf edge above their heads.*

Pepper (*returning*)   String, Captain.

Salt   Splendid. Thank you, Miss Pepper. Now, everybody, I'll show you the Captain's Capstan!

Music – shanty-style, the intro to the next song, as **Salt**, *helped by the other two, prepares the capstan. First he throws the string over the cup hook, above. Then he gives one end to the* **Gingerbread Man**, *showing him how to tie it round his waist as a kind of sling-hoist. (The slip-knot could already be there.) The other end of the string is tied round the thick part of the rolling pin, which should be up stage. The string should be taut. Then* **Salt** *and* **Pepper** *roll the rolling pin forwards (downstage), having the effect of lifting the* **Gingerbread Man** *off the ground. He will probably have to help himself, by using the side of the dresser, and finally helping himself climb on to the shelf.*

SONG: **Heave-Ho, A-rolling Go**

Salt	Haul on the halyard, hard as we can
All	Heave-ho, a-rolling go
Salt	Hup, mates, and hoist the Gingerbread Man
All	Way hay and yo ho ho.

Salt	Lifting our load and taking the strain
All	Heave-ho, a-rolling go
Salt	Turning the capstan, cranking the crane
All	Way hay and yo ho ho.
Salt	Higher and higher, t'ward the crow's nest
All	Heave-ho, a-rolling go
Salt	Fair wind and fortune follow the quest
All	Way hay and yo ho ho.

The music continues as the **Gingerbread Man** *removes the loop of string and hangs it from the hook, and waves down to* **Salt** *and* **Pepper***, who then sit and wait on the rolling pin. Lighting changes to the shelf area only. Tension music as the* **Gingerbread Man** *sets off towards the honey, treading on tiptoe.*

Suddenly the door of the cottage teapot creaks menacingly open, and the **Old Bag** *peeps out, then seeing the invader of 'her' territory, surreptitiously creeps out and starts stalking the* **Gingerbread Man.**

The audience will pretty certainly react, by shouting a warning to the **Gingerbread Man***, who by this time has reached the honey and is starting to remove the lid. The* **Old Bag***, looming like a ghost, advances and the* **Gingerbread Man** *senses danger; he mimes to the audience 'Is there someone behind me?'; 'Yes', comes back the reply. He works himself up to a sudden quick turn; but the* **Old Bag** *has been too quick for him, and hidden behind other jars and bottles. The* **Gingerbread Man** *assumes the audience is leading him up the garden path, and returns to the honey jar. The business is repeated as the* **Old Bag** *creeps out and advances again. This time, encouraged by the audience, he turns suddenly, and sees the* **Old Bag** *– surprising her at the same time. Both scream and run to hide in opposite directions. They re-emerge and go into a panto-style stalking – the* **Gingerbread Man** *never seeing the* **Old Bag** *and vice versa –*

back to back, until they bump into each other, jump violently, and
confront one another.

Old Bag (*sharply*)   Who are you?

Gingerbread Man   The G-G-G-Gingerbread Man.

Old Bag   Never heard of you.

Gingerbread Man   I was only b-b-baked today. By the
Big Ones.

Old Bag   You're trespassing.

Gingerbread Man   But . . .

Old Bag   This is *my* shelf.

Gingerbread Man   But this is an emergency. Herr Von
Cuckoo . . .

Old Bag   What about him?

Gingerbread Man   He's lost his voice.

Old Bag   You mean he can't 'cuckoo'?

Gingerbread Man   Yes. I mean no.

Old Bag (*with a sudden cackle*)   Ha, ha, ha.

Gingerbread Man   So I thought . . .

Old Bag (*with a sudden change back to sharpness*)   What did
you think?

Gingerbread Man   I thought I'd get him some honey. It
might help him.

Old Bag   You thought wrong.

Gingerbread Man   You mean honey won't help him?

Old Bag   I mean you're not getting him any. I'm glad,
delighted he's lost his voice. I've always hated that stupid
noise every hour of the day and night. 'Cuckoo, Cuckoo,
Cuckoo.' Now perhaps I can get a bit of peace and quiet.

Gingerbread Man   But the Big Ones may throw him in the Dustbin.

Old Bag   Good riddance. And good riddance to you, too. Clear off. (*To the audience.*) And *you* can clear off too. All of you.

Gingerbread Man   What have *they* done?

Old Bag   They don't like me.

Gingerbread Man   How do you know?

Old Bag   Nobody likes me. I'm all alone. All the other tea bags in my packet were used up ages ago. The Big Ones missed me and I hid in the teapot. No-one ever visits me.

Gingerbread Man   Well, it's not easy getting here.

Old Bag   It's not easy *living* here.

Gingerbread Man   Are you lonely?

Old Bag   I never said that.

Gingerbread Man   I'll be your friend, if you like.

Old Bag   Huh. Bribery. Get round me. Let's be friends. Then I give you the honey. Whoosh, down. Never see you again.

Gingerbread Man   I don't think you want a friend.

Old Bag   I never said that. I'm quite enjoying a bit of company.

Gingerbread Man   Good (*Indicating the honey.*) Then will you let me take some . . .

Old Bag (*interrupting*)   I'll tell your fortune for you, if you like.

Gingerbread Man   Will you? How?

Old Bag   Tea leaves have always had special magic fortune-telling properties. They send messages through my perforations. Show me your hand.

Gingerbread Man   Well . . .

The **Gingerbread Man** *tentatively stretches out his hand.*

Old Bag   Come along. Don't be shy.

SONG: **The Power of the Leaf**

Old Bag

If you want to know the future
You don't need a horoscope
You don't need to study stars
Through a telescope
You don't need a pack of tarot cards
You don't need a crystal ball
For the power of the tea leaf
Is more potent than them all.

So
Put your belief
In the power of the leaf
It can tell you things you never knew
before
Put your belief
In the power of the leaf
If you want to know what lies in
store.

No, there isn't any secret,
There's no club you have to join
And you needn't cross my palm
With a silver coin
You don't need to say a magic word
You don't need a medium
Through the power of the tea leaf
See the shape of things to come.

So
Put your belief

Gingerbread Man   *(spoken echo)* Put your belief
Old Bag   In the power of the leaf

Gingerbread Man   (*spoken echo*) In the power of the leaf
Old Bag   It can tell you things you never knew
                      before
Both   Put your belief
                In the power of the leaf
                If you want to know what lies in
                      store.

The music continues.

Old Bag   I can see! I can see!

Gingerbread Man (*speaking*)   What can you see?

Old Bag   A message.

Gingerbread Man   For me?

Old Bag   Yes. Listen and learn.
   'When trouble comes, if you can cope,
   Three lives will shortly find new hope.'

Gingerbread Man
   'When trouble comes, if I can cope,
   Three lives will shortly find new hope.'

What does it mean?

Old Bag   You'll find out – soon.

Gingerbread Man   Thank you, Old Bag.

Old Bag   Don't thank me, thank the power of the leaf.

Old Bag   ⎫ So
Gingerbread Man   ⎬ Put your belief
(*singing*)   ⎭ In the power of the leaf
                It can tell you things you never knew
                      before
                Put your belief
                In the power of the leaf
                If you want to know what lies in
                      store.

                Put your belief

> In the power of the leaf
> It can tell you things you never knew
>   before
> Yes! Put your belief
> In the power of the leaf
> If you want to know what lies in
>   store.

Old Bag   Don't forget.

Gingerbread Man   Thank you, Old Bag. Well, it's time for me to go down again.

Old Bag (*sharply*)   Why? Don't you enjoy my company?

Gingerbread Man   Yes, but the others are . . .

Old Bag (*charmingly*)   Let me show you round my shelf. (*She grabs him by an arm, and leads him across.*) See my herb garden? Bay, cinnamon, mint, rosemary.

Gingerbread Man   What are they for?

Old Bag   They contain remarkable medicinal powers. I have studied them hard and long. They can cure diseases, make sick folk better.

Gingerbread Man   Nobody told me you could do that.

Old Bag   Nobody else knows.

Gingerbread Man   But think of the good you could do for the dresser folk. The help you could be.

Old Bag   Nobody's ever asked for my help.

Gingerbread Man   I'm asking you now. To help Cuckoo.

Old Bag   That noisy bird?

Gingerbread Man   Just a small lump of honey . . .

Old Bag   No, no, no! I must be getting senile. Soft. I was beginning to like you. But you weren't being friendly at all.

Gingerbread Man   I was!

Old Bag   All you want is your rotten honey. And if I give you some I'll never see you again.

Gingerbread Man   You will.

Old Bag   Clear off.

Gingerbread Man   I'll come back.

Old Bag (*shouting*)   Get off my shelf.

Furious, the **Old Bag** *stomps back to the teapot and goes inside.*

Music, as the **Gingerbread Man** *considers what to do. He looks at the honey, then at the place of descent, perhaps checking for confirmation with the audience.*

Gingerbread Man (*whispers to audience*)   Shall I?

He makes his mind up, and, having checked that the teapot door is still closed, he tiptoes to the honey jar and steals a chunk. He checks once more that the coast is clear, then creeps to where he left his string harness. He looks over the edge.

Gingerbread Man (*whispering*)   Salty. Pepper. Psssst. Salty.

Salt and **Pepper** *are dozing on the rolling pin.* **Salt** *stirs and wakes up. The lighting changes to reveal below.*

Pssst.

Pepper (*waking*)   A-a-a-tishoo!

Salt   What? What?

Gingerbread Man (*whispering*)   Up here!

Salt (*looking up; loudly*)   It's Gingerbread Man!

Gingerbread Man   Shhhhh!

Music. The **Gingerbread Man** *shows* **Salt** *the honey, and mimes throwing it down.* **Salt** *understands, wakes up* **Pepper**, *hushing her and pointing up to the* **Gingerbread Man**.

They whisper briefly, then go to the back and bring forward a plate. Meanwhile, the **Gingerbread Man** *looks anxiously back at the teapot door.* **Salt** *and* **Pepper** *hold the plate underneath, and the* **Gingerbread Man** *prepares to throw down the honey. At this point the teapot door creaks open. The audience will probably shout a warning, as a result of which the* **Gingerbread Man** *throws the honey down on to the plate, and desperately puts on the string harness. Meanwhile, below,* **Salt** *and* **Pepper** *place the plate down, out of the way, and return to the 'capstan' rolling pin. With a cry of 'anchors away', they lower him to their level.*

During this, the **Old Bag** *emerges, shouting abuse. She reaches the edge of the shelf and very nearly catches the* **Gingerbread Man**.

Old Bag   You double-crossing little thief! I saw you! Let me get my hands on you! I'll make you squirm! Stealing deserves punishment and punished you will be! You evil little trickster. Come back.

By this time the **Gingerbread Man** *has reached the floor and* **Salt** *and* **Pepper** *help him off with the string harness. During the next speech the* **Gingerbread Man** *becomes subdued. Music to heighten the situation.*

(*With a deliberately nasty change of tack.*) You won't get away with it, you know. Gingerbread Man. Can you hear me? You'll soon suffer. You won't be around much longer. The Big Ones bake Gingerbread Men – to eat them. While they're fresh and crisp and tasty. Eat them. Good-bye, Gingerbread Man. Good-bye for ever.

Laughing, the **Old Bag** *backs away and returns inside the teapot.*

The **Gingerbread Man***, stunned by her words, is led to the rolling pin by* **Salt** *and* **Pepper***; they sit him down.*

Gingerbread Man   Is it true?

Salt   Well, shipmate, we can't say for certain . . .

Pepper   But – well, normally, if the Big Ones bake anything . . .

Gingerbread Man   I see.

Salt   Sorry, shipmate.

Pepper   We didn't say anything because – well, you seemed so happy. And you cheered all of us up.

Salt   *And* you were brave enough to answer Cuckoo's S.O.S.

Gingerbread Man   Cuckoo! (*He jumps up.*) I must tell him we've got his honey. (*He sets off, then stops and looks back.*) And don't worry about me! (*He smiles.*) I'm not beaten – till I'm eaten! And I won't be eaten – till I'm beaten!

Music as the **Gingerbread Man** *leaves* **Salt** *and* **Pepper** *to relax on the rolling pin, and crosses to the cuckoo clock, on the way possibly placing the plate in a central position. He reaches the clock and knocks on the door.*

Herr Von Cuckoo!

The door opens. The sickly **Herr Von Cuckoo** *emerges. He starts to speak.*

Don't speak! Save your voice! Look what I've got for you. (*Pulling the plate towards* **Herr Von Cuckoo**.) Honey. For your throat.

Herr Von Cuckoo *takes in the news, then grabs the startled* **Gingerbread Man** *and kisses him on both cheeks, making husky noises meaning 'Danke, danke!'*

Gingerbread Man   My pleasure, Cuckoo.

Herr Von Cuckoo *turns.*

Don't go! Aren't you going to eat some?

Herr Von Cuckoo *shakes his head and points to the clock face, which says ten to two. Then he mimes 'cuckoo, cuckoo'.*

You've got to do some 'cuckooing' first?

Herr Von Cuckoo *nods.*

Can't you give it a miss this once? You're not well.

Herr Von Cuckoo *shakes his head effusively. He must do his duty.*

All right. But you'll try the honey afterwards?

Herr Von Cuckoo *nods and grunts, 'Ja, danke.'*

Fine. Your throat is sore, you're feeling sick –
A dose of honey will do the trick!

Herr Von Cuckoo *goes back into the clock. Music as the* **Gingerbread Man** *leaves, and returns to* **Salt** *and* **Pepper***, on the rolling pin. He yawns, and sits on the floor, against the rolling pin, as if to go to sleep.* **Salt** *and* **Pepper** *smile at him.*

Pepper   Goodnight. (*She yawns and nods off.*)

Salt   Goodnight. (*He yawns and nods off.*)

Gingerbread Man   Goodnight. (*He yawns and nods off.*)

Pause. Suddenly there is a loud noise, scratching and scuffling. The **Gingerbread Man** *jumps awake and listens. The noise stops. He settles again. The noise starts again. He listens again. He decides to investigate. Meanwhile* **Salt** *and* **Pepper** *have gone to sleep.*

The **Gingerbread Man** *halts in his tracks. The noise stops. He takes a couple of steps. The noise starts again. He listens. It stops. Two steps. It starts again. The* **Gingerbread Man** *tracks down the noise to behind a plate, which stands vertical in the corner of the back of the dresser. Inquisitively, he tentatively slides the plate to one side. A hole is revealed in the back of the dresser.*

Sleek the Mouse *enters, sniffing hungrily, at the same time looking around to make sure the coast is clear.*

The **Gingerbread Man** *watches, half hidden behind the plate.*

Sleek (*to nobody in particular*)   O guys you K – I mean, OK, you guys. This is a raid. One move and you'll feel my false teeth – no, I mean, one false move and you'll feel my teeth.

SONG: **Sleek the Mouse**

N.B. To prick the balloon of **Sleek***'s cool exterior, the song should be staged in such a way that little things suddenly frighten him or go wrong — then he has to work hard to cover his embarrassment and preserve his image.*

Sleek

You hear scratching
In the skirting
In the kitchen
Of your house –
Then it's odds on
That you're list'ning
To your truly –
Sleek the Mouse.

I mean business
No-one bugs me
I'm not playing
Hide and squeak
Double-cross me
At you peril
I'm the boss mouse –
Call me Sleek.

I went raiding
In the pantry
In the middle
Of the night
When the Big Ones
Caught me nibbling
Pink blancmange
They got a fright.

Tried to catch me
In a mouse trap
But I fooled them
With such ease
And next morning
Trap was empty
No-one told them –

I hate cheese!

Any showdown
I can handle
With a human,
Mouse or cat
And my whiskers
Start to tremble
If you call me –
(A) dirty rat!

I'm a hungry
Desperado
So I'm forced to
Use my nouse
That comes easy
To the ruthless
One and only
Mafia mouse.

Super-mouse
Call me Sleek
Sleek the Mouse
Pretty chic

Sleek!

He goes to lean nonchalantly in a final position, against the mug – but misses it and falls to the ground.

Sleek *gets up and sniffs hungrily again.*

Somewhere I snack a sniff – sniff a snack. A lip-smackin', paw-lickin', whisker-itchin', nose-twitchin' supersnack. And I'm gonna track it down. For days my belly's been empty and I've had a bellyful! (*He sniffs.*)

The **Gingerbread Man** *emerges. Not suspecting danger, he approaches and stands by* **Sleek** *during the following.*

I'm gonna nose my follow and nothing's gonna stand in my way . . . (*He turns and bumps into the* **Gingerbread Man**.) Aaaaaah!

Gingerbread Man   Hallo.

Sleek   You're standing in my way, stranger.

Gingerbread Man   I'm the Gingerbread Man.

He shakes hands with **Sleek**.

Sleek   Hi, Ginger. I'm Sleek the Mouse. And I'm telling you this dresser ain't big enough for both of us.

Gingerbread Man   I don't know what you mean.

Sleek *sniffs, realizes the scent is near, sniffs his hand which was shaken by the* **Gingerbread Man**'s – *and realizes.*

Sleek   Hey. It's you! You're my little snackeroo!

Gingerbread Man   What?

Sleek   You smell good enough to eat, Ginger.

Gingerbread Man (*realizing the threat*)   I am, (*Suddenly.*) but not by you! Look! (*Points up, distracting* **Sleek***, then dashes off.*)

Music, as a chase starts.

The **Gingerbread Man** *escapes through* **Sleek**'s *legs, possibly making him fall over. The* **Gingerbread Man** *runs back to the plate and hides behind it.* **Sleek** *follows, and goes behind the plate. As he does so, the* **Gingerbread Man** *emerges from the other side of the plate and runs round it.* **Sleek** *follows. The chase round is repeated.*

The **Gingerbread Man** *emerges, and stops, then gingerly backs towards the other side of the plate. Suddenly* **Sleek** *comes out from that other side, having tricked the* **Gingerbread Man** *by not going the full circuit. He pounces. The* **Gingerbread Man** *manages to struggle free, but is forced to back away to the edge of the dresser.* **Sleek** *pounces again, but the* **Gingerbread Man** *slips sideways out of the way, leaving* **Sleek** *perilously near falling off. He teeters and totters alarmingly. Meanwhile, the* **Gingerbread Man** *dashes back to the rolling pin and wakes up* **Salt** *and* **Pepper***, who react animatedly to the situation. They quickly decide that the*

Gingerbread Man *should go aloft to the shelf. So* **Salt** *helps him up, winding the capstan.*

Meanwhile, **Sleek** *recovers his balance and turns to be faced by* **Pepper**. *They size each other up, then* **Pepper** *twists her grinder, picks up some pepper and throws it towards* **Sleek**, *who sneezes violently, but half-heartedly carries on the chase, which continues in the rolling pin area, involving* **Salt** *too. Up on the shelf, the* **Gingerbread Man**, *supposedly out of harm's way, watches and shouts encouragement.*

Suddenly the teapot door opens, and a furious **Old Bag** *pops out, screaming vengeance.*

The **Gingerbread Man** *senses her approach and a mini-chase starts. Everyone is in motion on both levels when we hear, as before, the loud noise of the door opening. Then the violent lighting change up to a blinding full. All except* **Sleek** *pause frozen for a second, realize what has happened and dash to their normal positions. The* **Old Bag** *returns in the teapot,* **Salt** *and* **Pepper** *to their spot, and the* **Gingerbread Man**, *not being able to climb down in time, lies flat on the shelf.* **Sleek**, *unaware of what has happened, stands transfixed and wide-eyed. Then we hear the voices of the* **Big Ones**.

Mrs Big One   There was no need for you to come down, dear.

Mr Big One   But you said you heard noises, darling.

Mrs Big One   I did, dear, funny scuffling noi . . . Aaaaaaah! Look.

Mr Big One   Heavens. A mouse!

Mrs Big One (*screaming*)   Aaaaaah!

Mr Big One   Shoo, shoo, you verminous little rodent. Shoo, shoo.

The 'Aaaaaaahs! And the 'Shoo shoos' continue ad-lib, until **Sleek** *comes to his senses and scurries to shelter – towards his hole behind the plate.*

He's gone, darling.

Mrs Big One   He hasn't, he's hiding! Ughhh!

Mr Big One   All right, all right. I'll put some poison down.

We hear noises of, say, a cupboard door and a tin opening.

Here you are. Here's some poison. This'll teach you. One gulp and you're a gonna.

Music, as from above the stage some poison (glitter?) floats down on to the plate on which the honey waits for **Her Von Cuckoo.**

Mrs Big One   Thank you, dear.

Mr Big One   Come on, darling, (*Yawn.*) let's go back to bed.

At this moment **Herr Von Cuckoo** *slowly and painfully comes out of his clock. It is two o'clock. He sadly croaks.*

Herr Von Cuckoo   Cuckoo, cuckoo. (*Hardly any noise comes out. He shakes his head.*)

Mr Big One   Huh. That cuckoo's no better. Hopeless.

Mrs Big One   I'll deal with it in the morning, dear.

The door slams shut, and the bright light goes out. Everybody except **Herr Von Cuckoo** *remains frozen after all the panic.* **Herr Von Cuckoo**, *reacting to the last words of the* **Big Ones**, *looks over to the plate, and smiles.*

Herr Von Cuckoo (*huskily*)   Herr Von Cuckoo will show you. In ze morning, thanks to ze Gingerbread Man's honey, ich will quite better be! (*Happily, he leaves the clock, arrives on the dresser and starts walking towards the poisoned plate of honey. He was in his clock when the* **Big Ones** *put down the poison, and therefore has no idea there is any danger.*

The audience, hopefully, scream a warning, and as he reaches the plate and prepares to eat –

Curtain.

Act Two

Act Two begins where Act One ended. It is suggested, to avoid the possibility of the audience missing the vital first minutes of this act (because of late return to seats, taking time to settle, etc.) that an entr'acte be played, after *the houselights go down and* before *the curtain rises.*

The curtain rises. A smiling **Herr Von Cuckoo** *rubs his hands in anticipation, bends down – and eats some of the poisoned honey. The audience may shout out another warning. The* **Gingerbread Man***, still flat out following the* **Big Ones***' visit, opens his eyes and sees* **Herr Von Cuckoo** *eat just too late. He shouts down to him.*

Gingerbread Man   Cuckoo!

Herr Von Cuckoo   Mein friend. How can ich danke you? Ich better already feel!

He goes to take more. The **Gingerbread Man** *stops him, shouting.*

Gingerbread Man   No!

Salt *and* **Pepper** *bustle across and pull away the plate. Then* **Salt** *helps the* **Gingerbread Man** *down, using the string.*

Salt   Did he eat any?

Gingerbread Man   One mouthful.

Herr Von Cuckoo   Was is ze matter? You honey fetchen me, zen away taken.

Pepper   It was poisoned, Cuckoo. Poisoned by the Big Ones.

Herr Von Cuckoo (*disbelieving*)   Nein. (*He laughs.*) You make ze bit of a joke with me, hah? Listen. (*He happily shows how improved his voice is.*) Cuckoo! Cuckoo! Cuckoo! (*But after a couple of smiling 'Cuckoos', he clutches his stomach and sways. He goes on cuckooing, but it becomes more and more painful, until finally* *he faints backwards into the arms of* **Salt** *and the* **Gingerbread Man**.

Pepper   Quick, lie him down.

Salt   Aye, aye, ma'am.

Pepper   Where's the tea cloth?

Salt   Behind the rolling pin.

Pepper *fetches the tea cloth and covers* **Herr Von Cuckoo** *to keep him warm.*

Gingerbread Man   What are we going to do?

Salt *listens to* **Herr Von Cuckoo**'s *heart.*

Pepper   Nothing much we *can* do. Just wait and hope he didn't eat too much.

Salt   He's still breathing. Just. If only we had a ship's doctor.

Pause.

Gingerbread Man   But we have!

Salt   What?

Gingerbread Man   Well, not a doctor exactly, but she could help.

Pepper   Who?

Gingerbread Man   The Old Bag. With her herbs. 'They can cure diseases, make sick folk better', she said.

Salt   She won't help. Never has before. Remember that jelly mould, Miss Pepper?

Pepper   Yes. Top shelf she was. In the shape of a rabbit.

Salt   She was made of metal – one day she started getting rusty.

Pepper   Next day. Bang. The Dustbin.

Salt   The Old Bag never lifted a leaf to help.

Gingerbread Man   Did anyone ask her to help?

Pepper   Huh. No-one dared to go near her.

Salt   Waste of time, anyway.

Gingerbread Man   If you didn't ask her, you could hardly expect her to help. (*He turns and looks up to the shelf, and the teapot.*) Hey! Old Bag. Can you hear me? (*Pause.*) Old Bag! We need your help. Please.

No response.

Salt   It's no use, shipmates.

Herr Von Cuckoo *groans with pain.* **The Gingerbread Man** *hears; it makes up his mind for him. He goes to the string hoist and starts putting it on.*

What are you doing?

Gingerbread Man   Come on. Hoist me up again. The Old Bag is Cuckoo's only chance.

Salt   But . . .

Pepper   He's right, Mr Salt. Let him try.

Gingerbread Man   Quick.

Salt (*after a pause*)   Aye, aye, sir!

Salt *and* **Pepper** *man the rolling pin capstan.*

SONG: **Heave-Ho, A-Rolling Go** (*reprise*)

Salt	Haul on the halyard, hard as we can
All	Heave-ho, a-rolling go
Salt	Hup, mates, and hoist the Gingerbread Man
All	Way hay and yo ho ho.
Gingerbread Man	S.O.S. – urgent! I'll do my best,
All	Heave-ho, a-rolling go

Salt   Fair wind and fortune follow your
                                                   quest
All   Way hay and yo ho ho.

*The **Gingerbread Man** arrives on the shelf. Below, **Salt** and*
Pepper** sit on the rolling pin, looking at the prostrate **Herr Von
Cuckoo**. The lighting intensifies on the shelf as the **Gingerbread
***Man** takes off his string hoist and leaves it on the cup hook. Music*
continues as he approaches the teapot. He is determined, though not
over-confident. He knocks on the door, turning away from it as he waits
for a reply. Nothing. He knocks again, and again turns away. No
*response at first, but then silently the door opens. The **Gingerbread***
***Man** is unaware of this.*

*The **Old Bag** slowly emerges.*

*The **Gingerbread Man** goes to knock on the door again, but in*
*fact knocks the **Old Bag** on the nose.*

Old Bag   Ow!

*The **Gingerbread Man** jumps with surprise.*

Gingerbread Man   Ooh!

Old Bag (*furious*)   First you pinch my honey, now you
knock me on the nose.

Gingerbread Man   I'm sorry. I didn't hear you.

Old Bag   Clear off!

Gingerbread Man   No, please.

Old Bag   Clear off! And if you ever come on my shelf
again, I'll . . .

Gingerbread Man (*shouting*)   I need your help.

Pause.

Old Bag   What?

Gingerbread Man (*sincerely*)   I need your help.

Old Bag (*softening*)   What for?

Gingerbread Man   It's Cuckoo.

Old Bag   That noisy bird again? I helped him when you helped yourself to my honey.

Gingerbread Man   He's been poisoned –

Old Bag (*losing her temper*)   How dare you? My honey is pure and healthy-giving . . .

Gingerbread Man   – by the Big Ones.

Old Bag   The Big Ones? Why?

Gingerbread Man   They put poison on his honey –

The **Old Bag** *looks indignant for a second.*

– I mean *your* honey. Look.

He leads the **Old Bag** *to the edge of the shelf and shows her the sight of the prostrate* **Herr Von Cuckoo** *below.*

Old Bag   But why?

Gingerbread Man   They wanted to get rid of Sleek the Mouse.

At the mention of **Sleek the Mouse**, *the* **Old Bag** *becomes nervous.*

Old Bag   Mouse? What mouse?

Gingerbread Man   Sleek. The mouse that's trying to eat me.

Old Bag   Eat you? Where? Has he followed you? (*She looks around, wild-eyed.*)

Gingerbread Man   No. Probably went home when he saw the poison pouring down.

Old Bag   I hate mice. Vicious creatures. They try to chew my perforations.

Suddenly, from a hole behind the herb jars, if necessary pushing between them, comes **Sleek the Mouse**.

Sleek   OK, Ginger, don't move.

The **Old Bag** *screams.*

Show for a timedown – time for a showdown.

Old Bag   Aaaaah. A mouse! Help! Help! (*She gathers in her perforations in terror.*)

Gingerbread Man   Shhh! Go away, Sleek. I'm not frightened of you. (*He does not sound convincing.*)

Meanwhile, **Salt** *and* **Pepper** *have heard the* **Old Bag**'s *screams and stand below, looking at the scene above.*

Sleek   No? Reckoned you were safe up here, huh? Reckoned I couldn't climb dressers too? Think again, Ginger. I used the back entrance.

Old Bag (*wailing*)   Get rid of him! (*Pushes the* **Gingerbread Man** *towards* **Sleek**.)

Sleek *cannot see the* **Old Bag** *behind the* **Gingerbread Man**.

Sleek   You've had your fun, Ginger. Now it's my turn. I'm starving.

Gingerbread Man   You may be hungry, but try as you can, you'll never eat the Gingerbread Man.

Music. **Sleek** *and the* **Gingerbread Man** *move towards each other 'High Noon' style. Left on her own, the* **Old Bag** *trembles at the edge of the shelf.* **Sleek** *and the* **Gingerbread Man** *circle each other. Then, say, three times* **Sleek** *lunges at the* **Gingerbread Man**, *who steps aside to avoid him. Then they clasp hands in a trial of strength. Slowly but surely* **Sleek** *gains supremacy till the* **Gingerbread Man** *is down. Then Sleek sniffs hungrily at the* **Gingerbread Man**'s *arm, and prepares to bite it. He has his back to the* **Old Bag**. *Very bravely, seeing the situation, the* **Old Bag**, *who has started to creep home to her teapot, decides she should help the* **Gingerbread Man**. *She looms up on* **Sleek**, *and pulls his tail.*

Sleek   Aah!

In this second or two of panic, the **Gingerbread Man** *rolls away from* **Sleek**'s *grasp and dashes to the hole behind the herb jars. He disappears.*

Sleek (*realizing what has happened*)   You miserable Old Bag. You'll pay for that.

Music continues as they stalk each other. Finally, the **Old Bag** *is backed towards the edge of the shelf. The* **Gingerbread Man** *arrives below (through the mouse hole behind the plate). He rushes to* **Salt** *and* **Pepper***, who have been watching. They consult in a huddle, then grab the tea cloth off the prostrate* **Herr Von Cuckoo***, and hold it under the shelf (firemen's blanket-style). Alternatively the others position the upturned mug for her to step down on. The tension builds as* **Sleek** *advances and finally the* **Old Bag** *jumps or falls from the shelf into the tea cloth. She is taken care of, as the lights focus on the furious* **Sleek** *above. During his next speech, the* **Gingerbread Man***, taking the tea cloth with him, goes back through the hole behind the plate.*

I've been boozlebammed! Bamboozled! You dirty, stinking rats! (*Petulantly whining.*) There were two of you against one of me. (*He suddenly cries with frustration and injustice, the aim being to get the audience to laugh at him.*) It's not fair! Boo hoo hoo hoo! (*He hears the audience laughing at him and looks up, furious.*) Hey! It's not funny. Nobody laughs at me, OK? I'm the baddie. The tough guy. A savage brute. And I'm telling you – (*He crumples again.*) – it wasn't fair! Boo hoo hoo!

Hopefully the audience are laughing again.

Shut up! I'm warning you. I'm a mouseless ruth – ruthless mouse – (*He has an idea.*) – and I'm so hungry that one more squeak from you and I'll be down there – raiding your sweets. All those toffees, and sherbet lemons and chocolate eclairs . . . (*He laughs and sniffs greedily. His sniffs suddenly change as he realizes he can detect something tasty nearby.*)

Through the hole, carrying the tea cloth, the **Gingerbread Man** *appears.*

Gingerbread Man   Coo – ee!

Music, as **Sleek** *sees the* **Gingerbread Man** *and prepares to attack. He charges a few times, warded off by the* **Gingerbread Man***, who uses the tea cloth like a bullfighter's cape – with appropriate music. Finally the* **Gingerbread Man** *manoeuvres himself to the teapot, the door of which is still open. With a final flourish he makes* **Sleek** *charge him and steps aside, forcing* **Sleek** *to run into the teapot. Swiftly, the* **Gingerbread Man** *slams the door shut, and either locks it or places something against it to stop it opening. (In the original production, a matchbox was used.) The others below have been watching, and now applaud. The* **Gingerbread Man** *bows graciously and throws down the tea cloth to be put back on* **Herr Von Cuckoo**. **Pepper** *returns to tend* **Herr Von Cuckoo**.

Thank you, thank you. (*Looking over the edge.*) All right, Old Bag?

Old Bag   No. You've shut him in my teapot. (*Wailing.*) There's a mouse in my house!

Gingerbread Man   Oh, sorry. I'll let him out, shall I?

Old Bag   What?

Gingerbread Man   Let him come down and nibble your perforations.

Old Bag   No, no. Leave him.

Gingerbread Man   Some folk are never satisfied. (*He sits on the edge.*)

Old Bag   I am. I am. Thank you. Thank you *all* for saving me.

Salt (*uncomfortably*)   Our duty, ma'am. Anyone in danger on the High Shelf . . .

Old Bag   But you'd rather it hadn't been me, eh?

Salt   No, but . . .

Old Bag   You don't like me, do you?

Salt   I . . .

Old Bag   You think I'm a miserable Old Bag who doesn't deserve saving! Eh?

An embarrassed pause.

Well, you're right. All this time I've kept myself to myself and then complained that I was lonely. Stupid. I can see that now.

Salt   Well, ma'am. Crisis brings folk together, so they say! (*He offers his hand.*)

Old Bag   Thank you.

Salt *and the* **Old Bag** *shake hands. A sickly groan comes from* **Herr Von Cuckoo**.

Pepper   I hate to interrupt your touching little scene, but Cuckoo is getting worse.

Salt   I'm sorry, Miss Pepper. Excuse me, ma'am.

Salt *hastens to help, leaving the* **Old Bag** *on her own, thinking.*

Old Bag (*after a pause, whispering to the shelf above*)   Psst. Gingerbread Man.

Gingerbread Man   Yes?

Old Bag   You said that bird was poisoned?

Gingerbread Man   By the Big Ones. And they'll chuck him in the Dustbin if he's not better when they come down. But, as you said, his cuckoos are very noisy. Good riddance.

Pause. **Salt** *and* **Pepper**, *who have heard this exchange, look on in anticipation.*

Old Bag (*to everybody*)   May I examine Herr Von Cuckoo? I may be able to help.

Music starts as the **Old Bag** *goes and looks at* **Herr Von Cuckoo**. *Then after a quick examination . . .*

SONG: **Herbal Remedy**

Old Bag

I can cure this malady
With a pure herbal remedy
I will effect it
With expedience
When you've collected
The ingredients.

Dill
Helps you sleep when you're ill
Horseradish
Eradicates the pain
Sage
Helps you live to old age
Rosemary
Strengthens the brain.

Chives
Are the savers of lives
Sweet Basil
A pow'rful antidote
Bay
Makes the aches go away
Bilberry
Soothes a sore throat.

Thyme
Puts you back in your prime
Witch Hazel
The antiseptic brew
Mint
Gives the eyes a fresh glint
Cinnamon
Fends off the 'flu.

All

Dill, Horseradish, Sage, Rosemary,
Chives, Sweet Basil, Bay, Bilberry,
Thyme, Witch Hazel, Mint,
    Cinnamon

Old Bag   Tarragon, and lastly
                               Parsley.

The music continues. **Herr Von Cuckoo** *groans and writhes in pain.*

Old Bag (*rushing to him*)   It's all right, Herr Von Cuckoo. It's only me!

Herr Von Cuckoo *raises his head and sees who it is. He groans even louder – in horror and fright; he knows how unpleasant the* **Old Bag** *can be.*

(*Calming him.*) Don't flap. I'll get your voice back for you – (*Turning from him; in a cross sotto voce.*) – even if it *does* upset my nerves.

Herr Von Cuckoo *half sits up, having heard this remark. He looks with inquisitive worry.*

(*Correcting herself.*) I said – I'll just get my herbs . . .

Herr Von Cuckoo *is satisfied by this and lies flat again. The song continues. During the next section, the* **Gingerbread Man** *throws down the ingredients; the others place them in the egg cup which they drag forward for the purpose. (N.B. In the first production,* **Salt**, **Pepper** *and the* **Gingerbread Man** *all went to the top shelf (using the back entrance) and sang the names of the herbs as solo lines while finding the herbs and throwing them in the egg cup below. The* **Old Bag** *therefore sang the lines describing the herbs' properties. This may or may not be practical in other productions.)*

Gingerbread Man	Dill
All	Helps you sleep when you're ill
Gingerbread Man	Horseradish
All	Eradicates the pain
Gingerbread Man	Sage
All	Helps you live to old age
Gingerbread Man	Rosemary
All	Strengthens the brain.
Gingerbread Nan	Chives
All	Are the saver of lives

Gingerbread Man	Sweet Basil
All	A pow'rful antidote
Gingerbread Man	Bay
All	Makes the aches go away
Gingerbread Man	Bilberry
All	Soothes a sore throat.
Gingerbread Man	Thyme
All	Puts you back in your prime
Gingerbread Man	Witch Hazel
All	The antiseptic brew
Gingerbread Man	Mint
All	Gives the eyes a fresh glint
Gingerbread Man	Cinnamon
All	Fends off the 'flu.

Old Bag   A final touch of Tarragon,
Soon you'll be the paragon
Of health, once again, fighting fit.

Lastly
Pass me
The Parsley . . .

The **Gingerbread Man** *throws it. The* **Old Bag** *adds it to the other ingredients. (N.B. In the original production* **Pepper** *and* **Salt** *arrived back down below in time for* **Pepper** *to pop it in the egg cup.)*

That's it.

Old Bag   It is ready. Herr Von Cuckoo must now drink.

Tension music as **Salt** *and* **Pepper** *help* **Herr Von Cuckoo** *up and lead him to the egg cup. The* **Gingerbread Man** *watches from the shelf above.*

Salt   Come on, shipmate.

Herr Von Cuckoo *groans.*

Pepper   Drink this, Cuckoo.

Herr Von Cuckoo (*recoiling from the smell of the brew*)   Ugh!

Old Bag   The nastier is smells, the more good it does you. Drink. It will make you sleepy.

Herr Von Cuckoo *drinks, helped by the others. He makes faces at the taste.*

Do you feel sleepy?

Herr Von Cuckoo *shakes his head and shrugs his shoulders. Then suddenly he relaxes into sleep as if by magic.*

That's good. Mr Salt, please help me lead him home.

Salt   Aye, aye, ma'am.

They set off for the clock.

Pepper   Will he get better?

Old Bag   I think so. But not for a few hours. I'll stay with him.

Salt   As long as he's shipshape by eight o'clock. The Big Ones will be down by then. They'll expect to hear him cuckoo.

Old Bag   I'll do my best.

Salt   Thank you, Old Bag.

Old Bag   Thank me when he's better.

*The **Old Bag** takes **Herr Von Cuckoo** inside. The door shuts. **Salt** returns to **Pepper**.*

Salt   Well, Miss Pepper, something exciting, out of the ordinary; that's what you wanted.

Pepper   And that's what I've had. Those shivers of terror. That awful uncertainty. The dreadful frights. My, it's been a wonderful night. (*She grins.*) I do hope it hasn't finished yet!

Gingerbread Man (*from the shelf above*)   It's hardly started.

Salt *and* **Pepper** *jump.*

Pepper   I'd forgotten you were up there.

Gingerbread Man   You've forgotten something else as well.

Pepper   What's that?

Gingerbread Man   Sleek the Mouse is up here too! (*He indicates the teapot.*) In there.

Salt   Can't we leave him there?

Gingerbread Man   In the Old Bag's teapot?

Pepper   Give him the poison.

Gingerbread Man   He wouldn't fall for that. He saw it being put down.

Pepper   You'll just have to let him out and order him home.

Gingerbread Man   I can't do that. He's starving. He won't stop to listen. He'll just start nibbling. Me.

Salt   Where does he live, anyway?

Gingerbread Man   Behind the dresser. (*He has an idea.*) Wait a minute. He's only here because I was curious and let him in. If we could get him back through this hole (*Indicating the hole on the shelf.*), block it up, *and* push the plate back down below, he'd be shut out.

Salt   He'd never fall for that! You just said, he's starving. He won't disembark from this dresser till he's had his nibble.

Gingerbread Man   Well, he's not nibbling *me*.

Pepper   No. We won't let him. We'll have to catch him and *then* force him back through the hole.

Salt   But how?

All think and look around.

Gingerbread Man (*suddenly*)   Your mug!

Salt (*thinking he means 'face'*)   What?

Gingerbread Man   Your mug!

Salt   What about it?

Gingerbread Man   It's big enough.

Salt   Are you being cheeky?

Gingerbread Man   No. You've got a big mug.

Salt   How dare you?

Gingerbread Man   Over there. (*He points.*) We could use it.

Salt   Oh. *That* mug.

Gingerbread Man   Yes. When he comes down, drop it over him.

Pepper   Yes, that could work. (*She goes to fetch the mug.*) Then push him to the hole, let him go through and block it up again. How thrilling!

Gingerbread Man   Exactly.

Pepper   But how do we drop the mug over him? He'll see it coming.

Pause.

Salt   Got it. Watch, shipmates!

Music, as **Salt** *takes the string from the rolling pin and attaches it to the handle of the upturned mug. He then mimes to the* **Gingerbread Man** *to throw down the sling hoist end, keeping the rope passing over the hook (or another hook if this is more convenient). By hauling on the string, the mug will rise – at least, the* handle *side will, leaving the opposite side still on the deck.*

(*Excitedly.*) Demonstration.

Gingerbread Man   Roll up, roll up. See Mr Salt's Patent Mug Mouse Trap.

Music, as **Salt** *pulls the string, and makes the mug rise.*

Salt   Now, Miss Pepper, could you hang on to the halyard please?

Pepper   Certainly. What do I do?

Salt   Nothing, ma'am, till I give the order. Then let down the mug.

Pepper   I hope I don't get too excited.

Salt   Now. I'm Sleek.

Tension music, as **Salt** *goes to his starting position and does a* **Sleek** *impersonation, sniffing towards the mug.*

OK, you guys, I'm the boss around here. Go, Miss Pepper!

Salt *stands under the inverted mug.* **Pepper** *lets the string up, which brings the mug down over* **Salt**.

Gingerbread Man   Bravo, bravo. (*He applauds from the shelf above.*)

Pepper   Congratulations, Mr Salt. (*She comes forward, leaving the string, and joins the applause.*)

Salt   Hey! Let me out!

Pepper   Oh! (*Loudly.*) Sorry.

She returns to the string, pulls, the mug rises, **Salt** *comes out.*

Salt   Right. Let him out, Gingerbread Man, and I'll stand by on the Mug Trap.

Gingerbread Man   Hang on.

Salt   Exactly. Hang on the halyard.

Gingerbread Man   No. Hang on. Problem.

Salt   Problem?

Gingerbread Man   How do we make sure Sleek gets in the right position for the trap to work?

Pepper   He's right. We can't just expect Sleek to happen to arrive there.

Gingerbread Man   No. What would make Sleek want to go under the mug?

Salt   Food! Cheese?

Gingerbread Man   He hates cheese.

Pepper   Something sweet. (*Idea.*) A sweet? (*Excited.*) A sweet!

Gingerbread Man   Of course! A sweet! Under the mug. Any sweets on the dresser, Salty?

Salt   Sorry, shipmate.

Gingerbread Man   Has *anyone* got a sweet we could use? Hands up. Don't throw them. Miss Pepper, perhaps you could select one!

Pepper   Certainly. Now, let's see. (*She looks at the audience, and selects a donor.*) You. Could we use your sweet? . . . Thank you. Can you throw it to me? (*She receives it.*) Oh yes, this should work. It looks very tempting. Smells it too. (*She describes the sweet.*)

Salt   Right, Miss Pepper. Under the mug. Heave-ho!

Salt *raises the mug, and* **Pepper** *carefully positions the sweet.*

Pepper   Ready.

Salt   Gingerbread Man, let him out!

Gingerbread Man   Hang on.

Salt   Again?

Gingerbread Man   Yes. We need something else to make the plan foolproof.

Salt   Go on then.

Gingerbread Man   Something to make sure that Sleek doesn't fool us by grabbing the sweet very quickly – before the mug has time to catch him.

Salt   Yes. Something to make him freeze, still as a statue, perhaps.

Pepper   Of course! He did that when the Big Ones came in.

Salt   What?

Pepper   Stood transfixed. They were shouting at him.

Gingerbread Man   What were they shouting?

Pepper   They were going 'Aaaah' and 'Shoo, shoo, shoo!'

Gingerbread Man   That's it, then. We'll go 'Aaaah' and 'Shoo, shoo shoo!'

Salt   I doubt if we can do it as loud as the Big Ones . . .

Gingerbread Man   Perhaps – (*To the audience.*) – would *you* help us again? You will? Thank you.

Pepper   Splendid. Now, if some of you could scream very loudly, the moment Sleek arrives under the mug . . .

Salt   I could use my whistle as a signal!

Pepper   Yes.

Salt   So, when I blow my whistle, some of you scream and some of you go 'Shoo, shoo, shoo'. Let's try it. All together. After the whistle.

Pepper   I'll pretend to be Sleek.

Pepper *acts as* **Sleek** *approaching the mug.* **Salt** *blows his whistle. The audience practise their noises and* **Salt** *encourages.* **Pepper** *acts transfixed.*

(*When satisfied.*) Thank you. Excellent.

Salt (*manning the string*)   Ahoy there, Gingerbread Man. Let him out!

Salt *hauls up the mug. Tension.*

Gingerbread Man (*breaking the tension*)   Hang on!

Salt   Not again!

Gingerbread Man   Last time.

Pepper   Go on, then.

Gingerbread Man   Well, if – (*Indicating the audience.*) – everybody is going to be kind enough to help us, we ought to make sure they're protected.

Salt   How do you mean?

Gingerbread Man   Suppose Sleek decides to leave the dresser and invade *them*?

Pause.

Pepper   Got it! When he goes to the mug, they – (*Indicating the audience.*) – make him freeze; if he goes to the edge – *I* make him *sneeze*! Mr Salt! Twist my grinder!

Salt   Oh, Miss Pepper. You're hot stuff!

SONG: **Hot Stuff**

During the song, **Salt** *and* **Pepper** *place pepper all around the edge of the dresser, and* **Salt** *acts out the effects of pepper mentioned in the lyrics.*

Pepper

I can make him sneeze
Like a tickle with a feather
I can make him sneeze
Like a change of weather
I can make him sneeze
Just a sniff's enough
Ev'ryone agrees
I'm
Hot stuff.

I can make him sneeze
Like a duster that is dusty
Splutter like a breeze
When it blows up gusty
I can make him sneeze

With a huff and puff
Ev'ryone agrees
I'm
Hot stuff.

First his nose will itch
On his brow a puzzled frown
Then his nose will twitch
Atishoo atishoo
And all fall down.

I can make him sneeze
Like the pollen in the summer
Ev'ryone agrees
I'm a red hot Momma
I can make him sneeze
Like a pinch of snuff
Ev'ryone agrees
I can make him sneeze
Make him cough and make him
   wheeze
Ev'ryone agrees
I'm
Hot stuff.

Atishoo!

Salt   Gingerbread Man, can we set sail now?

Gingerbread Man   Aye, aye, sir! You two keep out of sight as much as you can. (*To the audience.*) And don't forget, everybody . . .

Salt   Wait till Sleek is under the mug, then . . . (*He blows his whistle; the audience screams and shoos.*)

Gingerbread Man (*calming the audience*)   But wait till you hear the whistle. Good luck.

Tension music, as the **Gingerbread Man** *creeps to the teapot, removes whatever he has blocked the door with, and gingerly opens the door an inch; then he runs to hide. Below, all is set:* **Salt** *has hauled*

on the string, the mug is in the up position; and the sweet is in position.
Pause.

Suddenly, **Sleek the Mouse** *enters.*

Sleek   OK, Ginger, I've had enough of your tricks.
Prepare to beat your maker – I mean prepare to meet your
baker . . . (*He sees the audience.*) And as for you – you're the
creepiest, crawliest critters I've ever sniffed. Did you stop
laughing at me when I asked? Not on your life! When
Ginger shut me up, did you warn me? Not on your life! And
do you think I'm gonna forgive and forget? Not on your life!
You've asked for a sweetie raid and a sweetie raid you're
gonna get. I'm coming down! Yes I am!

Audience   No you're not!

Sleek   Oh yes I am!

Audience   Oh no you're not!

Sleek   On yes I am!

Audience   Oh no you're not!

Sleek   You just watch this!

Sleek *jumps, or slides down, from the shelf to the stage level. The*
Gingerbread Man *quickly blocks the mousehole with a herb jar*
or the honey pot, then hides again, occasionally peeping out to survey the
scene.

Sweetie raid! (*He advances towards the audience, sniffing all the*
while.) You just rustle 'em up ready or I'll nibble *you* instead.
Mmmm. Caramel whirls, fruit gums, gob stoppers . . . (*He*
reaches the edge of the dresser, sniffs and . . .) A . . . a . . . a . . .
tishoo! (*He backs away a little, then comes forward, at a different*
angle.) Chewy bullseyes, liquorice sticks, peppermints . . .
(*The sniffing of pepper is repeated.*) A . . . a . . . a . . . tishoo! (*He*
backs away again, then chooses another angle to go. As he starts, he
suddenly reacts to a new scent, and stands, excitedly sniffing and trying
to place the smell.) Oh! That sure is a swell smell! Kind of juicy
and crunchy and – (*Etc., improvising to describe the type of sweet*

under the mug – which will vary from performance to performance.) – my favourite sweetie! Where is it, where is it?

The audience should lead **Sleek** *to the mug. He can veer the wrong way a couple of times, but eventually he reaches the mug, and spots the sweet.*

Mmmmm! There it is! (*He starts to creep under the mug, then stops.*) This isn't a trick, is it?

Audience (*encouraged by the* **Gingerbread Man** *above*) No.

Sleek   It's not a trap?

Audience   No.

Sleek   'Cos if it *is* – you've had it!

The tension music builds as **Sleek** *goes under the mug and reaches for the sweet. At the appropriate moment,* **Salt** *blows his whistle.*

Audience (*encouraged by the* **Gingerbread Man** *above*) Aaaaaah! Shoo! shoo! Aaaaaah! Shoo, shoo! etc.

Sleek, *as expected, reacts by staring transfixed. After enough time to establish this,* **Salt** *lowers the mug, enveloping* **Sleek**. **Salt**, **Pepper** *and the* **Gingerbread Man** *cheer. The* **Gingerbread Man** *triumphantly jumps down from the shelf on to the mug.*

Gingerbread Man   Well done, everyone! Thank you.

Suddenly he nearly falls as **Sleek** *causes the mug to move like a bucking bronco. The* **Gingerbread Man** *jumps off. The mug darts about on the worktop.* **Salt**, **Pepper** *and the* **Gingerbread Man** *chase it and eventually push it to the corner, where the hole is, and carefully line it up in the correct position.*

Salt   One more time! (*He blows his whistle.*)

Audience   Aaaaaah! Shoo, shoo! Aaaaaah! Shoo, shoo!

Salt, **Pepper** *and the* **Gingerbread Man** *tip up the mug,
allowing* **Sleek** *to scuttle out. He reacts terrified to the audience's
noises and runs to and then through the mousehole.*

The **Gingerbread Man** *slides the plate to its original position.
All is safe. All cheer. Victory! They shake hands and thank the
audience for their help.*

The door of the cuckoo clock opens, and the **Old Bag** *comes out.*

Old Bag   Shhh! Quiet! Herr Von Cuckoo is asleep.

Gingerbread Man   Sleek's gone home!

Old Bag   My home!

Gingerbread Man   No, behind the dresser.

Old Bag   Good riddance.

Salt   How is Cuckoo?

Old Bag   Much better. But he must have hush. If he can
sleep till just before eight o'clock he should be fine again.

Pepper   And his cuckoos?

Old Bag   Back to their irritating, noisy selves!

Gingerbread Man   Hooray!

Salt, **Pepper** and **Old Bag**   Shhh!

(*Optional line to help calm the audience for the song.*)

Old Bag   We must have quiet! For Cukoo.

SONG: **Come the Light**

Salt	
Pepper	Come the light
Gingerbread Man	The light of day
Old Bag	The problems of the night
	May fade away
	Faint ray of hope
	May you shine bright
	Making ev'rything come right

Come the light.

Hear the tick tick tock
Of the cuckoo clock
Ticka taking us towards the dawn
Hear the time tick by
Hear the seconds fly
Ticka telling us tomorrow's born.

And
Come the light
The light of day
The problems of the night
May fade away
Faint ray of hope
May you shine bright
Making ev'rything come right
Come the light.

Hear the tick tick tock
Of the cuckoo clock
Ticka tocka never going wrong
Hear the time tick by
Hear the seconds fly
Ticka telling us it won't be long.

And
Come the light
The light of day
The problems of the night
May fade away
Faint ray of hope
May you shine bright
Making ev'rything come right
Come the light.

Come the light
Come the light,
May ev'rything come right
Come the light.

At the end of the song, they all fall fast asleep.

Tick-tocking music is heard, to suggest a time lapse. If possible, the lighting narrows to the face of the cuckoo clock, where the hands turn round till they reach about ten minutes to eight. (During the next scene they creep up to eight o'clock.) The lighting changes to suggest the early morning. **Salt**, **Pepper**, *the* **Gingerbread Man** *and the* **Old Bag** *are still asleep.*

The music continues as the door of the cuckoo clock opens, and **Herr Von Cuckoo** *emerges, yawning and tentative at first, as though testing himself to make sure he is better. He checks the time on the clock face. He clears his throat . . .*

Herr Von Cuckoo   Mi, mi, mi, mi. (*He is pleased. He yodels – without difficulty.*) La, la, la, la, la, te, teeeee. (*He smiles, delighted. Then, as a final test, he sings.*) Cuck – oo! Cu – ckoo! (*They sound back to normal.*) Ze toad has flown! My voice is found!

SONG: **Toad in the Throat** (*reprise*)

Herr Von Cuckoo   I was made in the mountains of
　　　　　　　　　　　　Switzerland
　　　　　　　　　　　(*Yodel.*)
　　　　　　　　　　　From a fine piece of pine I was
　　　　　　　　　　　　carved by hand
　　　　　　　　　　　(*Yodel.*)
　　　　　　　　　　　With all
　　　　　　　　　　　My power
　　　　　　　　　　　I call
　　　　　　　　　　　The hour
　　　　　　　　　　　On a clear and unwavering note
　　　　　　　　　　　It's my
　　　　　　　　　　　Belief
　　　　　　　　　　　To my
　　　　　　　　　　　Relief –
　　　　　　　　　　　I haven't a toad in my throat.
　　　　　　　　　　　(*Yodelling chorus.*)

During the chorus, the others wake up, and, pleased and relieved to see
Herr Von Cuckoo *is better, gather round the clock. The music
continues as they applaud him. He sees them.*

Herr Von Cuckoo   My friends. Ich danke you much for
better me making. (*He bows politely.*)

Gingerbread Man (*indicating the audience*)   Everybody
helped.

Herr Von Cuckoo (*to the audience*)   My friends. Ich danke
too you. (*He bows to the audience.*)* Ich would like to danke you
all, as is ze custom in Switzerland, by inviting you all to join
me in my yodel! You all will do zat, ja?

All including audience   Ja/Yes!

Herr Von Cuckoo   Danke. After drei – three. Eins, zwei,
drei . . .

*All sing the yodelling chorus – those on stage should find it difficult.
The audience will probably not be very good either!* . . .

(*After a while.*) Nein, nein, nein. Das ist *horrible*! Listen, I teach
you.

Herr Von Cuckoo *teaches everyone line by line. If it is thought
desirable, he could pull down a roller-blind-style song sheet from above
his door, with the 'words' on it.*

Yodel oddle oddle
Yodel oddle oddle
Yo ho ho
Yodel oddle oddle
Yodel oddle oddle
Yo tee hee
Yodel oddle oddle
Yodel oddle oddle
Yo yoo hoo
Yodel oddle oddle
Yodel oddle oddle
Dee.

*Optional cut between asterisks; see note in introduction.

Depending on audience response, **Herr Von Cuckoo** *leads everyone in the whole chorus, once or twice. He then sings a verse to lead into a chorus sung by everyone. The audience are encouraged to cough and 'Mi, mi, mi' before they sing.*

Herr Von Cuckoo   I was made in the mountains of
                            Switzerland
                       (*Yodel.*)
                       From a fine piece of pine I was
                            carved by hand
                       (*Yodel.*)
                       With all
                       My power
                       I call
                       The hour
                       On a clear and unwavering note
                       It's my
                       Belief
                       To my
                       Relief –
                       I haven't a toad in my throat.

Herr Von Cuckoo *sings the chorus with the audience.*

Bravo, bravo.*

All on stage clap the audience. Suddenly a loud door noise stops everyone in their tracks, and a bright light snapped on tells us that the **Big Ones** *have arrived. Tension music. All scuttle to their number one positions –* **Herr Von Cuckoo** *in his clock, and* **Salt** *and* **Pepper** *below the shelf, if possible with the letter between them. The* **Gingerbread Man** *and the* **Old Bag** *both go behind the rolling pin – the* **Gingerbread Man** *flat out as he was at the beginning.*

We hear the voices of the **Big Ones***. The clock points to eight o'clock. The shadows of the* **Big Ones** *are seen against the dresser.*

Mrs Big One   Hurry up, dear. We'll be late.

Mr Big One   Sorry, darling. I must have overslept.

Mrs Big One   Well, I've got to be at work by nine.

Mr Big One   No time for breakfast then.

Mrs Big One   Any sign of that mouse?

Mr Big One   No. I should think he's gone for good.

Indignantly, the **Gingerbread Man** *pops up for a second, as if to say 'You* sent *him packing? We* did!' *Realizing what he is doing, he stops and drops down again.*

Mrs Big One   Thank heavens.

Herr Von Cuckoo *enters from his door, and with great confidence, proclaims the time.*

Herr Von Cuckoo   Cuckoo! Cuckoo! Cuckoo! Cuckoo!
                        Cuckoo! Cuckoo! Cuckoo! Cuckoo!

He stands there, listening.

Mr Big One   Did you hear that, darling? Eight perfect working order cuckoos.

Mrs Big One   He's not past it after all! No Dustbin for him!

Herr Von Cuckoo *smiles radiantly. He has forgotten to go back inside.*

Mr Big One   Probably a bit of fluff in his works.

Herr Von Cuckoo *looks indignant.*

Come on, darling.

Mrs Big One   Do you want the Gingerbread Man to nibble in the car?

Mr Big One   Yes, that's an idea.

The **Gingerbread Man**'s *head emerges nervously from behind the rolling pin.*

Mrs Big One   Otherwise you'll be hungry with no breakfast.

Mr Big One   Hang on. No. He's probably all germy –

The **Gingerbread Man** *looks indignant.*

– that mouse's dirty paws must have run all over him.

Mrs Big One   Ugh, you're right. Don't eat him. Might make yourself ill.

*The **Gingerbread Man** looks relieved. The **Old Bag** pops her head up to congratulate him.*

Mr Big One   No. I'll throw him in the Dustbin.

Their reactions change to fright.

Mrs Big One   Oh no, don't do that. He's nice. He's got a cheeky face. Let's keep him – as a sort of decoration. He can stand on the shelf next to the teapot. Come on, dear, we'll be late.

*The bright light is switched off, and a door slam tells us the **Big Ones** have gone. Pause. Then all five emerge cheering, and converge centre, shaking hands with each other, and **Herr Von Cuckoo** kissing cheeks.*

Salt   Congratulations, Cuckoo. You've never sung better.

Herr Von Cuckoo   Danke. Danke you all.

Pepper   Gingerbread Man . . .

Gingerbread Man *(fiercely)*   Don't come near me!

Pepper   Why not?

Gingerbread Man *(laughing)*   I'm all germy and nasty and horrible – *(He jokingly advances on her like a monster.)*

All laugh.

– but I'm not to be beaten, and not to be eaten!

Salt   A happy end to the voyage.

Old Bag *(angrily)*   Happy? First that bird is better, and second, I have to share my shelf with *him*! *(She indicates the **Gingerbread Man**.)* You think I'm *happy*? *(Awkward pause. Then she breaks into a huge smile.)* I'm delighted, thrilled . . .

*The **Gingerbread Man** runs to the **Old Bag**.*

And if you don't visit me at least twice every day, there'll be trouble!

Gingerbread Man   Trouble! I can cope with trouble. Your fortune telling was right.

Old Bag   Of course!

Gingerbread Man
  'When trouble comes, if you can cope
  Three lives will shortly find new hope.'

Herr Von Cuckoo   One is me. I escaped the Dustbin.

Gingerbread Man   Two is me. I escaped being eaten!

Salt   And three?

Old Bag   Three is – me!

Pepper   What did you escape?

Old Bag   I escaped – from myself. And found you – my friends.

All cheer.

Herr Von Cuckoo   And who do we owe it all to?

All   The Gingerbread Man!

SONG: **The Gingerbread Man** (*reprise*)

Pepper	Ginger
Salt	Ginger
Old Bag	Ginger
Herr Von Cuckoo	Ginger
Gingerbread Man	Ginger?
All	Ginger, ginger,
	Gingerbread Man.
	Soon as you arrived the
	Dresser party began
	Hey hey
	You're the Gingerbread Man

Ginger you're the greatest
I'm your number one fan
Hey hey
You're the ginger, ginger
Ginger, ginger, ginger
Ginger, ginger,
Gingerbread Man.

Ginger, ginger
Ginger, ginger, ginger
Ginger, ginger,
Gingerbread Man.

Gingerbread Man   Newly baked this morning
Take a look at my tan
Hey hey
I'm the Gingerbread Man
Like a magic spell I
Just appeared with a bang
Hey, hey
I'm the ginger

All   Ginger
Gingerbread Man   Ginger
All   Ginger
Gingerbread Man   Ginger
All   Ginger
Gingerbread Man   Ginger, ginger,
Gingerbread Man.

All   Ginger, ginger
Ginger, ginger, ginger
Ginger, ginger,
Gingerbread Man.

Gingerbread Man   One more time

All   Ginger, ginger
Ginger, ginger, ginger
Ginger, ginger,
Gingerbread Man.

Curtain.

The See-Saw Tree was originally commissioned by the Redgrave Theatre, Farnham. The first performance was given by the Farnham Repertory Company, sponsored by Arundell House Securities, on 18 March 1986, with the following cast:

Mrs Wise/Owl	Patricia Samuels
Mrs Dunnock/Dunnock	Alex Kingston
Mr Storer/Squirrel	Christopher Reeks
Mr Jay/Jay	Kit Thacker
Mr Batty/Bat	Paul Benzing
Mrs Thrush/Mistlethrush	Brenda Longman
Mrs Cook/Cuckoo	Sharon Courtney
Mr Bunn/Rabbit	Andrew Sargent

Directed by Stephen Barry and Kit Thacker
Designed by Juliet Shillingford
Musical direction by Peter Pontzen
Lighting by Vincent Herbert

The play was subsequently presented at Sadler's Wells Theatre, London, and on tour by Whirligig Theatre in the autumn of 1987, with the following cast:

Mrs Wise/Owl	Susannah Bray
Mrs Dunnock/Dunnock	Mary Ann Coburn
Mr Storer/Squirrel	Mike Elles
Mr Jay/Jay	Richard Hague
Mr Batty/Bat	Michael Seraphim
Mrs Thrush/Mistlethrush	Caroline High
Mrs Cook/Cuckoo	Shelaagh Ferrell
Mr Bunn/Rabbit	David Bale

Directed by David Wood
Designed by Susie Caulcutt
Musical supervision by Peter Pontzen
Musical direction by Michael Haslam
Lighting by Roger Frith

For Common Ground, the conservation group who sowed the seed

& THE GREEN MAN ·

TREES, WOODS · COMMON GROUND

IMAGE BY BEN NICHOLSON

I wish to acknowledge with gratitude the helpful advice given me by Jim Flegg, whose excellent book *Oakwatch* (published by Pelham Books) confirmed my belief that here was subject matter for a play, and encouraged me to proceed. The subsequent use of Jim Flegg as a sounding-board for ideas and as an oracle of the oak has been not only extremely useful but also most enjoyable. Thank you, Jim!

D.W.

Characters

Each actor plays two parts, the human role linked with the animal role.

ACTOR 1: **Mrs Wise**, *the Chairperson of the Parish Council. Solid, fair and authoritative.*
Owl, *the leader of the oak community.*

ACTOR 2: **Mrs Dunnock**, *Secretary of the Parish Council. Keeps a low profile. Efficient, helpful, knowledgeable, but unshowy.*
Dunnock, *a rather drab, hardworking bird, willing to perform menial tree tasks, cleaning, taking messages, etc.*

ACTOR 3: **Mr Storer**, *businesslike, financially orientated Treasurer of the Parish Council.*
Squirrel, *home-loving, conservative, occasionally excitable member of the tree community.*

ACTOR 4: **Mr Jay**, *rather flashy supermarket owner, smarmy businessman, ingratiating.*
Jay, *a flash itinerant member of the tree community, popping in and out almost as a travelling salesman, on the lookout for a good opportunity.*

ACTOR 5: **Mrs Thrush**, *a fairly outspoken woman, who takes public service seriously and loudly espouses a cause.*
Mistlethrush, *a strident member of the tree community, builder of untidy nests, not afraid to be outspoken.*

ACTOR 6: **Mrs Cook**, *not a local person, but not afraid to put her views. Might be regarded as somewhat common by the residents.*
Cuckoo, *an itinerant visitor to the tree, a colourful character from Africa, whose sole motive for visiting is to dump her egg in some unsuspecting bird's nest.*

ACTOR 7: **Mr Bunn**, *a concerned conservationist. Outspoken.*
Rabbit, *a member of the animals' underground movement. Resistance leader. Practical.*

ACTOR 8: **Mr Batty**, *entrepreneur, whizz-kid smooth operator.*

Bat, *hi-tech way-out member of the tree community. His radar comes in useful. He has big headphones connected to a 'Walkman' style radio.*

The play takes place in three locations:

1) A Village Hall
2) The Bottom of an Oak Tree
3) Further up the Oak Tree

Act One

As the audience arrives, the stage resembles a public platform with table and chairs.

Mrs Dunnock, *a few minutes before 'curtain up', sweeps the platform.*

Mrs Wise, *the Chairperson, arrives and bids 'Good-day' to* **Mrs Dunnock**, *then settles herself in the chair.*

Mr Jay *and* **Mr Storer** *also arrive, greet each other and* **Mrs Wise**, *then sit down.* **Mr Jay** *prepares some maps and pictures.*

In the auditorium, **Mr Batty**, **Mrs Thrush**, **Mrs Cook** *and* **Mr Bunn** *sit amongst the audience, near the front.*

When the play is due to start, **Mrs Dunnock** *rings a small bell, and takes her seat at the table, as Secretary, taking notes. The house lights stay up.*

Mrs Wise   Welcome, everybody, to this public meeting. Thank you for taking the trouble to come along to discuss the future of Turner's Field, the patch of waste land next to Jay's Supermarket. As Chairperson of the Parish Council, I invite you to make your views known. Mrs Dunnock, our Secretary, will make notes on the proceedings.

Mrs Dunnock (*shyly*)   Thank you, Mrs Wise. (*Correcting herself.*) Madam Chairman.

Mrs Wise   First, the Treasurer, Mr Storer, will outline our proposals.

Mr Storer   Thank you, Madam Chairman. As you may know, Turner's Field was left in his will to the Council by Farmer Turner, who died last year. For a long time it has been unused – except as an unofficial unsightly rubbish tip, and we feel the time has come to decide its future. We are pleased that Mr Jay, here –

Mr Jay (*smiling broadly, almost smarmily*)   Good afternoon.

Mr Storer   – the owner of the supermarket, has offered a substantial sum for the land, and, let's face it, the Council desperately needs the cash to help improve local services . . .

Mrs Thrush (*from the floor, standing*)   Hear, hear. They could do with it. Our road's in a shocking state. Like driving on cobblestones . . .

Mr Storer   Yes, indeed. So, Mr Jay, please reveal your plans.

Mr Jay (*rising*)   Certainly, Mr Storer. As you know, Jay's Supermarket aims to provide a service. High quality, low prices, that's our motto. For some time, in our quest to make shopping a happy, *family* experience, we have improved our facilities – more tills for speedier checkouts, easy-push trolleys, music to soothe the harassed housewife. And now, in our usual caring way, we propose to create, (*Showing a map.*) on Turner's Field . . . guess what?

Mrs Cook (*from the floor, standing*)   More car parking space. That's what's needed. I'm not a local, but I come here to shop and it's always a dreadful problem finding a space, then humping the shopping to the car . . .

Mr Jay   Maybe, Mrs er –

Mrs Cook   Cook.

Mr Jay   Cook. Maybe. But, may I be so bold – do you have children?

Mrs Cook   Yes, but I never bring *them* here. They get bored. I leave them with a friend.

Mr Jay   Exactly. They get bored. That's why we propose to create a children's playground, where our customers' children can safely play till the shopping is successfully accomplished.

Mrs Thrush   I support that. There's so little for the kids to do in this place. Not even a cinema any more.

Mrs Wise   Yes, well, Mrs er –

Mrs Thrush   Thrush.

Mrs Wise   Mrs Thrush. Thank you. Let's have a vote.
Please raise your hands if you like Mr Jay's idea of a
children's playground. (*She encourages the audience to raise their
hands.*) Fine. Thank you.

Whatever the outcome . . .

Mr Bunn (*from the floor, standing*)   Madam Chairman,
before I vote, could I know more of what this playground
will be like? Will it be an adventure playground? Swings,
slides, that type of thing?

Mrs Wise   Mr Jay.

Mr Jay   Ah, yes, well to answer that, may I, Madam
Chairman, invite Mr Batty to speak? I will be giving Mr
Batty the concession to create the playground and operate
it.

Mr Bunn   Concession? You mean this is a business deal?

Mr Jay   Well, life's a business, Mr er –

Mr Bunn   Bunn.

Mr Jay   Mr Bunn. Mr Batty, please . . .

Mr Batty *joins the others on the platform. He displays a diagram.*

Mr Batty   Yes, well, like I'm going to clear the land and
have an open play area with swings and slides, all free for
the use of, plus a special building for the machines.

Mr Bunn   Machines?

Mr Batty   Yes. The space invaders, the pin tables, the
fruit machines . . .

Mrs Wise   And, Mr Batty, will these be er . . . free for the
use of?

Mr Batty   Ah. Well. No. Like I've got to make a living,
Madam Chairman.

Mr Jay   Seems fair enough to me. Only providing what the kids of today really want.

Mr Bunn   So, Mr Batty, you are going to clear the land, are you?

Mr Batty   Yes.

Mr Bunn   On that land are several trees. Healthy trees.

Mr Batty   Can't help that. They'll have to come down.

Mr Bunn   But one of those trees is an oak. It's been there for nearly three hundred years.

Mr Batty   So what?

Mr Bunn   So what? (*He goes on to the platform.*) That tree has a history. In the old days people called it the See-Saw Tree.

Mr Batty   The See-Saw Tree?

Mr Bunn   The See-Saw Tree.

Lighting changes. **Mr Bunn** *remains in a pin-spot, while the rest of the stage grows dark. The actors clear the stage as* **Mr Bunn** *speaks.*

One of its branches grew straight out, near to the ground. Children used to balance a plank over the branch and use it as a see-saw. The villagers loved that oak. And the tree was itself like a village. A living community of animals, birds and insects, going about their daily business. It still is.

During the following speech, an actor hands **Mr Bunn** *his 'Rabbit' costume and, if necessary, helps him on with it.*

Just imagine what that community will feel like should it be threatened. Just imagine what might happen if Mr Jay's plan went ahead and Mr Batty was allowed to cut down that oak tree, that special oak tree. Just imagine. (*Echo effect.*) Just imagine, just imagine . . .

The lighting changes as the curtains part to reveal the base of the oak tree. The trunk is wide, bearing in mind that the characters are small. Various knob-like shapes and root formations sprout from the bottom, which might be used as 'seats'. The entrance to **Rabbit**'*s burrow is incorporated. Ivy climbing the tree could afford masking for scaffolding or ladder-like rungs, down which and up which the characters can climb. Foliage is visible above. A few acorns lie on the ground. Grass grows around the roots. A large white cross has been painted or chalked on the trunk.*

Mr Bunn *becomes* **Rabbit**.

It is dawn. A chorus of birdsong is heard.

Rabbit *chooses a likely blade of grass and begins eating it. He makes for his burrow, but suddenly sees the white cross. Mystified, he approaches it and stretches up to feel it. It is still wet. He examines the paint on his paw, then looks at the cross again.*

Suddenly **Dunnock**'*s head peers through the foliage above.*

Dunnock   Morning, Rabbit.

Rabbit *jumps and turns.*

Rabbit   Oh it's you, Dunnock. Morning. You're up early.

Dunnock   Lots to do, Rabbit. A Dunnock's work is never done. Owl's hollow to clean, Squirrel's drey to muck out . . .

Rabbit (*idea*)   Squirrel?

Dunnock   Yes, he's doing his annual acorn tally. Stock-taking. Takes it so seriously . . .

Rabbit   Dunnock, give him a message, will you? It's urgent.

Dunnock   S'pose so. If he's in.

Rabbit   Please. There's a mystery to solve.

Dunnock   How exciting. The only mystery I've got to solve is how I'm going to get all my jobs done. You've no idea how –

Rabbit   Go. Now. Tell Squirrel to meet me here. As soon as possible.

Dunnock   All right, all right. Keep your fur on. (*Disappearing.*) Dear oh dear oh dear.

Dunnock *exits.*

Rabbit (*to himself*)   Silly little bird.

Sudden noises from a distance make **Rabbit** *turn and listen eagerly. Heavy vehicles approaching. Headlamps swing across the stage momentarily dazzling* **Rabbit**. *The vehicles stop. Doors bang. Distant voices are heard.*

Voice 1   Right, lads. Cup of tea. Then unload.

Voice 2   OK. Brew up, Charlie.

Voice 3   Righto.

Voice 4 (*singing*)   Charlie put the kettle on . . .

Laughter. **Rabbit** *listens transfixed.*

Rabbit (*to himself*)   Big Ones.

He scuttles to his burrow and disappears.

The noises of the **Big Ones** *recede.*

Squirrel *descends the tree.*

Squirrel   Make it snappy, Rabbit. I can't afford to dilly dally, shilly shally, mystery or no mystery. (*He notices* **Rabbit** *is not there.*) Rabbit? Rabbit. (*He goes to the burrow entrance. Calling.*) Rabbit? (*Louder.*) Rabbit? (*He gives up and calls up the tree.*) Dunnock?

Pause.

Dunnock!

Dunnock *appears through the foliage.*

Dunnock   Dear oh dear oh dear. What is it, Squirrel?

Squirrel   Play a little game with me, would you?

Dunnock   I beg your pardon?

Squirrel   Play a little game with me, would you?

Dunnock   Sorry, Squirrel, too busy. Didn't know you liked games. Ask Rabbit to play with you.

Squirrel   No!

Dunnock   He likes games.

Squirrel   No, you bird of little brain. I mean, is this your idea of a joke?

Dunnock   Joke?

Squirrel   Leading me on a wild rabbit chase.

Dunnock   Sorry, you've lost me.

Squirrel   I've lost Rabbit.

Dunnock   Him too? Dear oh dear. Where is he?

Squirrel   If I knew that, I wouldn't be saying I'd lost him. He's not here. You really are very thick, Dunnock.

Dunnock   There's no call for rudeness. Rabbit wanted to see you about some mystery.

Squirrel   The mystery is, where's Rabbit?

Dunnock   Search me, Squirrel.

She disappears.

Squirrel *tries the burrow again.*

Squirrel (*calling*)   Rabbit!

No reply. **Squirrel** *goes to leave. He spies an acorn.*

Ah!

(*Picking it up.*) At least it's not a totally wasted journey. (*He goes to climb the tree, and suddenly sees the white cross. He reacts mystified, then, like* **Rabbit** *earlier, stretches up to feel it. He, too, gets paint on his paw. Bemused, he climbs back up the tree, carrying his acorn. As he climbs.*) Out of my way, Dunnock.

Squirrel *disappears.*

Dunnock (*off*)   Charming. (*Calling after him.*) It's not my fault he's not there.

Dunnock *reappears through the foliage and climbs down the trunk.*

(*To herself.*) Hope he's all right. It's not like him to be unreliable. He did seem in a bit of a state, though. (*She goes to the burrow and calls down it.*) Rabbit? Rabbit! Are you there? I took your message. Rabbit!

Rabbit *enters from off-stage – from the direction in which the* **Big Ones**' *voices came from. He is breathless and agitated.*

(*Still looking down the burrow.*) Rabbit!

Rabbit   What are you doing?

Dunnock (*turning*)   Looking for Rabbit. (*Turning back and calling down the burrow.*) Rabbit!

Rabbit   Yes?

Dunnock   What? Oh it's you! Silly me. Where did you spring from?

Rabbit   My back door. Over there. Where's Squirrel?

Dunnock   He's been and gone.

Rabbit   Been and gone?

Dunnock   Arrived and departed.

Rabbit   But I haven't spoken to him yet.

Dunnock   That's on account of the fact that you weren't here when he arrived. He arrived after you departed. *You* arrived after *he* departed. A matter of bad timing, if you ask me.

Rabbit   I'm not asking you, Dunnock, I'm telling you, to get Squirrel down here. Now.

Dunnock   Again?

Rabbit   Quickly, please. It's serious.

Dunnock   It *is*. I'll never get my jobs done at this rate.

Rabbit   Go!

Dunnock   Oh, all right.

Rabbit   Hurry!

Dunnock (*climbing the tree*)   Dear oh dear oh dear oh dear.

Dunnock *disappears.*

As **Rabbit** *watches her depart, the noises of the* **Big Ones** *return.*
Rabbit *freezes.*

Voice 1   Right, lads, the party's over. We got a job to do.

Voice 2   OK. Unload the gear.

Voice 1   Shift yourself, Charlie!

Laughter.

Rabbit *reacts frightened and scampers down his burrow.*

*As he does so, the lights fade. The noise of heavy mechanical gear being
unloaded, and an engine being turned on, fills the air and increases in
intensity as the scene change takes place. The base of the tree disappears
(flown or revolved) and the main set, halfway up the tree, is revealed.*

*It incorporates several levels, dominated by, at stage level, the 'hollow'
– the home of* **Owl***. This should include a closed-off section, which
could be like a hut, complete with door; however, it might be more
appropriate, and less fantasy-orientated, to have a section partitioned off
by a leafy equivalent of a bead curtain.* **Owl***'s hollow becomes the
dominant acting area, in which meetings of the tree community take
place. Other important locations are a hole in the trunk, in which*
Squirrel *has his drey, an upper level, partly covered with foliage,
where* **Mistlethrush** *has her nest, and a branch the other side from
which* **Bat** *can 'hang'. The actor playing* **Bat** *should appear to be
upside down, with his head on his arms. Branches should provide
walkways between these locations, perhaps using scaffolding and steps
disguised with leaves and ivy.*

As the noises of the **Big Ones**' *working recede, lighting reveals*
Dunnock *climbing towards* **Squirrel***'s drey. She carries cleaning*

implements — brush (made of twigs) and dusters (made from leaves).
The brush could be strapped on her back. She whistles as she climbs.

As **Dunnock** *reaches* **Squirrel**'s *drey, we hear his voice from*
inside.

Squirrel (*inside*)   Twenty-three, twenty-four, twenty-five . . .

Dunnock   Excuse me. Squirrel.

Squirrel (*inside*)   Twenty-five, twenty-six . . .

Dunnock (*louder*)   Squirrel!

Squirrel   What is it? I'm busy. Twenty . . .

Dunnock   It's Rabbit.

Squirrel (*popping out, carrying acorns, or perhaps an improvised*
abacus)   Rabbit? Where?

Dunnock   Down there.

Squirrel   Down where?

Dunnock   Down there. Waiting.

Squirrel   Oh not again. Where was I? Twenty-five?
Twenty-six? I've lost count now. I'll have to start all over
again.

Dunnock   Sorry, Squirrel.

Squirrel   *You're* sorry? My annual acorn tally's important,
Dunnock. I don't do it for fun. Winter has a nasty habit of
creeping up on us. I must be prepared. It's serious.

Dunnock   I know, Squirrel. But Rabbit's serious too. I've
never seen him so serious.

Squirrel   Oh, very well. But this is the last time. Up,
down, up, down.

Dunnock   Life's full of them, they say.

Squirrel   What?

Dunnock   Ups and downs. Shall I clean out your drey while you're gone?

Squirrel   Yes, please, Dunnock. But don't interfere with my acorns, please. They're all sorted.

Dunnock   Right. Mind how you go.

Squirrel *climbs down, round the trunk and out of sight.*

Squirrel (*as he goes*)   Dilly dally, shilly shally . . .

Squirrel *disappears.*

Dunnock *starts sweeping the entrance to the drey. Suddenly, from above her, comes a strident, shrill, out-of-tune singing, the sort of singing that human beings might practise in the bath. It is* **Mistlethrush**.

Mistlethrush   La la la la laaaah!
                   La la la la laaaah!

A bundle of nesting material falls from above on or near **Dunnock**. *She reacts irritated, and sweeps it up.*

                   Spring, spring
                   Makes me sing
                   My happy tuneful song.

More nesting material descends on **Dunnock**.

Dunnock   What's going on up there? (*She clears up the nesting material.*)

Mistlethrush   La la la la laaaah!
                   La la la la laaah!

More nesting material falls.

Dunnock (*calling*)   Hey! Up there, whoever you are.

Foliage parts, revealing **Mistlethrush** *in the throes of making her nest. She untidily builds it around her in a slap-dash manner. She leans out.*

Mistlethrush   'Allo, dearie.

Dunnock   Oh it's you, Mistlethrush. Morning.

Mistlethrush   Nice one! (*She sets to work on her nest again, slapping on grass and twigs and odd shreds of Polythene bag material. She sings even more stridently.*)

> Spring, spring
> Makes me sing
> 'Cos summer won't be long!

More nesting material gets flung out on to and around **Dunnock***, who gamely tries to collect it.*

Dunnock   Mistlethrush, must you be so messy?

Mistlethrush   Sorry, dearie, I'm building my nest.

Dunnock   I can see that. (*Holding up the fallen nesting material she has collected.*) I thought you were building it down here for a moment.

Mistlethrush   Sorry, dearie. Just getting sorted out. Be a love and bring me those bits back.

Dunnock (*resigned*)   On my way. (*She climbs up to* **Mistlethrush***'s nest.*)

Mistlethrush   Got some lovely bits of plasticy stuff this year. Big Ones leave it behind after their picnics. Very good stuff for insulting, that, my fella says.

Dunnock   Insulting?

Mistlethrush   Yeah, insulting, infiltrating, something like that.

Dunnock   Insulating.

Mistlethrush   Exactly! Keeps the eggs warm. And the babies when they hatch. (*Receiving the nesting material from* **Dunnock***.*) Ta, dearie. You're a treasure. (*She starts building again, making a terrible mess.*) Now, this bit here, that bit there. Whoops! Lost that bit.

Dunnock   Do you want a bit of help?

Mistlethrush   Oh, would you? I'm not much good at it, am I? Funny, I'm not what you'd call domesticized . . .

Dunnock   Domesticated.

Mistlethrush   Exactly. But come springtime I get this feeling, all warm and cosy and material . . .

Dunnock   Maternal.

Mistlethrush   Exactly. And I fling myself into a flavour of activity getting ready for the big day. Oo, I can't wait. What about you, dearie? Are you laying this year?

Dunnock   In a few weeks, I expect.

She works away. **Mistlethrush** *does very little.*

Mistlethrush   Lovely. Listen, I've written this pretty little lullaby for my babies. I'll teach it to you. Might come in useful. (*She sings, loudly and off-key.*)

> Hush your beak
> Close your eyes
> Go to sleep
> And rest all the rest of you
> Mum is tired
> Don't squawk or squeak
> Hush your beak.

Dunnock *has listened with a pained, patient expression.*

Good, innit? That'll nod 'em off in no time.

Dunnock   I think it might keep them awake!

Mistlethrush   Eh?

Dunnock   It's excruciating.

Mistlethrush   Exactly. Knew you'd like it. (*Looking at her nest.*) Oo, you are getting on a treat. A palace! Ta, dearie, everso. (*She starts to sing again – a dreadful din.*)

> Spring, spring –

Dunnock (*interrupting*)   I'd, er, better be off. Squirrel's drey to muck out. (*She starts to leave.*)

Mistlethrush   Bye, dearie. (*Singing.*)

> Spring, spring
> Makes me sing
> My happy tuneful song

She works away on her nest again as **Dunnock** *descends and enters* **Squirrel**'s *drey. More nesting material falls down.*

> Spring, spring
> Makes me sing
> 'Cos summer won't be looooooooong!

Suddenly **Jay** *arrives – on the branch below, near* **Squirrel**'s *drey. He is brashly confident, and carries a kind of 'suitcase' for his wares.*

Jay   What music fills my ears?

Mistlethrush (*looking down*)   Who's that?

Jay   Such tone. Such pitch. Such artistry.

Mistlethrush   Ooh! You flashy flatterer.

Jay   Jay's the name, madam. Travelling salesbird supreme.

Mistlethrush   I know you! Long time no see.

Jay   I have been on a flight of exploration, madam, spreading my wings far and wide in search of marketable merchandise. Scouring the countryside for new and exciting lines to offer my lucky customers at bargain prices. What do you fancy?

Mistlethrush   Nothing, dearie. I'm too busy building my nest.

Jay   Aha! See my selection, perfect for the use of. (*He opens his coat. Inside his wares are neatly displayed.*) Dried grasses, bracken, quality mosses, badger hair, sheep's wool for extra warmth, polythene and paper. Pick your own, mix 'n' match, yours for the modest sum of two acorns. Can't say fairer than that.

Mistlethrush   Not today, thank you, Jay.

Jay   Do me a favour.

Mistlethrush   I've got all I need, dearie. I'm almost ready to lay.

Jay   Aha! Think ahead, madam. Think of when your eggs hatch. Think of all those hungry little beaks to feed. No problem. (*He opens the other side of his coat, revealing more merchandise.*) I've got crab apples, juicy slugs, calorie-stuffed caterpillars, mouthwatering worms, specially selected spiders, meaty maggots and crunchy moths. Take your pick.

Mistlethrush   Sorry, dearie, come back next week.

Jay   Your loss, dear lady, not mine. Happy laying.

Mistlethrush   Tata, Jay.

She disappears into her nest, dropping more nesting material by **Jay**. *He eagerly picks it up, then drops it.*

Jay   Ugh. Most inferior. (*He thinks again.*) Might sell it second-hand. (*He approaches* **Squirrel**'s *drey.*) Wakey, wakey! Anyone at home?

Dunnock *appears, carrying rubbish from the drey.*

Dunnock   Not today, thank you, Jay.

Jay   Give a bird a chance, Dunnock! Where's Squirrel?

Dunnock   Out. I'm doing his cleaning.

Jay   Aha! Glad you said that. Ideal for the use of. (*He opens his suitcase, displaying more wares.*) Look at this little lot. Bark scourer, lichen loosener, fungus flusher, mildew stripper, leafmould remover. Tried and tested. Satisfaction guaranteed.

Dunnock   No thanks.

Jay   I'm only asking one acorn per item.

Dunnock   I've got no acorns. Squirrel's your best bet for acorns. He's got stacks of them in there.

Jay   Really?

Dunnock   Nightmare it is trying to clean round them, believe you me.

Jay (*apparently sympathetic*)   I'm sure, I'm sure.

Dunnock   Now, if you'll excuse me, I must get rid of Squirrel's rubbish. (*She sees* **Mistlethrush**'s *nesting material.*) Oh, no. (*To herself.*) Mistlethrush, I've just cleaned this branch. Dear oh dear oh dear.

She passes **Jay** *and starts clearing up. She doesn't notice* **Jay** *take the opportunity to enter* **Squirrel**'s *drey. He checks no-one is looking, then darts inside, returning almost immediately carrying two acorns.* **Dunnock** *finishes clearing and turns round.* **Jay** *hastily hides the acorns.*

You still here?

Jay   Er . . . thought I'd wait for Squirrel. Any idea when he'll be back?

Dunnock   Anybody's guess. I must get on, anyway. Owl's hollow to muck out yet. See you.

Jay   Good day, dear lady.

Dunnock *sets off for* **Owl**'s *hollow. When she arrives, she disappears inside the inner sanctum.*

Jay *stows away the two acorns in his suitcase or in his pockets. He checks the coast is clear and pops back inside* **Squirrel**'s *drey.*

Suddenly **Squirrel** *appears, scrambling up from behind the tree. He is breathless and agitated.*

Squirrel (*calling*)   Owl! Owl!

He goes towards **Owl**'s *hollow, as* **Jay** *emerges from the drey with two more acorns.* **Squirrel** *doesn't see* **Jay**, *who nervously pops back in the drey.*

Owl!

Dunnock *appears from* **Owl**'s *inner sanctum.*

(*Shouting.*) Where's Owl?

Dunnock   Owl's out.

Squirrel   She would be.

Dunnock   See Rabbit?

Squirrel   Yes, yes. Where is she?

Dunnock   Still hunting, I dare say.

Squirrel   Never around when she's needed.

Dunnock   Don't blame me, Squirrel. I only work here.

Squirrel   I know, Dunnock. I'm sorry, but it's urgent.

Jay *sees his chance. He hurries out with two acorns, grabs his things and hides behind the trunk, unseen by* **Squirrel**.

Dunnock   It's always urgent.

Squirrel (*shouting*)   It's *very* urgent.

Mistlethrush (*leaning out of her nest*)   Excuse me. Could I ask you to lower your voices?

Squirrel   Don't you start, Mistlethrush.

Mistlethrush   That's just it, dearie. I *have* started. My eggs are coming and I have to conserve.

Dunnock   Concentrate.

Mistlethrush   Exactly. So, please. A bit of hush for Mistlethrush. (*She disappears.*)

Squirrel (*in a loud whisper*)   Dunnock! Please. Let me know the moment Owl gets back.

Dunnock   Right. (*She goes back into* **Owl**'s *inner sanctum.*)

Squirrel (*muttering as he returns to his drey*)   What a day! (*He enters his drey.*) What a – (*With a shriek.*) What on earth? (*He darts out again. Calling.*) Dunnock! Dunnock!

Mistlethrush *leans out of her nest.*

Mistlethrush   Hush, please!

Squirrel   Sorry, Mistlethrush.

Mistlethrush *flounces out of sight.*

(*Calling.*) Dunnock!

Dunnock *emerges from* **Owl***'s inner sanctum as* **Squirrel** *arrives.*

Dunnock   Not again. I told you. Owl's out.

Squirrel   I know, I know, you silly little bird. Listen, I thought I asked you not to interfere with my acorns.

Dunnock   You did and I didn't. Devil of a job I had cleaning round them.

Squirrel   They're not all there.

Dunnock   *You're* not all there, if you ask me. Been funny all morning.

Jay *creeps back from behind the tree, and enters* **Squirrel***'s drey again.*

Squirrel   Come with me. I'll show you. (*He drags* **Dunnock** *towards his drey.*)

Come on.

Dunnock   Oh dear, oh dear. Calm down, Squirrel.

Squirrel   I'm perfectly calm. I –

He is cut short by the sight of **Jay** *emerging from the drey, carrying another two acorns.*

Thief! Thief!

Jay   Ah! No! I can explain.

Squirrel   Caught in the act!

Jay   No, no. Listen, Squirrel. I er . . . I lost my way.

Squirrel   Lost your way? I've lost my acorns. You've stolen them!

Jay   No, no, no. These are *my* acorns.

Squirrel   Your acorns?

Jay   Yes. I was hoping to sell them to you. You're one of my best customers.

Squirrel   Liar!

Jay   Squirrel, please! My reputation!

Squirrel   Clear off!

Jay   You're making a big mistake!

Squirrel   Clear off!

Dunnock *looks on philosophically as* **Mistlethrush** *looks down from her nest.*

Mistlethrush (*shrill*)   Will you shut up!

The others freeze in surprise.

Have a little consternation.

Dunnock   Consideration.

Mistlethrush   Exactly.

Squirrel   Sorry, Mistlethrush. Serious business down here.

Mistlethrush   It's not exactly a barrel of laughs up here! Laying eggs is a very painful progress.

Dunnock   Process.

Mistlethrush   Exactly. And you can shut up too, cleverdick Dunnock. Ooh! (*A cry of pain as her labour pains force her back into the nest.*)

Dunnock   I'd better go up and help her.

Dunnock *climbs up to* **Mistlethrush**. *Both remain hidden behind the foliage.*

Squirrel (*to* **Jay**)   You see the havoc you cause?

Jay   Havoc? Have a heart, Squirrel. Just a bit of honest trading.

Squirrel   Honest? You stand there holding my acorns and call it honest?

Jay   Yes. Well. Perhaps I overstepped the mark. Call it quits, eh? (*He hands the acorns back to* **Squirrel**.)

Squirrel   Call it what you like. Just flap your wings and fly away. (*He throws an acorn at* **Jay**.)

Jay   All right. All right. Keep calm.

Squirrel   I'm perfectly calm! (*He throws another acorn.*)

Jay   Ow! You've made your point!

Squirrel *quickly gets more ammunition from inside the drey, and throws it.*

Squirrel   Scarper!

Jay   Ow!

Squirrel   Now!

(*N.B. In the original production, to really throw the acorns proved impractical:* **Squirrel** *mimed throwing in threatening fashion, and* **Jay** *reacted.*)

He has forced **Jay** *back towards* **Owl***'s hollow.*

Suddenly they are both frozen by the appearance of **Owl** *from her inner sanctum.*

Owl   Enough!

Both **Squirrel** *and* **Jay** *react nervously.*

Squirrel   Sorry, Owl.

Jay   No harm meant.

Owl   I will not suffer brawling. This is a civilized tree.

Squirrel   Yes, Owl.

Owl   We are a civilized society.

Jay   Yes, Owl.

Pause.

Squirrel   Good hunting, Owl?

Owl   Disastrous. (*Threateningly.*) I'm starving.

Squirrel   Oh dear.

Jay   May I be of service, Owl? (*He opens his coat.*)
Caterpillar? Slug? Very tasty.

Owl   Insubstantial. Junk food. Do you have a mouse?

Jay   Er, no. But I could do you a vole.

Owl *advances, as* **Jay** *starts to delve in his suitcase.* **Owl** *simply takes the suitcase, calmly turns and heads back to her hollow.*

Owl   Thank you, Jay.

Jay   That's four acorns, please.

Owl (*turning threateningly*)   I beg your pardon?

Jay (*nervously*)   Four acorns?

Owl   No, thank you.

Jay   I meant . . .

Owl (*charmingly threatening*)   But I'm sure Squirrel would
appreciate four acorns.

Jay   But Owl!

Owl   Now.

Jay (*defeated*)   Yes. Yes. My pleasure. Here you are,
Squirrel. (*He hands over the acorns he stole earlier.*) One, two,
three, four.

Squirrel   Thank you, Jay. How generous. Good day.

Owl   Good day, Jay.

Jay *mumbles and disappears behind the tree.*

Squirrel   Thanks, Owl.

Owl   I think justice prevailed.

Squirrel   Yes, indeed. Er . . . Owl, could I have an urgent word? You see . . .

Owl   Not now, Squirrel. Hunting makes me tired. Unsuccessful hunting makes me exhausted.

Squirrel   Yes, but –

A sudden scream of pain from **Mistlethrush***'s nest above.*

Mistlethrush   Aaaaagh!

Owl (*with a jump*)   What on earth's that?

Squirrel   Mistlethrush laying. It's a painful process.

Owl   I know the feeling.

Dunnock *leans from above, by the nest.*

Dunnock (*excited*)   One egg laid. Number two coming! (*She sees* **Owl**.) Morning, Owl, I've cleaned your hollow.

Owl   Thank you, Dunnock.

Another shriek from **Mistlethrush***.*

Mistlethrush   Aaaaaah!

Dunnock   Excuse me. (*She disappears to help* **Mistlethrush**.)

Owl (*yawning*)   See you later, Squirrel. (*She turns to go.*)

Squirrel   But please, Owl, it's important. Let me –

Owl   Later, Squirrel, later.

Squirrel   But *please*, you see, Rabbit –

Another interruption. Loud singing:

Bat (*from behind the tree*)
> You gotta keep
> Hanging on
> Baby
> Gotta keep

> Hanging on . . .

Owl   Oh no, Bat's back!

Bat *enters, heavily 'into' the rock song playing (unheard by us) through his large headphones. A 'Walkman'-style battery pack is attached to his belt.*

Bat   You gotta keep
Hanging on
Baby
Gotta keep
Hanging on . . .

As though in a trance, he jigs up and down, making loud percussion-type noises in accompaniment to the music.

> Shubba dubba boom boom
> Shubba dubba wow!

Owl   He's in one of his trances again. Wake him up.

Squirrel *goes to* **Bat** *and waves frantically at him.* **Dunnock** *peers down to see what all the noise is about.*

Squirrel   Bat! Bat!

Bat   Be-dum dum dum dum
Pow!

He nearly knocks **Squirrel** *over.*

> You gotta keep
> Hanging on –

In desperation **Squirrel** *pulls the plug out of the battery pack.* **Bat** *immediately stops dancing.*

Hey, Squirrel, baby, you turned me off! I was all turned on and in the groove. In the groove and on the move. Pow! Pow! Pow! My, what a night! (*He sees* **Owl**.) Hi, Owl, baby!

Owl   Don't baby me, Bat. Where have you been? You stink.

Bat I've been raving, Owl baby. Down the Battery Disco Tree. Where all the best bats hang out. The joint was jumping and I was flying.

Owl He's high as a kite. Go to your perch and sleep it off. Help him, Squirrel.

Bat I'd far sooner swing in your cosy little hollow, Owl baby.

He tries to reach it, but **Squirrel** *leads him away to his perch.*

Owl You come near my cosy little hollow and I'll swallow you for breakfast.

Bat OK, Owl baby. Don't get uptight, right? (*He tries to perch upside down.*) Let it all hang out, like little old me.

He keeps losing his balance. **Squirrel** *tries to help him. He sings jerkily.*

> You gotta keep . . .
> Hanging on . . .
> Baby . . .
> Gotta keep . . .
> Hanging . . . on . . .

He finally balances and starts snoring. **Squirrel** *returns to* **Owl**.

Owl Did I say this was a civilized tree? A civilized society? Sometimes I wonder.

Squirrel *I* wonder, Owl, if you could please listen . . .

Owl I've told you, Squirrel.

Squirrel ⎫ But it's vital that you listen. Rabbit has
news. *The Big Ones* . . .
⎬ (*together*)
Owl ⎭ I want some rest. Now go away and
leave me alone –

Owl The Big Ones? (*She pays attention immediately.*)

Squirrel Yes.

Owl What? Where?

Squirrel   I don't know, but Rabbit says please come.

Owl   Why didn't you tell me before?

Squirrel   I tried, Owl, I did try.

Owl (*preparing to leave*)   I'll meet you down there. I don't like flying so low in broad daylight, but it's a risk I'll have to take.

She disappears round the trunk, preparing to fly down.

Squirrel   Thank you, Owl.

Squirrel *hastens to climb down the tree. He disappears.*

Jay *emerges from hiding. He checks the coast is clear, laughs softly, retrieves his suitcase from* **Owl***'s hollow, then enters* **Squirrel***'s drey.*

Bat *wakes and looks at* **Owl***'s hollow.*

Bat (*delighted*)   Owl's out! Groovy! (*He goes down to it and settles upside down, enjoying the comfort.*)

Suddenly a shriek from above – **Mistlethrush.**

Mistlethrush   Aaaaaah!

Bat *loses his balance and topples.* **Jay** *pops his head out of the drey in alarm.* **Dunnock** *leans out over* **Mistlethrush***'s nest.*

Dunnock   Two!

Black-out.

As the scene changes back to the base of the tree, we hear the grating mechanical sound of a digger. The sounds continue as the lights come up on the base of the tree.

Squirrel *is descending. He goes to* **Rabbit***'s burrow.*

Squirrel (*calling*)   Rabbit! Owl's coming! Rabbit!

Owl *arrives, as though she has just landed.*

Owl (*tense*)   Where is he?

Squirrel   He'll be here. Look, Owl. The mystery. (*He shows* **Owl** *the white cross.*) What does it mean?

Owl   I wish I knew, Squirrel. (*Suddenly.*) What's that noise?

The digger noise increases. **Owl** *and* **Squirrel** *listen intently. Then, distant voices.*

Voice 1   Another one over here, Tom.

Voice 2   OK. (*Calling.*) Charlie. More earth. Get a move on.

Voice 3   Coming.

Owl   Rabbit was right. Big Ones.

Suddenly **Rabbit** *emerges from his burrow, caked with earth and terrified.*

Rabbit (*breathless and almost hysterical*)   No! No! Please! No!

Squirrel   Rabbit, Owl's here.

Rabbit   Owl, Owl. Tell me I'm dreaming. Tell me it's not true. It can't be true! Help me! Help me!

Owl   Pull yourself together, Rabbit. What's happened?

Rabbit   I tried. I did try. There was nothing I could do. Murderers! Murderers!

Owl   Rabbit! Tell us. Calmly.

Rabbit   Big Ones. Filling in the burrow. Earth pouring down. Friends and relatives struggling, suffocating. Buried alive. (*He breaks down, sobbing, and collapses into* **Squirrel***'s arms.*)

Squirrel   He's fainted. Oh, Owl, what are we going to do?

Owl   Back up the tree, quick.

Squirrel   What about Rabbit?

Owl   Him too.

Squirrel   Up there? But how, Owl, how?

Owl   Like before.

Squirrel   Before?

Owl (*taking hold of* **Rabbit**)   Before you were born,
Squirrel. One winter it rained for days. The waters rose and
flooded out Rabbit's burrow. I lifted Rabbit and his friends
and relatives to safety in the tree till it was over. Emergency
rescue. Like this one.

The noise of the digger and earth pouring into the burrow interrupt.
Owl *and* **Squirrel** *react.*

See you at the hollow. And Squirrel.

Squirrel   Yes, Owl?

Owl   Get Dunnock to call a crisis meeting!

Squirrel *starts to climb.* **Owl** *prepares for take-off, grasping*
Rabbit *firmly.*

*The lighting fades and the scene changes back to half-way up the tree.
Meanwhile, noises increase and become more menacing. Regular beat of
the generator. Then voices.*

Voice 1   Ready for the main action, Tom?

Voice 2   Ready, boss.

Voice 1   Got enough cable?

Voice 2   Reckon so.

Voice 3   Where do we start, boss?

Voice 1   Small ones first. Work up to the big one, eh?

Voice 3   Right.

Laughter.

The lights fade up. **Bat** *is snoring, asleep in* **Owl**'s *hollow.* **Jay** *is
stuffing acorns into his suitcase. Suddenly,* **Mistlethrush** *bursts
into song.*

Mistlethrush (*hidden*)
                    La la la la laaaaah!

Jay *and* **Bat** *react.*

(*Appearing, jubilant.*)

La la la la laaaaah!
Spring, spring
Makes me sing
A celebration song.

Jay (*wincing*)   Wish I had your headphones, Bat!

But **Bat** *is asleep again.*

Mistlethrush   Spring, spring
My eggs are laid
And they'll hatch before too long.

Dunnock *appears by the nest.*

Dunnock   Congratulations, Mistlethrush. Four eggs!

Mistlethrush   Ta, dearie. And thanks for all your help.

Dunnock   Fancy a bite to eat?

Jay (*who has been listening*)   How's about some fresh mistletoe berries, Mistlethrush?

Mistlethrush   Oo, my favourites. How much?

Jay   No charge, Mistlethrush. My present to congratulate you on a safe delivery.

Mistlethrush   Oo, ta. (*Imitating him.*) Can't say fairer than that!

Dunnock   I'll get them for you.

She starts to go down to **Jay**, *who finds the berries.*

Squirrel *scampers up to the hollow.*

Squirrel   Right. Action stations, everyone!

Dunnock   You still at it, Squirrel? Up, down, up, down.

Squirrel   Dunnock, Owl says you're to call a meeting.

Dunnock   A meeting? Why?

Squirrel   You'll find out. It's an emergency.

Dunnock   Oh dear. Right. Come on, everybody.
Meeting. (*She goes to* **Bat**.) Wake up, you smelly Bat. (*Lifting
one of his earphones.*) Wake up! Meeting.

Bat *overbalances.*

Bat   OK, OK. Stay cool, Dunnock.

Squirrel (*to* **Jay**)   You still here?

Jay   Just on my way.

Squirrel   You'd better stay. (*Calling up.*) Mistlethrush!

Dunnock   She's just laid her eggs.

Squirrel   Can't help that. (*Calling.*) Mistlethrush! Down
here.

Mistlethrush (*leaning out*)   Don't be daft, dearie. Can't
leave my eggs.

Squirrel   Owl's orders.

Mistlethrush   But –

Squirrel   Emergency.

Dunnock   Cover the eggs up. Keep them warm.

Jay (*seeing the seriousness of the situation*)   Take her all this stuff.
That'll help. (*He opens his coat, revealing the nesting material.*)

Dunnock   Thank you, Jay.

She takes the nesting material and hurries up to **Mistlethrush**.
*During the next section we see both birds carefully covering the eggs in
the nest.*

Squirrel (*to* **Bat**, *who has gone back to sleep*)   Bat!

Bat   I'm up! I'm up!

Owl *and* **Rabbit** *enter round the trunk to the hollow.* **Rabbit** *is
conscious but weak. He crumples into the hollow, watched by the
others.*

Owl   Everybody here?

Squirrel   Mistlethrush and Dunnock are on their way.

Owl   Now, you all know Rabbit.

Bat   He looks rougher than I feel.

Owl   He's in a bad way, I'm afraid.

Jay   Here. Try this. (*He produces a sprig from his suitcase, and puts it under* **Rabbit***'s nose.*) Garlic mustard. Sniff this, Rabbit.

Rabbit *sniffs, then sneezes violently. He recovers somewhat.*

Dunnock *and* **Mistlethrush** *arrive in the hollow.*

Mistlethrush   What is all this? If my eggs don't hatch, Owl, there'll be trouble.

Owl   Hush, Mistlethrush.

Mistlethrush *sees* **Rabbit**.

Mistlethrush   What's that Rabbit doing here?

Owl   Hush! Rabbit, can you hear me?

Rabbit (*nodding*)   Where am I?

Owl   Safe. Up the tree. Among friends. Now tell us all what happened. Calmly.

Rabbit   Noises. Big Ones. Voices. Machines. Went to look. Met my friends and relatives other side of the field.

Squirrel   What did you see?

Owl   Quiet, Squirrel. Take your time, Rabbit.

Rabbit   Big machines. Sharp metal. With pointed teeth. Wire. Then one machine clears Big Ones' rubbish. I thought, 'Good. Rubbish dangerous.' But then . . . then . . .

Owl (*gently*)   Yes?

Rabbit   Another machine digs earth . . . and comes towards us. Panic. Fear. Down burrow. Then earth pouring down on us. Run through burrow. Scrabble to survive.

Many friends and relatives can't make it. Buried alive . . .
(*He breaks down.*)

A shocked pause.

Mistlethrush   But why?

Owl   Who can fully understand the Big Ones? Not us.

Jay   Butchers.

Bat   You stick with us, Rabbit, baby. You'll be OK.

Dunnock   You're safe up here.

Rabbit   No. White cross.

Squirrel   Yes! Tell them about the white cross.

Rabbit   On the tree. Paint. Still wet.

Owl   I saw it too.

Mistlethrush   What does it mean?

Rabbit   Others. Other white crosses. On the other trees.
Danger! Danger!

Owl   All right, Rabbit, relax. (*To the others.*) We must find
out more. Bat, how's your radar?

Bat   A-one, Owl. Shall I tune in? See what I can suss?

Owl   Please.

Bat *goes to his perch and 'tunes in'. A sudden noise interrupts.*

Cuckoo (*from behind the tree*)   Yoo-hoo! Yoo-hoo! Yoo-hoo!

Cuckoo *enters. She is loud and colourful and very tanned. She
carries a travelling bag.*

> Well, hi there, fans, I'm here to say
> I've just flown in on my holiday
> From Africa is many a mile
> So now I'm here I'll stay awhile
> Yoo-hoo!

Mistlethrush *springs up.*

Dunnock   Oh dear, oh dear. It's Cuckoo.

Mistlethrush (*fury rising*)   This is the last straw!

Cuckoo   Mistlethrush! Yoo-hoo!

Mistlethrush (*rushing to her nest*)   Get rid of her! Get rid of her!

Cuckoo   Aren't you glad to see me? I sure am glad to see you!

Mistlethrush   I bet you are.

Owl   Cuckoo. You've chosen a bad time. You're welcome, but –

Mistlethrush (*leaning out from her nest*)   Welcome? She's about as welcome as a bolt of lightning.

Cuckoo   That's not nice.

Mistlethrush   And you think what you did to me was nice? Last year? You sly bird. You dumped your egg in my nest, scarpered back off to the sun, and left me to bring up your brat.

Cuckoo   And a fine job you made of it. Then he flew right back to his momma in Africa.

Mistlethrush   And that's what you can do. Fly right back to Africa! Now!

All try to placate **Mistlethrush**. *Suddenly a loud noise interrupts and freezes everyone into silence. The savage, harsh grating noise of a chainsaw.*

Squirrel   Shhhhhh!

All look, horrified. After ten seconds or so, the sound of a falling tree.

Owl   Bat?

Bat (*tuned in to his radar*)   No echo! I'm getting no echo!

Owl   Explain.

Bat   The tree the other side of the field. (*Realizing.*) The
Battery Disco Tree. Like it's gone. Disappeared.

*The noise of the chainsaw returns and increases to an almost painful
level as the characters look at each other in fear and the lighting fades to
black-out.*

The noise of the chainsaw suddenly cuts out.

Curtain.

Act Two

As the house lights fade, the screech of the chainsaw is heard. It rises in intensity.

Then the sound of another tree falling. Nearer than the earlier one.

The lights come up on the hollow. All except **Mistlethrush** *are gathered as at a meeting, with* **Owl** *'in the chair'.* **Rabbit** *is recuperating.* **Mistlethrush** *is in her nest, visible. All listen, horrified.*

Squirrel How many's that?

Bat Five trees down. And they're getting nearer.

Owl Bat, how many trees before they reach ours?

Bat Two. Three. Depends on which direction they take.

Cuckoo I don't see what all the fuss is about. We're quite safe here, aren't we?

Squirrel Don't be stupid, Cuckoo. The Big Ones are clearing the land, the trees. *Our* tree, maybe.

Mistlethrush Anyway, it's all right for her. She doesn't live here. This is our home, Cuckoo.

Dunnock We'll have to move.

Squirrel Why should we move? Mistlethrush is right. This is our home. It's always been our home.

Owl There must be something we can do.

Rabbit The white cross.

Owl What about it?

Rabbit The Big Ones painted white crosses on lots of trees. Why?

Jay As a sign, if you ask me. To remind them which ones to remove, so to speak.

Owl   That means they wouldn't cut down our tree . . .

Bat   . . . if it didn't have a white cross on it! Yeah! Yeah!

Owl   Exactly. Dunnock, could you clean it off?

Dunnock   I could try.

Jay   Take my samples, Dunnock. Only the best. No rubbish. Clean off anything with that lot. (*He gives her his suitcase.*)

Dunnock   Thanks, Jay.

Jay   All part of the service.

Rabbit   Let me help. I'm better now, Owl. Take me down. I can do a bit of scouting too.

Owl   Good idea . . .

Sudden interruption – nearer.

Voice 1   OK, Charlie. Turn on.

The noise of the chainsaw. All freeze.

Owl   Bat!

Bat (*tuning in*)   After this one, we're next in line.

Owl   Quick! Before it's too late.

Owl, **Rabbit** and **Dunnock** (*grabbing cleaning things*) *go behind the trunk, preparing to fly down, as the lighting fades and the chainsaw noise increases.*

Then, in the black-out . . .

Voice 3   Here she goes!

Crashing noise of a tree falling.

The scene changes back to the base of the tree.

Dunnock *and* **Rabbit** *are scrubbing out the cross. Already much of it has gone.* **Jay**'s *suitcase lies open.*

Voice 1   OK, lads, chain her up.

Noises of chains being attached to the next-door tree. **Dunnock** *and* **Rabbit** *scrub furiously.* **Dunnock** *tires.*

Dunnock Oh dear, oh dear.

Owl (*whispering*) Keep going, Dunnock. Here, let me. (*She desperately joins in.*)

Voice 1 Right, lads, take her away.

The noise of a heavy vehicle dragging the tree away.

Next one, Charlie.

Heavy footsteps of two men approach. There is one area of white paint still visible, near the bottom of the trunk.

Dunnock I can't do it, Owl. This bit's dried solid. I can't . . .

Owl Too late! Retreat!

Owl *and* **Dunnock** *escape behind the tree, remembering to take* **Jay**'s *suitcase.* **Rabbit** *starts to go, then, realizing white paint is still visible, flings himself against it. He lies motionless.*

The footsteps stop.

Voice 3 Funny. Where's the cross?

Voice 1 Let's have a bit more light on the subject.

A sudden flash of light illuminates the trunk, moving up, down and across.

Nothing.

Voice 3 This one staying, then, boss?

Voice 1 Must be, Charlie.

The light finds **Rabbit**.

What's that?

Voice 3 Rabbit. Dead by the look of it.

Voice 1 Died of fright, I dare say.

Laughter.

Fancy a rabbit stew for your supper, Charlie?

Voice 3   No, no!

Voice 1   I'll get it for you.

Footsteps, plus shadows in the torchlight.

Suddenly, from behind the tree, **Owl** *hoots, menacingly.*

Stone the crows, what's that?

Owl *hoots again.*

Voice 3   An owl, I reckon, boss.

Voice 1   Don't like owls. Spooky creatures. Come on.
We'll do the next one.

Voice 3   Right.

The light and footsteps recede, as the **Big Ones** *go.*

Owl *and* **Dunnock** *hurry round to see* **Rabbit**.

Dunnock   Well done, Rabbit! You really fooled them.

Owl   Congratulations, Rabbit. That was very brave.

Rabbit   Thanks, Owl. Your hoot really got 'em going . . .

Footsteps returning.

Look out, they're coming back!

Owl *and* **Dunnock** *dash behind the tree.* **Rabbit** *throws himself
against the remains of the cross and feigns dead.*

Voice 3 (*calling*)   It's over here somewhere!

Voice 2 (*from a distance*)   Trust Charlie to leave the saw
behind!

Voice 1 (*from a distance*)   Ha, ha.

Voice 3   I'll give you a sore behind in a minute! Here it is.
Sorry, boss.

The footsteps recede. Pause.

Rabbit *gets up and looks tentatively off. Then . . .*

Rabbit (*in a loud whisper*)   All clear!

Owl *and* **Dunnock** *emerge.*

Owl   Thanks again, Rabbit.

Rabbit   A bit close that was, Owl.

Dunnock   I'd better finish scrubbing off this paint. (*She starts work again.*)

Owl   Good idea, Dunnock. Can't be too careful. Then we'd better go back up. Report to the others. A celebration is called for. You come too, Rabbit.

Rabbit   I don't think I'd better . . .

Owl   You must. You are the hero of the hour. Thanks to you, our home is safe. We are safe.

Rabbit   Well, it's very kind of you, Owl, but I'd rather not. I think I'd better see what's left of the burrow.

Owl   Of course. Very selfish of me. Your friends and relatives haven't been as lucky as us.

Rabbit (*quietly*)   No.

Dunnock   Finished!

Owl   Excellent. Up we go, then, Dunnock.

Dunnock   'Bye, Rabbit. Thanks again.

Rabbit   'Bye, Dunnock. 'Bye, Owl.

Owl   Goodbye, Rabbit.

Rabbit *starts to go.*

And Rabbit!

Rabbit *stops.*

Rabbit   Yes, Owl?

Owl   I hope you find at least some of your friends and relatives safe. I really do.

Rabbit   Thanks, Owl.

Rabbit *goes.*

The noise of the chainsaw attacking the next tree makes **Owl** *and* **Dunnock** *get moving.*

They disappear, preparing to fly back up the tree, as . . .

The lighting fades and the noise intensifies.

The scene changes back to half-way up the tree. The noise continues as the lights come up.

Bat, **Jay**, **Cuckoo** *and* **Squirrel** *wait tensely in the hollow.* **Mistlethrush** *looks down anxiously from her nest.*

A tree is heard to fall. All react, nervous and powerless.

Cuckoo   I don't understand your Big Ones. Why do they cut down your trees?

Mistlethrush   What's it matter to you, Cuckoo? You're only here a couple of weeks a year.

Cuckoo   It matters much. In Africa there are so few trees. They say Big Ones die because of this. Here they have trees. Why do they cut them down?

Squirrel   The Big Ones move in mysterious ways, Cuckoo. Who are we to reason why?

Bat   Cut the homespun philosophy, Squirrel, baby. I've got a sounding on the airwaves.

All attend.

(*Tuned in.*) Gotta work this out. The tree that's just fallen was west, right?

He points. The others agree.

The one that fell before was east, right?

He points in the opposite direction. The others agree.

Then, my, my, I think we've done it. The Big Ones have missed our tree out. Yippee!

Relief and general cheers.

Jay Snack, anyone? (*He takes food from inside his hat or pockets and offers it round.*) Caterpillar, slug? First-class festive fare.

They accept gratefully.

Squirrel I have to admit I misjudged you, Jay. I'm sorry. You've been very helpful.

Jay That's big of you, Squirrel. I appreciate that. Fancy an acorn? (*He gives him one.*)

Squirrel Thank you.

Jay It's one of yours anyway.

Squirrel *goes to react, but thinks better of it and smiles. All laugh.*

Cuckoo Come on down, Mistlethrush! It's party time!

Mistlethrush Thanks, dearie, I'd love to, but I can't leave my eggs.

Cuckoo I'll egg-sit for you. Very good egg-sitter I am.

Mistlethrush Oh, would you? I could do with a stretch . . . (*Realizing.*) . . . hang on, not blooming likely! Don't you come anywhere near my nest, Cuckoo. I know your game. Get up here, get rid of one of my eggs, lay one of your own and leave me to do the dirty work. Egg-sitter indeed!

Cuckoo Only trying to help.

Mistlethrush Ha!

Bat (*suddenly tuning in*) Hey, hey! Cool it, you chicks. Something on the line.

All attend.

(*Eventually.*) It's OK. It's Owl.

Owl and **Dunnock** *enter from behind the trunk.*

Owl   Emergency over! Celebration!

All cheer.

Squirrel   What happened, Owl? Did you manage to clean off the white cross?

Owl   Well, yes . . .

Jay   Jay's classy cleaning products up to scratch, eh?

Owl   Yes, thank you, Jay. But it was Rabbit who truly saved the day.

Dunnock   We hadn't finished scrubbing off the paint, so Rabbit covered it up by pretending to be dead. And the Big Ones couldn't see it!

Squirrel   Good for Rabbit! Hip, hip, hip . . .

All   Hooray.

Bat   On with the party!

Music starts.

Come on, Owl baby, let's let it all hang out! (*He starts gyrating.*)

Owl (*looking shocked, then melting*)   Why not? Go, Bat, go! Groovy, groovy!

Bat *sings. The others pick up the song and dance with wild enthusiasm.* **Mistlethrush** *jogs about above.*

Bat	You gotta keep hanging on
All	Baby, gotta keep hanging on
	You gotta keep hanging on
	Baby, gotta keep hanging on.
	You gotta keep hanging on
	Baby, gotta keep hanging on
	You gotta keep hanging on
	Baby, gotta . . .

Suddenly noises of the **Big Ones** *make all freeze. First a loud whistle – a piercing human whistle to attract attention.*

Then . . .

Voice 1   Oy! Charlie! Shift yourself.

Running footsteps. Breathless arrival of **Charlie**.

Voice 3   What is it, boss?

Voice 2   Look here.

Rustle of paper.

I thought there was something fishy going on.

Voice 3   What do you mean?

Voice 1   Of course this tree has to come down. It's on the plan, see? Clear as daylight. No question.

Voice 3   Then why no white cross?

Voice 1   Don't ask me. Administrative error. Who cares?

Voice 3   What do we do, then, boss?

Voice 1   Don't be stupid, Charlie. It's marked on the plan so down it comes.

Voice 3   Right, boss.

Voice 1   Now, it's the biggest of the lot, right? I want the chainsaw, the most powerful one we've got, with the yellow cable. And we'll need the generator. Tell Tom.

Voice 3   Right, boss.

Voice 1   And get a move on. We don't want to be here all night.

Footsteps recede.

A shocked hush on the tree. Eventually . . .

Squirrel   That's it, then.

Pause.

Owl   We should have known. We can never beat the Big Ones.

Dunnock   Bring them with you!

Mistlethrush   I can't!

Cuckoo   You can, Mistlethrush! Let me help.

Mistlethrush   You?

Cuckoo   Please!

All are affected by the smoke, which becomes thicker.

Squirrel (*who has rushed to his drey*)   What about my acorns?

Owl   You'll have to leave them.

Squirrel   But we'll starve! And I've been storing them for days.

Jay   Take them with us, Squirrel. Drop them down the tree! Bat, give us a hand!

Squirrel *passes out acorns to Jay, who passes them to* **Bat**, *who throws them down the tree. Meanwhile,* **Mistlethrush** *hands down two eggs to* **Cuckoo***, or even drops them down. Or maybe* **Dunnock** *works a relay system up and down. Two eggs go in* **Cuckoo***'s bag, packed with nesting material that* **Mistlethrush** *flings down.* **Dunnock** *takes* **Jay***'s 'suitcase' for the other two eggs. In the confusion, perhaps an egg is mistakenly thrown to* **Bat** *as an acorn – then carefully passed back down to* **Cuckoo** *and* **Dunnock***. In the midst of this hive of activity,* **Bat** *freezes.*

Bat (*tuning in*)   Big Ones returning! Big Ones returning!

Owl   Hurry! Hurry!

Noises of vehicles, burning logs, and chainsaws intensify as the lighting fades on the scene of urgent activity.

The scene changes back to the base of the tree.

As the light fades up, there is still smoke, but not as much.

The evacuees arrive. **Squirrel** *climbs down the tree.* **Owl**, **Dunnock**, **Mistlethrush**, **Bat**, **Cuckoo** *and* **Jay** *come round the trunk, having flown down.* **Bat** *uses his radar to check for safety.* **Cuckoo** *and* **Mistlethrush** *immediately improvise a nest*

in the root formations, checking that the eggs are well wrapped.
Dunnock *helps.*

All here? Mistlethrush?

Mistlethrush   Here.

Owl   Jay?

Jay   Here.

Owl   Bat?

Bat   Here.

Owl   Cuckoo?

Cuckoo   Here.

Owl   Dunnock?

Dunnock (*returning* **Jay**'s 'suitcase' *to him*)   Here.

Owl   Squirrel?

Squirrel   Here.

Owl   Any sign of Rabbit?

Squirrel   No, Owl. Shall I go and look for him?

Owl   No. We stick together. Wait for Rabbit. He knows
the field better than us.

They huddle together.

Jay   Anyone hungry?

All (*muttering*)   No, thank you, Jay.

Mistlethrush *perches on her improvised nest.* **Dunnock** *and*
Cuckoo *fuss around her.*

Mistlethrush   I think the eggs are OK. Ta everso,
Dunnock. (*To* **Cuckoo**.) And you, dearie.

Cuckoo   Quiet, Mistlethrush. Try to rest.

Mistlethrush   No, I'm very grateful. And if we come through all this, Cuckoo, feel free to dump your rotten egg on me as usual.

Cuckoo   Thank you.

Bat (*tuned in*)   Owl! (*After a pause.*) Rabbit.

Rabbit *enters, breathless.*

All listen eagerly.

Owl   Well?

Rabbit (*not defeated*)   The field's a right old mess, Owl. They've filled in the burrow. Killed all my friends and relatives. They're burning the trees. Chaos it is, chaos.

Bat (*tuned in*)   Big Ones approaching.

The rumble of a heavy vehicle approaching.

Owl   We'd better move on.

Rabbit   No. There's nowhere to move on to. And this is the last tree. We can't let it die like the others.

Squirrel   Hear, hear!

Owl   But we can't stop the Big Ones.

Rabbit   Maybe not. But we can show a bit of resistance. Stand up for our home.

Jay   Go down fighting, eh?

Bat   Right on!

Mistlethrush   We can't fight them.

Dunnock   But we can't desert our home.

Rabbit   Good for you, Dunnock. What do you say, Owl?

The heavy vehicle stops. Doors slam. As voices are heard approaching, **Owl** *makes her decision. Standing centre, she stretches out her hands. The others, as if mesmerized, join her. They defiantly, bravely, form a chain in front of the tree.*

Voice 2   Right, boss. Let's get it down. Charlie, how are you doing?

Voice 3   Nearly ready.

The sound of machinery being unloaded.

Voice 2   Big one, this. What do we do, boss? Start up top?

Voice 1   I reckon.

Voice 2   Polish this one off, be home in time for tea, eh?

Laughter. Suddenly a yellow cable swings into view.

Voice 3   Chainsaw ready, boss.

Voice 1   Electrics ready?

Voice 2   Ready!

Voice 1   OK, Charlie. Turn on.

The ghastly noise of the chainsaw. Reflections from the savage metal glint on the faces of the tree folk. Suddenly, accompanied, as it were, by the noise of the chain-saw, they sing, loudly and defiantly.

Tree Folk   Save our tree
Don't let it fall
Save our tree
Save us all.

Save its trunk
And leafy dome
Save our tree
Save our home.

Can't you see
This tree
Has a history
Its own traditions
And laws
Can't you see
This tree
Is a community
A world as alive

As yours.

Save our tree
Please set it free
Save our tree
Let it be.

This tree's ours
But it's your tree too
Share it, care for it
The way we do.

Save our tree
Don't let it fall
Save our tree
Save us all.

The singing stops.

Voice 2   What's all this, then?

Voice 1   Some sort of demo?

Laughter.

Clear off, the lot of you. Vermin, that's what you are. Dirty, stinking vermin. Go on, Charlie, do your worst.

The noise of the chainsaw increases. Suddenly **Owl** *leaps forward as though to attack. She is followed by* **Jay** *and* **Cuckoo**. *But in vain. They mime being beaten back.* **Mistlethrush** *screams. The noise of the chainsaw attacking wood. The cable swings. The tree folk look upwards. A branch crashes down from above. The tree folk huddle against the trunk.*

(Optional: More branches crash down, hopefully identifiable – **Bat**'s *'perch', part of* **Owl**'s *hollow,* **Mistlethrush**'s *nest.)*

Light increases to suggest that the chainsaw is coming lower. The wretched tree folk cower and maybe scream, clinging on to each other for dear life.

Suddenly **Rabbit** *breaks out. As though in a trance of defiance. He moves to the cable, grabs it and bites it.*

A flash. The fuse has blown. The noise of the chainsaw cuts out.

Rabbit *shudders with the force of the electricity, then crumples in a heap. The others look on aghast.* **Squirrel** *approaches* **Rabbit,** *puts his ear to* **Rabbit***'s heart, then turns to the others and shakes his head.* **Rabbit** *is dead.*

The tree folk sadly hum the tune of their 'Save Our Tree' song, backing away, holding hands. The lighting narrows to a pin-spot on **Rabbit.** *The others melt into the background.*

Rabbit *stirs, gets us and begins to take off the rabbit parts of his costume. He becomes* **Mr Bunn** *again.*

Mr Bunn   Will Mistlethrush's eggs ever hatch? Will Cuckoo lay her egg in Mistlethrush's nest and fly back to Africa? Will Bat find another Battery Disco? Will Owl, Dunnock and Squirrel ever lead a normal life again? Will Jay find other trees on which to carry out his business? Who knows? It's all in the imagination, anyway. Just a story. Who cares? Well, I care. And perhaps it *could* happen. It *will* happen if Mr Jay and Mr Batty have their way, if they do as they want and clear Turner's Field for their children's playground.

Mr Bunn *has wandered to the side of the stage, still in his pin-spot, as the scene is changed back to the public platform in the village hall.*

The other characters return to take their places as at the beginning of the play – **Mrs Wise, Mrs Dunnock, Mr Storer, Mr Jay, Mr Batty, Mrs Cook** *and* **Mrs Thrush.**

So, I put it to the meeting. What right have we to kill the See-Saw Tree, a tree that has lived longer than any of us? It would take three minutes, with a chainsaw, to destroy the work of three hundred years. And jeopardize the lives of all its inhabitants. Animals, birds, insects. And for what? So that Mr Batty and Mr Jay can line their pockets with the pocket money of our children.

The lighting comes up on the meeting, and in the auditorium.

Mr Jay   Madam Chairman, I object to that. We are providing a much-needed amenity in this area, and all this sentimental twaddle is totally irrelevant.

Mr Batty   Hear, hear.

Mrs Thrush   Hear, hear. We want that playground.

Mrs Cook   I agree. You can't stop the wheels of change. It's called progress.

Mrs Wise   Thank you. Well, we've heard the arguments. Earlier your votes suggested a children's playground was a good idea. But, please, let's vote again, this time on whether Mr Jay and Mr Batty should be allowed to cut down the See-Saw Tree. Please raise your hands if you want it cut down.

Mrs Dunnock *counts hands. They include* **Mr Jay**, **Mr Batty**, **Mrs Thrush** *and* **Mrs Cook**. **Mrs Dunnock** *gives the number 'for'.*

Mrs Wise   Now please raise your hands if you do *not* want the See-Saw Tree cut down.

Hopefully the audience unanimously raise their hands. **Mrs Dunnock** *starts to count.*

The result, I think, can be said to be unanimous. The See-Saw Tree must stay.

Mr Bunn *and others lead applause. (For alternative endings to suit any eventuality on the voting, see end of play.)*

Mr Jay   Now hang on a minute. Earlier on you said you wanted the children's playground. Now you say you want the See-Saw Tree. You can't have it both ways.

Mr Storer   I think, if I may be allowed to speak, Madam Chairman, we *can*.

Mrs Wise   Go ahead, Mr Storer.

Mr Storer   Of course Mr Jay should have his children's playground – it's an excellent idea. But why can't the See-

Saw Tree be part of it? For the children, indeed for all of us, to see and enjoy.

Mrs Dunnock   And why shouldn't Mr Batty provide a plank and give the tree a see-saw, as in the old days. Then today's children can play on it.

Mrs Wise   Well, Mr Batty?

Mr Batty   Ah. Well, it's not as simple as that. All the plans'll have to be redrawn. That costs money.

Mr Jay   I think it's fair enough, Batty. You've still got your video games and fruit machines, and they've got their tree.

Mr Batty   Well . . . I suppose . . . it's quite a neat idea . . . (*Visualizing a sign over the entrance to the playground.*) 'The See-Saw Tree Children's Playground' . . . it's good! Yes! OK, I agree!

Applause, led by **Mr Bunn**.

Mrs Wise   Good. Thank you all for coming. I declare the meeting closed. And I suggest a celebration. To celebrate the saving of . . .

Mr Bunn   The rebirth of . . .

All   THE SEE-SAW TREE!

All happily sing and dance, encouraging the audience to join in each chorus.

SONG: **The See-Saw Tree**

An actor accompanies the song on guitar or piano (the piano could be part of the village hall set).

All   Sing the story of
                 The See-Saw Tree
                 Standing proud and free
                 Such a sight to see.
                 May we always share
                 With the creatures living there

The story of
The glory of
The See-Saw Tree.

The verses could be sung by all in unison, or solo lines could be allocated if required.

All (*or solos*)

A long time ago a squirrel found
An acorn and buried it in the ground
Came the rain and the sun
On the fertile earth
And the story had begun
With an oak tree's birth.

Using a song-sheet, the actors encourage the audience to join in the chorus.

All (+ *audience*)

So
Sing the story of
The See-Saw Tree
Standing proud and free
Such a sight to see.
May we always share
With the creatures living there
The story of
The glory of
The See-Saw Tree.

All (*or solos*)

As the seasons changed and the years
    went by
The oak tree flourished and soared up
    high
So its trunk and its branches
And its roots could give
The animals and birds
A place to live.

All (+ *audience*)

So

Sing the story of
The See-Saw Tree
Standing proud and free
Such a sight to see.
May we always share
With the creatures living there
The story of
The glory of
The See-Saw Tree.

All (*or solos*)

The tree looked down on the old high
    street
The local landmark, the place to meet.
And ev'ry May Day
It set the scene
For the singing and the dancing
On the village green.

All (+ *audience*)

So
Sing the story of
The See-Saw Tree
Standing proud and free
Such a sight to see.
May we always share
With the creatures living there
The story of
The glory of
The See-Saw Tree.

All (*or solos*)

A tree with a future, witness of the past
Steadfast and stable in a world changing
    fast
Let the sun shine down
Let the see-saw sway
Long live our tree
As the children play.

All (+ *audience*)

So
Sing the story of
The See-Saw Tree
Standing proud and free
Such a sight to see.
May we always share
With the creatures living there
The story of
The glory of
The See-Saw Tree.

May we always share
With the creatures living there
The story of the glory of
The glory of the story of
The story of the glory of
The See-Saw Tree.

The characters freeze at the end of the song. We hear the creak of a see-saw. The lights slowly fade.

Curtain.

Alternative endings

Endings to suit (hopefully) any eventuality.

Each ending starts from **Mrs Wise**'s *invitation to vote* against *the cutting down of the tree.*

(1) If the vast majority of the audience vote against*:*

Mrs Wise   The result is virtually unanimous. The See-Saw Tree must stay. (*Etc. as before.*)

(2) If the audience are divided, but clearly more are against *than* for*:*

Mrs Wise   The majority are against. So the See-Saw Tree must stay. (*Etc. as before.*)

(3) If voting looks even:

Mrs Wise   We are divided. No clear majority.

Mr Storer   If I may be allowed to speak, Madam Chairman.

Mrs Wise   Go ahead, Mr Storer.

Mr Storer   We may be divided on whether or not to cut down the See-Saw Tree, but we all agree a children's playground is a good idea. Now, why can't the See-Saw Tree be part of the Children's Playground?

Mrs Dunnock   And why shouldn't Mr Batty . . . (*Etc. as before.*)

(4) *If all the audience vote* for *cutting down the tree (hopefully unlikely):*

Mrs Wise   Well, the meeting clearly decides to cut down the See-Saw Tree. Mr Jay, Mr Batty – you have your go-ahead.

Mr Jay *and* **Mr Batty** *shake hands, delighted.*

Thank you all for coming to the meeting. Good day.

All collect their papers and leave.

(N.B. The play would therefore finish without *the song.)*

The Ideal Gnome Expedition

The Ideal Gnome Expedition was first produced by the Liverpool Playhouse Company under the title *Chish 'n' Fips* on 3 December, 1980, with the following cast:

Mr Fisher	David Monico
Mr Wheeler	Alan Thompson
Baby Duck	Jane Egan
Chips	Richard Fox
Securidog	Frank Ellis
Wacker	Daniel Webb

Directed by William Gaunt and Peter Lichtenfels
Designed by Bim Hopewell
Choreography by Neil Fitzwiliam
Musical direction by Stuart Barham

The play was subsequently produced at Sadler's Wells Theatre, London, and on tour by Whirligig Theatre (sponsored by Clarks Shoes and subsidized by Arts Council Touring) in the autumn of 1981, with the following cast:

Mr Fisher	Mike Elles
Mr Wheeler	Gary Linley
Baby Duck	Melody Kaye
Chips	Keith Varnier
Securidog	Clive Mantle
Wacker	Clive Mantle

Directed by David Wood
Designed by Susie Caulcutt
Choreography by Sheila Falconer
Music arranged and supervised by Peter Pontzen
Musical direction by Paul Knight

Characters

Mr Fisher, *a garden gnome, whose usual function is to sit on a toadstool with his fishing-rod. Rather grumpy and dissatisfied with his lot; nevertheless, like all garden gnomes, he has a warm heart.*

Mr Wheeler, *a garden gnome who is normally to be seen holding his wheelbarrow. Dressed identically to Mr Fisher, he is more of an optimist and an adventurer. Very practical.*
N.B. Both gnomes have an olde worlde charm and quaint over-polite way of talking to each other and others.

Baby Duck, *a clockwork toy duck, complete with detachable key sticking out of his back. Could be dressed in a nappy. Waddles slightly stiffly. Cannot talk or sing – only quack. (Could be played by a male or female).*

Chips, *an alley-cat, who has learnt the hard way to survive in the concrete jungle of the town. Knows his way around and how to look after himself. Doesn't easily trust anyone, but once he has accepted someone as a friend, will stick by them. Quite a cool cat!*

Securidog, *night watchdog at the Adventure Playground. Unnecessarily unpleasant and rude. Also rather stupid. Could be wearing a kind of security officer's uniform or hat.*

Wacker *a pneumatic machine which bounces up and down flattening uneven road surfaces or tar. As a character he is bouncy and determined to flatten everything in sight – that is, for logical reasons, his reason for living. He should be considerably taller than the others – the actor encased in a high cylinder.*

(**Securidog** *and* **Wacker** *could be doubled by the same actor.*)

Off-stage (recorded) voices of the **Big Ones**, *the human beings in whose garden/back yard the gnomes live: mother, father and child. Also the voices of two policemen.*

Production Note

Most of the characters in the play would in reality be between eighteen inches and two feet high. Therefore the scale of the settings should be about three or four times 'human-size', i.e., the kerb of the pavement should be, say, two or three feet high; the dustbin, say, six or seven feet high. The environment throughout is urban, but the sets and costumes should still be very colourful and visually exciting.

Much use is made of lighting and sound effects, all of which help create a world in which human activities are seen through the eyes of animals and garden gnomes; so, for instance, the sound of a car and the glare of its headlights will be magnified for these smaller folk.

Scenes

Act One
Scene One	The Back Yard
Scene Two	The Alley
Scene Three	The Adventure Playground

Act Two
Scene One	The Street
Scene Two	The Island
Scene Three	The Back Yard

Act One

Scene One

The Back Yard.

After a short overture, the house lights go down, and the curtain rises on a darkened stage. Over loudspeakers, we hear the sound of a back door being unbolted, top and bottom. Then a key turns in the lock and the door opens. Now we hear the voices of the **Big Ones**, *the human beings whose back yard we are about to visit.*

Miss Big One (*who is about eight years old*)   But, Mum, it's my favourite.

Mrs Big One   I know, love, but it's broken.

Miss Big One (*shouting*)   Then mend it.

Mrs Big One   Don't talk to me like that. Your dad's tried to mend it, but he can't. He's going to buy you a new one.

Miss Big One   I don't *want* a new one.

Mrs Big One   Don't be silly.

Miss Big One   I want this one.

Mrs Big One   But it's broken. It's useless.

Miss Big One   But, Mum . . .

We hear a dustbin lid being removed, the metallic clang of something being thrown in, and finally the lid being slammed back down.

(*Shrieking.*) Mum! (*She starts crying.*)

Mrs Big One (*briskly*)   Come on. Inside. I've had enough.

We hear the slam of the back door as the **Big Ones** *return inside.*

Music as the lights go up on a corner of a back yard or urban back garden.

A wall: on it a tap with an attached hosepipe coiled round it. Maybe a flower-bed or a couple of tubs with plants in. A dustbin, the lid half on,

*half off. In prominent positions we see two garden gnomes, identically
dressed.* **Mr Fisher** *sits crosslegged on a stone toadstool; he holds a
fishing-rod.* **Mr Wheeler** *stands next to the toadstool. He holds his
wheelbarrow. Both* **Gnomes** *are in frozen positions.* **Mr Fisher**
*is asleep. Other items of garden / back yard dressing could be visible,
and it might be effective if the* **Gnomes** *were on a small patch of
grass. But it is important that the garden / back yard is noticeably urban
rather than rural. We imagine that the back door is off-stage, to one
side or out front, in the audience as it were. It is afternoon.*

*From the dustbin we hear a sort of quacking cry for help. Once. Twice.
On the third cry,* **Mr Wheeler** *'comes to life'. He registers concern,
checks that nobody is coming, leaves his wheelbarrow and scuttles over
to the dustbin. He listens, ear against the side. Another quacking cry.*
Mr Wheeler *nips back and looks up at* **Mr Fisher**.

Mr Wheeler (*in an urgent whisper*)   Mr Fisher!

No reaction.

Mr Fisher!

A loud snore from **Mr Fisher**. **Mr Wheeler** *tries another tack.
He pulls gently on the fishing line; this rings a little bell on the top of
the rod. Another snore. Another ring. Another snore. Another ring –
more vehement. This time* **Mr Fisher** *wakes up with a violent start.*

Mr Fisher   A bite! A bite! Heave! Heave! Come on, my
beauty!

Mr Wheeler *is still holding on to the line and is nearly pulled off
his feet as* **Mr Fisher** *pulls and tugs.*

Mr Wheeler   Mr Fisher!

Mr Fisher   My, it's a big 'un. A codfish at least! Heave!

Mr Wheeler   Mr Fisher!

He lets go of the line, making **Mr Fisher** *nearly fall off his
toadstool.*

Mr Fisher   Aaaah! (*Regaining his balance.*) Oh, it's you, Mr
Wheeler. I thought you were a codfish.

Mr Wheeler   Do I look like a codfish, Mr Fisher?

Mr Fisher (*disappointed*)   I must have been dreaming.

Mr Wheeler   Do I have a face like a codfish?

Mr Fisher   How do I know? I've never seen a codfish face, have I? Or a codfish fin. Or a codfish fillet. Or a codfish finger. I've never seen a *fish*!

Mr Wheeler   Please, Mr Fisher, don't start all that again . . .

Mr Fisher   What a joke! Stuck up here year after year, fishing-rod in fist, with no hope of usefully employing it. My life, Mr Wheeler, is a wasted life.

Mr Wheeler   Fiddle faddle, Mr Fisher. I've a job for you and your fishing-rod right now. Listen.

Another quacking cry from the dustbin.

Mr Fisher (*with a jump*)   What was that?

Mr Wheeler   An SOS call. From the dustbin.

Dramatic chord.

Mr Fisher   The dustbin?

Another quacking cry.

Mr Wheeler   Something needs our help. Come down, please.

Mr Fisher   No, no, no. Leave it there, Mr Wheeler. If the Big Ones throw something away, that's their business. Not ours. If something doesn't work; if it's useless – good riddance.

Mr Wheeler   The Big Ones may throw *you* away one day, Mr Fisher.

Mr Fisher   Me?

Mr Wheeler   And if they do, I won't lift a finger to rescue you.

Mr Fisher (*nervously*) Why should they throw me away?

Mr Wheeler (*imitating* **Mr Fisher**) 'If something doesn't work' . . . 'If it's useless' . . . Well, *you* don't work . . . 'My life, Mr Wheeler, is a wasted life' . . . (*Pointedly.*) Good riddance to *you*.

Another quacking cry. **Mr Fisher** *looks guilty.*

And besides, Mr Fisher . . .

Mr Fisher (*uncomfortable*) Besides, Mr Wheeler?

Mr Wheeler (*significantly*) The Code of the Gnomes.

SONG: **The Code of the Gnomes**

(*Singing.*)	If anyone's in trouble or in a mess
	If anyone's unhappy, unwell or in distress
	It's up to us
Mr Fisher (*reluctantly*)	It's up to us
Mr Wheeler	It's up to us
Mr Fisher (*nodding*)	It's up to us
Mr Wheeler	With no fuss
	It's up to us
	To help him on his way
	It's up to us
Mr Fisher (*more enthusiastic*)	It's up to us
Mr Wheeler	It's up to us
Mr Fisher (*whole-heartedly*)	It's up to us
Both	The Code of the Gnomes
	We must obey.

Mr Fisher *climbs down from his toadstool.*

	If ever you're in danger or need a friend
	Be sure that we'll stick by you until the bitter end
Mr Wheeler	It's up to us
Mr Fisher	It's up to us

Mr Wheeler	It's up to us
Mr Fisher	It's up to us
Both	We won't wait
	Or hesitate
	Just put us to the test
Mr Wheeler	It's up to us
Mr Fisher	It's up to us
Mr Wheeler	It's up to us
Mr Fisher	It's up to us
Both	The Code of the Gnomes
	We do our best.
	Gnomes know no
	Other way to live
	No gnome's slow
	His help to give
	The Gnomes' Code
	Is share the load
	And help one another
	Along life's road.
Mr Wheeler	It's up to us
Mr Fisher	It's up to us
Mr Wheeler	It's up to us
Mr Fisher	It's up to us
Both	We won't wait
	Or hesitate
	Just put us to the test
Mr Wheeler	It's up to us
Mr Fisher	It's up to us
Mr Wheeler	It's up to us
Mr Fisher	It's up to us
Both	The Code of the Gnomes
	We do our best.
	It's up to us
	It's up to us
	It's up to us
	It's up to us
	The Code of the Gnomes

U.P.T.O.U.S.
Up to us
It's up to us
To do our best.

The music continues as **Mr Wheeler** *gives* **Mr Fisher** *a leg-up to the top of the dustbin. If necessary, they use the toadstool or the wheelbarrow to achieve extra height.* **Mr Fisher** *peers down inside.*

Mr Wheeler   Well?

Mr Fisher   Can't see a thing.

Another quacking cry. **Mr Fisher** *jumps. The* **Gnomes** *nearly lose their balance.*

(*Calling down.*) We're going to let you out. Don't move. Stay there.

Mr Wheeler   I don't think it has much choice, Mr Fisher.

Music as **Mr Fisher** *tries, unsuccessfully, to reach whatever it is out of the dustbin. Both* **Gnomes** *think; then* **Mr Fisher** *points to his fishing-rod.* **Mr Wheeler** *passes it to him. Carefully he lowers the line into the dustbin. Tension music as the line tightens. After a struggle, he manages to pull up and help out* **Baby Duck**, *who is virtually lifeless, though emitting the odd quack.* **Mr Wheeler** *helps him to the ground. Both* **Gnomes** *hold him up. Thinking he is balanced, they let go of him. He totters and nearly falls. The* **Gnomes** *catch him. Then balance him and leave go. Again he nearly falls. This time they hold on to him.*

Mr Wheeler   What is it?

Mr Fisher   No idea.

Mr Wheeler (*to the audience*)   Maybe you can help. Do you know what this is?

Audience   A duck.

Mr Wheeler   A what?

Audience   A duck.

Mr Fisher   Of course! A duck. A baby duck, by the look of it.

Mr Wheeler (*noticing the key sticking out of* **Baby Duck***'s back*) What's this?

Mr Fisher   A key.

Mr Wheeler   But what's it for? (*To the audience.*) Do you know? What's the key for?

Audience   To wind it up.

Mr Wheeler   To what?

Audience   To wind it up.

Mr Fisher   Of course! It's a toy, Mr Wheeler. You wind it up and it comes to life, I bet.

Mr Wheeler   Shall I try it?

Mr Fisher   Why not?

Mr Wheeler *tries to turn the key.*

Mr Wheeler   It won't budge. It's stuck.

Mr Fisher   Why? (*To the audience.*) Why?

Audience   It's broken.

Mr Fisher   Broken? Of course! That's why the Big Ones threw Baby Duck away. He doesn't work.

A weak quacking cry. **Baby Duck** *starts falling forwards in a faint. The* **Gnomes** *catch him.*

Mr Wheeler   He's very weak, Mr Fisher.

Mr Fisher (*idea*)   A drink of water.

Mr Wheeler   The tap!

They start to carry him. He is heavy.

Wheelbarrow.

They tip him into the wheelbarrow and wheel him to the tap and hose.

Jay   Evacuate. Leave the tree. That's the answer. The only answer.

Cuckoo   You could all come home with me. To Africa.

Mistlethrush   I don't want to go to bloomin' Africa. This is my home.

Squirrel   I agree, Mistlethrush. If my home is to die, I will die with it.

Mistlethrush   Well. I didn't say *that*, dearie.

Dunnock   Forgive me, Squirrel, but that's a silly attitude. Dear oh dear, we can't just give up! (*She is embarrassed by her own vehemence.*)

Bat (*urgently*)   Turn down the volume, Dunnock, I'm picking up . . . hey, that's crazy!

Owl   What?

Bat   Cloud. Low cloud. Very low.

Owl   Cloud?

Squirrel (*sniffing the air*)   What's that smell?

All sniff the air. Suddenly smoke begins to appear.

Jay   That's not cloud, Bat. It's smoke!

Dunnock and **Cuckoo** *begin to cough. Sound of burning wood.*

Owl   They're burning the cut-down trees. (*She coughs.*) We've no choice now. We'll suffocate if we stay. Everybody leave. Abandon tree!

The noise of flames increases. A red glow is seen to one side. More smoke.

Meet down the bottom!

Signs of panic as the creatures dash about.

Mistlethrush (*screaming*)   No. No. My eggs. I won't leave my eggs!

Carry on, Mr Fisher. Back in a jiff.

Mr Fisher Right, Mr Wheeler.

Mr Wheeler *exits.*

Mr Fisher *reaches up for the hose and positions it near* **Baby Duck**'s *mouth. Then he stretches to the tap and turns it very slightly, then turns it off again. He returns to the end of the hose and shakes a drop or two into* **Baby Duck**'s *mouth.*

There. Just a drop.

Baby Duck *utters a spluttering quack.*

It's all right. Keep calm. We're only trying to help you.

Mr Wheeler *returns carrying a large (for him) screwdriver.*

Mr Wheeler Found this in the Big Ones' shed.

Tension music as **Mr Wheeler** *'operates' on the key area. He carefully twiddles the screwdriver. After a few seconds of concentration . . .*

There.

Mr Fisher *gently pulls a dirty piece of fluff from the key area.*

Mr Fisher Ugh. No wonder.

Tension music continues as the **Gnomes** *carefully tip* **Baby Duck** *from the wheelbarrow.* **Mr Wheeler** *gingerly turns the key. A ratchet noise indicates it is now turning. Several turns. Then the* **Gnomes** *stand to one side and eagerly watch. Slowly a very excited* **Baby Duck** *comes to life and then starts waddling fast and furiously. The* **Gnomes** *have, perhaps, to jump out of his way. Joyfully he scuttles around exploring, then returns to the* **Gnomes** *to thank them for mending him, all the time quacking with delight. He bows up and down several times.*

What's he doing?

Mr Wheeler Saying thank you. Our pleasure, Baby Duck, our pleasure.

Now, **Baby Duck** *starts to run down. His movements become slow and jerky until he stops altogether.*

Mr Fisher   Has he conked out again?

Mr Wheeler   No. Just needs rewinding.

Ratchet noises as he does so. **Baby Duck** *comes to life again. He smiles at the* **Gnomes**.

Now, let's say hello properly.

Mr Fisher   Is that his name?

Mr Wheeler   What?

Mr Fisher   Properly. Funny name for a duck.

Mr Wheeler   No. Let's say hello properly. Introduce ourselves. Hello. (*He bows.*)

Baby Duck *quacks and bows.*

I'm Mr Wheeler. This is Mr Fisher.

Mr Fisher *bows.* **Baby Duck** *bows.*

Mr Fisher   How do you do?

Baby Duck *quacks.*

What's *your* name?

Baby Duck *shrugs.*

You don't know?

Baby Duck *shrugs again.*

You haven't got a name?

Baby Duck *shakes his head.*

Mr Wheeler. He hasn't got a name.

Mr Wheeler   That'll never do. Everyone should have a name.

Baby Duck *indicates the audience.*

What?

Baby Duck *indicates the audience and quacks again.*

Ask *them* to think of a name for you?

Baby Duck *nods.*

Good idea. Anyone got a good name for a baby duck?

Audience participation: the **Gnomes** *invite suggested names. After rejecting a couple,* **Baby Duck** *nods his acceptance of one. For the purposes of the script, let's call him 'Fluffy'.*

He likes it! (*To the audience.*) Thank you. Fluffy Duck!

SONG: **A Duck Called——?**

Mr Fisher ⎫ **Mr Wheeler** ⎬	Once there was a duck called Fluffy Went and got a bit of fluff in his works With a worried frown This duck ran down In a flurry of jiggles and jerks.
	But Fluffy Your problems are ended Fluffy You can waddle and quack Fluffy Your clockwork is mended Fluffy Welcome back.
	Fluffy Your problems . . .

Mr Wheeler   Wait a minute! Mr Fisher, I have an excellent idea.

Mr Fisher   Carry on, Mr Wheeler.

Mr Wheeler (*taking in the audience*)   Since *they* thought of
the name 'Fluffy', why don't they join in the song? Would
you do that?

Audience   Yes.

Mr Wheeler   Would you?

Audience   Yes.

Mr Wheeler   Splendid. Every time the word 'Fluffy'
crops up in the song, you shout it out. (*Demonstrating.*) Fluffy!
Yes? Have a go now. After three. One, two, three.

Audience   Fluffy!

Mr Wheeler   Excellent!

Mr Fisher   Mr Wheeler, I have an idea too.

Mr Wheeler   Carry on, Mr Fisher.

Mr Fisher   To give them a signal every time the word
'Fluffy' comes up, I'll lift my fishing-rod high in the air.

Mr Wheeler   Good.

Mr Fisher   Let's try it. Here we go. One, two, three. (*He
raises his fishing-rod.*)

Audience   Fluffy!

Mr Fisher   And again!

Into the song . . .

Audience	Fluffy
Mr Fisher **Mr Wheeler** }	Your problems are ended
Audience	Fluffy
Mr Fisher **Mr Wheeler** }	You can waddle and quack
Audience	Fluffy
Mr Fisher **Mr Wheeler** }	Your clockwork is mended
Audience	Fluffy

Mr Fisher } **Mr Wheeler**	Welcome back!
Audience	Once there was a duck called Fluffy
Mr Fisher } **Mr Wheeler**	In the bin the Big Ones threw him away But we heard him shout And fished him out So he'd live to see another day. So
Audience	Fluffy
Mr Fisher } **Mr Wheeler**	Your problems are ended
Audience	Fluffy
Mr Fisher } **Mr Wheeler**	You can waddle and quack
Audience	Fluffy
Mr Fisher } **Mr Wheeler**	Your clockwork is mended
Audience	Fluffy
Mr Fisher } **Mr Wheeler**	Welcome back!
All	Fluffy!

The music continues. They dance happily. Then, suddenly, we hear loud noises of the **Big Ones**. *Bolts being undone, key turning and the back door opening. A dramatic lighting change – perhaps human shadows towering over the characters on stage.*

Immediately the two **Gnomes** *expertly rush back to their places. If necessary they drag the toadstool back in place.* **Mr Fisher** *retrieves his fishing-rod and climbs back up.* **Mr Wheeler** *grabs his wheelbarrow.* **Baby Duck**, *unused to this ritual, stands uneasily.* **Mr Fisher** *and* **Mr Wheeler** *beckon or usher him to a position of safety – out of sight of the* **Big Ones**. *Behind the toadstool, perhaps.* **Baby Duck** *pops out again.*

Mr Wheeler   Back. Fluffy Duck, back.

Baby Duck *obeys.* **Mr Fisher** *and* **Mr Wheeler** *freeze.*

The voices of the **Big Ones** *boom out.*

Miss Big One   Come on. Granny will think we're never coming.

Mrs Big One   Have we got everything?

Mr Big One   Everything but the kitchen sink. Anyone would think we were going for six months, not just a weekend.

We hear the door shutting, and the key turning.

Mrs Big One   I've cancelled the milk, turned off the gas, shut the windows . . .

Miss Big One   Come on, Mum.

Mr Big One   Hey! Who's been playing around with my screwdriver?

The **Gnomes** *exchange worried expressions. They haven't had time to return the screwdriver to the shed. Tension music.*

Miss Big One   Not me.

Mrs Big One   Not me.

Mr Big One   I wish people would put things back where they found them. I s'pose *I'll* have to.

Miss Big One   Come on, Dad. We're late.

Mr Big One   Oh, all right. (*Tutting noise.*) Bet it gets all rusty.

We hear the sound of car doors slamming, the engine starting and the car driving off.

The lighting returns to normal. The **Gnomes** *unfreeze.*

Mr Wheeler   All clear, Fluffy Duck. They've gone.

Baby Duck *emerges.*

Mr Fisher   Trust him to notice that screwdriver.

Mr Wheeler   My fault for leaving it there.

Mr Fisher   The Big Ones notice everything.

Mr Wheeler   At least they didn't notice Fluffy Duck wasn't in the dustbin.

Baby Duck *quacks*.

Mr Fisher   My nerves won't stand it, Mr Wheeler. Being taken by surprise like that. Why can't they leave us in peace?

Mr Wheeler   They have. For the weekend, anyway. Didn't you hear, Mr Fisher? They've gone to see Granny. We're free! Free to do as we please.

Mr Fisher   Well, I shall go back to sleep. That will please me.

Mr Wheeler   No! This is a time for excitement! Adventure! Doing things we always wanted to do.

Mr Fisher   What things?

Mr Wheeler   Fishing! You've always wanted to fish.

Mr Fisher   I've never seen a fish. Fish don't live in back yards.

Mr Wheeler   Exactly. We'll go away. On holiday. For the weekend. Like the Big Ones. What do you say, Fluffy Duck?

Baby Duck *quacks*.

Mr Fisher (*getting interested*)   I once heard the Big Ones talk of things called 'islands'. It seems islands are holiday places in the sun, surrounded by sea water. Water in which fish swim. Hundreds and thousands of fish.

Mr Wheeler   We'll find an island, then. (*Reaching up to* **Mr Fisher** *on his toadstool.*) Come on.

Mr Fisher   But, Mr Wheeler, we've never left the back yard before. Who knows what dangers lie beyond that wall?

Mr Wheeler   Who knows indeed, Mr Fisher? But we'll
soon find out.

SONG: **Holiday Island**

(*Singing*)   Ev'ryone needs a change of
                                   scene
                            Including you and me
                            Year after year
                            We've not moved from here
                            Now is our chance to be
                                   free.

Mr Fisher *smiles and nods his agreement.*

Mr Wheeler ⎫   So
Mr Fisher   ⎭   Let's find our holiday island
                            Our holiday yours and my
                                   land
                            Where there's nothing to do
                            But enjoy doing nothing
                            Where there's nothing to do
                            But have fun
                            Let's find our holiday yours
                                   and my land
                            Island in the sun.

Mr Fisher   A quiet spot
                            Where a quiet spot of fishing
                            Would make my wishing
                            Come true

Mr Wheeler ⎫   Far away
Mr Fisher   ⎭   A place to play
                            Where the sky is always blue.

Mr Wheeler and **Mr Fisher**, *carried away by their thoughts,*
stop singing and gaze ahead in reverie. **Baby Duck** *quacks to*
'awaken' them.

Baby Duck   Quack, quack, quack.

Mr Wheeler ⎫
Mr Fisher ⎭
	Let's find our holiday island
	Our holiday pie in the sky land
	If we're feeling too warm
	We can splash in the water
	Then get dry in the sun's
	   golden beams
	Let's find our holiday yours
	   and my land
	Pie in the sky land
	Do or die land
	Island of our dreams.

They start preparing to go as the music continues. They go to the wall, throw the hose up and over the wall, like a rope. **Mr Wheeler**, *using the tap as a foothold, scrambles up.* **Mr Fisher** *hands him his wheelbarrow; or they use the hose to lift it. Then* **Mr Fisher** *hands up his fishing-rod. Helped by* **Mr Wheeler**, **Mr Fisher** *uses the tap and hose to climb up. Finally,* **Baby Duck**, *maybe reluctantly at first, climbs up. All three are now on top of the wall.*

> Let's find our holiday yours
>   and my land
> Pie in the sky land
> Do or die land
> Island in the sun.

They disappear over the wall. (N.B. **Mr Fisher** *leaves behind his fishing-rod.)*

The lights fade to a black-out.

Scene Two

The Alley.

This will most easily be a simple front cloth – in order to cover the scene change. It represents a wall, colourfully vandalized with graffiti or posters, spray paints, chalked cricket stumps, etc. (In one production of the play, the 'back yard' set was two revolving trucks, on the other side of which were the two sections of wall). Downstage is a street-lamp –

just the upright part; the lamp itself is out of view, up in the flies; it is not turned on yet. It is dusk.

From the shadows, or over the wall, **Chips** *enters, on the prowl. He sniffs around hungrily.*

SONG: **This Is My Patch**

Chips
When I'm out on the prowl
The other cats all fly
They wouldn't stop and sniff
    me
They wouldn't dare to try
No, *no* cat muscles in on me
'Cos I'm the Boss round here
And I can scratch –
This is my patch

Though I look sort of scruffy
Up top I'm sort of smart
The struggle for survival
Is really quite an art
So don't come interfering
    when
I'm scavenging for scraps
Don't try to snatch –
This is my patch.

Some cats
Lead a life of luxury
Cuddly and clean and pretty
But an alley cat
Can't be a pally cat
When he's starving
In the streets of the city.

Some nasty kids once caught
    me
And flung me down a hole
I've had to learn the hard way
So I don't trust a soul

> Right now I'm on the look out
>   for
> A juicy bite to eat
> A tasty catch
> May meet its match
> On this – my patch.

As the song ends, **Chips** *reacts to a voice off-stage.*

Mr Wheeler (*off*)   Forward, Mr Fisher. This way.

Chips *beats a hasty retreat.*

From the other side, **Mr Wheeler** *enters pushing the wheelbarrow.* **Baby Duck** *is inside, asleep.* **Mr Fisher** *follows a few paces behind. He is tired.*

Mr Fisher   Oooh! My legs.

Mr Wheeler   Ssh, Mr Fisher, *please.* Fluffy Duck's asleep. He's had a nerve-wracking day.

Mr Fisher   *He's* had a nerve-wracking day. *My* nerves have never been so wracked. I'm exhausted.

Mr Wheeler   Let's have a rest then.

They stop under the street-lamp. **Mr Wheeler** *sits on his barrow.*

Mr Fisher (*sitting down*)   Ohhh! I wasn't made for walking. I was made for sitting cross-legged. That's better.

Mr Wheeler   What an exciting journey. Aren't you glad we came, Mr Fisher?

Mr Fisher   I just hope it's safe here. It's getting quite dark.

A sudden burst of light hits them from above, making them jump.

Jumping toadstools! What's that?

Mr Wheeler   Lightning! Look out for the thunder.

They both cover their ears and close their eyes. Nothing happens. After a short while, they peep.

Mr Fisher   Can't have been lightning. Didn't flash. Still here, look.

Mr Wheeler   What is it then? (*To the audience.*) Anyone know?

Audience   A street-lamp.

Mr Wheeler   A what?

Audience   A street-lamp.

Mr Wheeler *looks up.*

Mr Wheeler   Of course. Look, Mr Fisher. This is a special lamp – it lights up the street when it gets dark.

Mr Fisher   How very thoughtful, I feel much safer now. Good-night, Mr Wheeler. (*He settles in his usual cross-legged position.*)

Mr Wheeler   Good-night, Mr Fisher.

Mr Fisher (*suddenly*)   Aaaaaaah!

Mr Wheeler   Quiet, please. You'll wake Fluffy Duck.

Mr Fisher   It's gone. It's gone.

Mr Wheeler   No, it hasn't. It's in my wheelbarrow.

Mr Fisher   Not Fluffy Duck, you noodly gnome. My fishing-rod! My fishing-rod! (*He jumps up and searches.*)

Mr Wheeler   Stop flappety flapping, Mr Fisher. Where is it?

Mr Fisher   If I knew where it was, I wouldn't be flappety flapping, would I? I've lost it.

Mr Wheeler   You must have left it behind.

Mr Fisher   Behind what?

Mr Wheeler   Not behind what. Behind. Back in the back yard.

Mr Fisher   Then back we must go for it, Mr Wheeler.

Mr Wheeler   We can't go back now.

Mr Fisher   I insist.

Mr Wheeler   You go back.

Mr Fisher   On my own? Certainly not. You come too.

Mr Wheeler   All that way? Just for a fishing-rod?

Mr Fisher   Just for a fishing-rod? Mr Wheeler, my fishing-rod is all I have in the whole world.

Mr Wheeler   Oh, very well. What about Fluffy Duck?

Mr Fisher   Leave him here. He's fast asleep. We won't be long.

Mr Wheeler   But my wheelbarrow . . . Oh, I suppose it'll be all right. (*To the audience.*) Will you keep an eye out for us, please?

Audience   Yes.

Mr Wheeler   Thank you. Thank you very much.

Mr Fisher (*impatient*)   Come on, Mr Wheeler.

They scuttle off.

Tension music as, from the other side, **Chips** *enters. He hungrily approaches the barrow, licking his lips when he sees* **Baby Duck** *inside.*

The audience may well shout a warning. Just as **Chips** *goes to pounce,* **Baby Duck** *wakes and sits up in the barrow with a loud quack.*

Thus taken by surprise, **Chips** *dashes off, or behind the wall.*

Baby Duck *looks around for the* **Gnomes***. He climbs out of the wheelbarrow and looks off-stage. He waddles towards the exit opposite to the one* **Chips** *has just left by. He looks off. Turns to the audience and shakes his head – nobody there. He starts waddling back towards the centre.*

Just behind him, echoing his movement, comes **Chips** *(having run round behind the front cloth or wall).*

The audience should shout a warning. **Baby Duck** *realizes something is amiss, stops and turns suddenly. But* **Chips** *does exactly the same, running round behind* **Baby Duck**, *unseen. This can be repeated. Then* **Baby Duck** *turns, sees* **Chips**, *who goes to grab him.* **Baby Duck** *neatly side-steps, and* **Chips** *crashes to the ground. Furious, he gets us and pursues* **Baby Duck**. *This becomes a chase – round the street-lamp a couple of times, round or over the barrow; perhaps* **Baby Duck** *side-steps the barrow, leaving* **Chips** *to fall over it. As* **Chips** *lies headlong,* **Baby Duck** *suddenly and dramatically starts to run down. Music echoes his struggling helplessness; almost in slow motion his limbs stretch hopelessly.* **Chips** *sees his chance, and, rubbing his paws with glee, advances menacingly, preparing to pounce.*

In the nick of time, the **Gnomes** *enter, returning with* **Mr Fisher***'s fishing-rod.*

The audience may well shout out to them, directing them to help **Baby Duck**, *but in any event, they speedily size up the situation, and wade in to help. They get the fishing-rod between* **Baby Duck** *and* **Chips**, *then drag* **Chips** *away, perhaps forcing him to stumble backwards into the wheelbarrow.* **Mr Fisher** *stands guard over him, while* **Mr Wheeler** *goes to* **Baby Duck** *and re-winds him. He 'wakes up' again and quacks his gratitude. The music ends.*

Mr Fisher (*prodding* **Chips** *with his fishing-rod*)   Now then.

Chips   Easy, man, easy.

Mr Fisher   Easy? What do you mean, easy?

Chips   Cool it.

Mr Fisher   Cool it? Cool what?

Chips   Just cool it. And blow.

Mr Fisher   Blow?

Chips   Blow.

Mr Fisher   Mr Wheeler, I need your assistance.

Mr Wheeler *and* **Baby Duck** *approach*.

Mr Wheeler   Yes, Mr Fisher?

Mr Fisher   This cat's talking fiddle-faddle. He says I have to cool something by blowing on it. He says it's easy.

Mr Wheeler   Explain yourself.

Chips   Like there's nothing to explain, man.

Mr Wheeler   There most certainly is. Why were you attacking this defenceless duck?

Chips   He looked sort of yummy.

Mr Wheeler   Yummy?

Chips   Scrummy.

Mr Wheeler   Scrummy?

Chips   Out of sight.

Mr Wheeler   But how could he look – er – yummy and scrummy if he was out of sight?

Mr Fisher   He talks fiddle-faddle. I told you.

Chips   He looks good enough to eat. Get it?

Mr Fisher   Eat? You wanted to eat him?

Chips   Did you think I wanted to dance with him? I'm starving.

Mr Wheeler   But you couldn't eat *him*?

Chips   You want to bet?

He advances towards **Baby Duck**, *who quacks and backs away*.

Mr Wheeler   But he's not a *real* duck. He's a toy.

Chips *stops*.

Chips   Huh?

Mr Wheeler   He's a toy.

Chips   You mean, one of those clockwork jobs?

Mr Wheeler   Yes.

Chips (*philosophically*)   Story of my life. Win some, lose some. (*Paw outstretched, he approaches* **Baby Duck**.) Sorry, Duck. Nothing personal.

Baby Duck *is unsure and doesn't reciprocate.*

Sorry, gents.

Mr Wheeler   Gnomes, actually. Mr Fisher. (*He bows.*)

Mr Fisher   Mr Wheeler. (*He bows.*)

Chips   Chips.

Mr Wheeler   I beg your pardon?

Chips   That's what they call me. Chips.

Mr Fisher   Funny name for a cat.

Chips   That's all he had left.

Mr Fisher   Eh?

Chips   The guy at the fish and chip shop. Like one day I went and begged for some fish. But he'd sold it all. Only had chips left. I was so hungry, I ate them. So people call me Chips. Well, I'd better blow – (*Seeing the* **Gnomes** *don't understand.*) – er – go.

Mr Wheeler   Where are you – er, blowing to? Where do you live?

Chips   Here. This alley is my home. This street is my home. This city is my home. Like I'm free. No ties, man. No responsibilities.

Mr Fisher   No food . . .

Chips   I get by.

Mr Fisher   If only I could catch you a fish – all my life I've wanted to – here's my rod, you see – listen, if I ever catch one, *you* shall have it.

Chips   Good on you, Mr Fisher, that's ace, really. Ace.

Mr Fisher   I don't know a fish called ace; a plaice, maybe?

Mr Wheeler   And who knows? Mr Fisher may catch it very soon. We're on holiday, you see, Chips . . .

Music for tension. **Chips** *suddenly changes. He shakes with fear and anger.*

Chips   Holiday? Holiday? Horrid things, holidays. I hate them. I hate them.

Mr Wheeler   But why? Holidays are for enjoying.

Chips   Not when you're left behind, they're not. Like I lived in a house once, with a family of Big Ones; they went on holiday. Like I never saw them again.

Mr Fisher   You mean they just left you? Without food or shelter?

Chips   They even nailed up the cat flap.

Mr Fisher   That's disgraceful.

Chips   Mm. Maybe. I don't care. All I know is that now I only have to hear the word 'holiday' and I freak out. My whiskers tremble and my fur stands on end.

Mr Wheeler   I'm so sorry. I should never have mentioned hol – well, you know – that word.

Chips   That's OK, man. You weren't to know. So where are you heading?

Mr Wheeler   To be honest, we don't really know.

Mr Fisher   We've never left the back yard before.

Chips   Well, why don't I show you around? I'll take you anywhere you want. I know this city like the back of my paw.

Mr Wheeler (*uncertainly*)   Well, that's most kind . . .

Baby Duck *quacks, alarmed.*

What's the matter, Fluffy Duck?

Baby Duck *mimes he isn't sure whether* **Chips**' *presence would be a good idea.*

I'm sure Chips won't hurt you now.

Baby Duck *still looks concerned.* **Mr Wheeler** *turns to* **Chips**.

Mr Fisher   Well, maybe . . .

Mr Fisher   It might be sensible –

Mr Wheeler   – to, er, press on alone.

Chips   Don't trust me, huh?

Mr Wheeler   It's not that, we – oh, dear, have we hurt your feelings?

Chips   No skin off my nose. But I tell you straight. The city's not safe to explore on your tod. You won't get far through the concrete jungle by yourselves. Still. Up to you. Good luck. See you. (*He casually leans against the street-lamp to watch them go.*)

The **Gnomes** *are a little uncomfortable, but decide to go.*

Mr Wheeler   Goodbye.

Mr Fisher   Goodbye.

Baby Duck *quacks 'Goodbye'. Music as they prepare to go – collecting wheelbarrow and rod. They start off towards the audience. Sudden frightening light hits their faces, accompanied by the loud noise of a car roaring past. The* **Gnomes** *and* **Baby Duck** *react terrified, and back away. After a moment to recover they gingerly set off again. Another dazzling light blinds them and another car roars past. Again the* **Gnomes** *and* **Baby Duck** *recoil, frightened.* **Chips**

remains impassive, watching from the street-lamp. **Baby Duck**
quacks in alarm.

What's happening, Mr Wheeler?

Mr Wheeler   I wish I knew, Mr Fisher.

Baby Duck *quacks and points to the audience.*

What? Ask them? Good idea? (*To the audience.*) Do you know
what's making all that noise and shining that light?

Audience   Cars.

Mr Wheeler   I beg your pardon?

Audience   Cars.

Mr Fisher   Of course, Mr Wheeler. Cars – like the Big
Ones' car. Big dangerous things that move very fast.

Mr Wheeler (*to the audience*)   Thank you. Would you be
kind enough to let us know if another's coming?

Audience   Yes.

Mr Wheeler   Thanks. Come on, Fluffy. Come on, Mr
Fisher.

*There is the noise of an approaching vehicle as the three creep forward.
The audience shout out a warning. The car flashes by. The* **Gnomes**
and **Baby Duck** *look relieved.*

(*To the audience, as they move off.*) Thanks.

*They try again. Another vehicle is heard approaching. Again the
audience shouts out a warning. The* **Gnomes** *and* **Baby Duck**
stop again in the nick of time. The light hits their faces.

Thanks again.

Mr Fisher   Mr Wheeler, this is absurd. We'll be here for
ever.

Baby Duck *quacks and indicates, with a little embarrassment, the
impassive* **Chips**.

What? Ask Chips to help? Trust him?

Baby Duck *nods.*

Mr Fisher   I agree. Mr Wheeler?

Mr Wheeler   So do I, but we may well have upset Chips by turning down his offer the first time. Let's try, anyway.

They go back to **Chips**.

Er . . . Chips.

Chips   Mmmmm?

Mr Wheeler   We – er . . .

Chips   Mmmmm?

Baby Duck *quacks, apologizing.*

Mr Wheeler   Fluffy Duck apologizes. We all apologize.

Mr Fisher   Please may we accept your earlier offer to show us around the city?

Chips   Mmm, well, like I'm a busy cat; I may have other – engagements . . .

Mr Wheeler   Please?

Chips (*after a pause*)   OK. Come on. (*He leads them back to the 'kerb'.*) Rule number one in the city coming up – crossing roads – stand, wait – then . . .

SONG: **Use Your Eyes and Ears**

(*Singing.*)
                    Use your eyes and ears
                    Before you use your feet
                    Look and listen
                    Before you cross the street
                    Double check and when
                        you're satisfied
                    Walk don't run
                    To the other side.

(*Speaking.*) OK? Do you think you can remember that?

Mr Fisher   Er . . . (*Singing unaccompanied.*)

> Use your ears and feet

Mr Wheeler   Before you blow your nose . . .

Chips   No!

Mr Fisher   Oh dear.

Mr Wheeler   You'd better teach us again, Chips, please.

Chips   OK. (*Idea, taking in the audience.*) We'll *all* teach you. (*To the audience.*) Will you help the Gnomes and sing it with me?

Audience   Yes.

Chips   You will?

Audience   Yes!

Chips   Great.

At this point **Chips** *teaches the song to the audience. A songsheet could be used, or* **Chips** *could chalk the words on the wall, but in the original production the audience picked up the song with ease, simply learning it from* **Chips**, *with actions to suit the words. The routine used was as follows.*

Right. Everybody, stand up.

The house lights come up as the audience is encouraged to stand.

Now, we're going to learn it in three chunks. I'll sing it first, and then you all sing it after me. First chunk coming up, after three. One, two, three . . .

(*Singing unaccompanied.*)

> Use your eyes and ears
> Before you use your feet

(*Speaking.*) Ready? One, two, three . . .

Chips ⎫
Audience ⎬   Use your eyes and ears
　　　　　　⎭   Before you use your feet

Chips   Very good. Don't forget the actions. Once more.
One, two, three . . .

Chips ⎫	Use your eyes and ears
Audience ⎬	Before you use your feet

Chips   Next bit.

(*Singing.*)
> Look and listen
> Before you cross the street

(*Speaking.*) Ready?

Chips ⎫	Look and listen
Audience ⎬	Before you cross the street

Chips   Very good. Just once more.

Chips ⎫	Look and listen
Audience ⎬	Before you cross the street

Chips   Last bit.
(*Singing.*)
> Double check and when
>   you're satisfied
> Walk don't run
> To the other side.

(*Speaking.*) Ready?

Chips ⎫	Double check and when
Audience ⎬	you're satisfied
	Walk don't run
	To the other side.

Chips   Just one more try.

Chips ⎫	Double check and when
Audience ⎬	you're satisfied
	Walk don't run
	To the other side.

Chips   Right. Now let's put it all together. After three.
One, two, three . . .

*The **Gnomes** join in the words and actions. **Baby Duck** does the actions.*

All   Use your eyes and ears
                                 Before you use your feet
                                 Look and listen
                                 Before you cross the street
                                 Double check and when
                                     you're satisfied
                                 Walk don't run
                                 To the other side.

Chips   Great! *They've* got it. How about you, Mr Fisher, Mr Wheeler?

Mr Fisher   Well, nearly, I think . . .

Mr Wheeler   Just once more, Chips, and we'll know it.

Chips   OK. Everybody. One, two, three . . .

All   Use your eyes and ears
                                 Before you use your feet
                                 Look and listen
                                 Before you cross the street
                                 Double check and when
                                     you're satisfied
                                 Walk don't run
                                 To the other side.

Mr Fisher   I think I've got it! (*To the audience.*) Thank you, everybody.

Mr Wheeler   So have I. (*To the audience.*) Thank you.

Chips   Terrific! Thanks, everyone. You can sit down now.

The house lights fade.

Mr Wheeler   Can we cross now, Chips?

Chips   OK. This time it's for real!

This time they sing the song, following each action on the 'real' road.

Mr Fisher   ⎫   Use your eyes and ears
Mr Wheeler ⎬   Before your use your feet
Chips   ⎭   Look and listen
                              Before you cross the street

Pause as they look and listen. No sound or light.

> Double check.

Another pause as they look and listen.

> And when you're satisfied

They nod to each other.

> Walk don't run
> To the other side.

Music continues as happily and confidently they 'cross the road'. The lights fade to a black-out.

Scene Three

The Adventure Playground.

(If at the end of the previous scene, the characters have crossed the road by walking 'out front' – towards the audience – into a black-out, it is suggested they stay on stage for the scene change, turn round, backs to the audience, and, when the lights come up, walk into the scene.)

Downstage we see a section of the wire-netting fence surrounding the playground. Also part of the entrance gate, which is closed, but under which there is just enough room for the characters to crawl. (In one production, a corner of the wire netting was loose, thus enabling the characters to creep in that way.) Signs and notices are visible in this area – 'ADVENTURE PLAYGROUND' above the entrance; 'KEEP OUT', 'BEWARE OF THE GUARD DOG', 'TRESPASSERS WILL BE PROSECUTED' on the gate or fence. A red burglar alarm system is attached to the fence, with 'BURGLAR ALARM' written on it.

Upstage of the fence and gate section is a corner of the playground itself. It has a large rubber tyre (from a bus or lorry?) suspended like a trapeze from the flies. (This could be a simple swing.) Also a tube of pipe lying horizontally on the ground. This should be about five feet long, with enough room for the characters to crawl through it, like a tunnel. Finally, we can see a dog kennel, marked 'SECURIDOG'. Its occupant is not visible. A food bowl is positioned just outside; it is marked 'Doggy Dins'.

The Adventure Playground should be as colourful as possible. It is still evening – atmospheric 'darkness'. Street-lamp-type lighting making things visible in shafts of light. In fact, in this scene, we need to see the action clearly.

The **Gnomes**, **Baby Duck** *and* **Chips** *arrive outside the Adventure Playground.*

Chips   OK, so now we've crossed the road, like where do we go from here?

Mr Wheeler   Well, Chips, our dream is to discover what the Big Ones call an island.

Mr Fisher   Sun and sea and fish.

Baby Duck *quacks.*

Chips   An island. No problem. Follow me.

He leads them a step or two. Then suddenly he stops dead. Perhaps the others concertina into him. **Chips** *sniffs – picking up a scent.*

Mr Wheeler   What is it?

Chips *moves fitfully, sniffing the air.*

Chips   Can't you sniff it?

Mr Wheeler   Sniff it? Sniff what?

Chips   A whiff.

Mr Fisher   Sniff a whiff? Sniff a whiff of what?

Chips   Sniff a whiff of yummy, scrummy – Doggy Dins!

Mr Wheeler   Doggy Dins?

Chips   Mm. Meaty, mouthwatering, magnificent Doggy Dins! One of my favourite-flavoured foods.

Mr Fisher   Where?

Chips (*after a big sniff*)   There. Over there. (*He turns, sees the kennel and bowl, and reacts angrily.*) Aaaaah! Typical. Typical. (*He stomps away.*)

The others follow.

Mr Fisher   Isn't the whiff you sniffed Doggy Dins after all?

Chips   Of course it's Doggy Dins. But look whose Doggy Dins it is.

They turn.

Securidog's!

Dramatic chord.

Mr Wheeler   Securidog's?

Chips   Isn't that just my luck? Starving. Get a sniff. Securidog's Doggy Dins.

Mr Fisher   I'm sorry, I don't get it.

Chips   *You* don't get it! *I* don't get it. I don't get any Doggy Dins. Look. Behind this fence is the Adventure Playground. Right?

Mr Wheeler   Er – right.

Mr Fisher   Sorry, but what's an Adventure Playground?

Chips   What's an Adventure Playground? Don't you Gnomes know nothing? And Adventure Playground is *ground* where children *play* and have *adventures*. Right?

Mr Fisher   Ah. Right.

Chips   At night, it's locked up, right?

Mr Fisher 〉 Right .
Mr Wheeler 〉

Baby Duck *quacks at the same time.*

Chips   Securidog guards it, right?

Mr Fisher } Right.
Mr Wheeler }

Baby Duck *quacks with them.*

Chips   Securidog loves Doggy Dins and hates cats, right?

Mr Fisher } Right.
Mr Wheeler }

Baby Duck *quacks with them.*

Chips   So no Doggy Dins for poor old Chips, right?

Mr Fisher } Right
Mr Wheeler }

Baby Duck *quacks with them.*

Mr Wheeler   Wrong. You've helped us, so we'll help you.
Or try to.

Chips   Help me?

Mr Wheeler   We'll crawl under here with my
wheelbarrow – (*He indicates the space under the gate.*) – and ask
Securidog, very politely, if he can spare some of his Doggy
Dins for a deserving cause. You.

Mr Fisher   But, Mr Wheeler, is it safe?

Chips   Like Securidog is pretty fierce.

Baby Duck *starts quacking excitedly. He has spotted the notices
hanging on the fence and gate.*

Mr Fisher   Mm? What?

Baby Duck *quacks, pointing at the signs.*

What are they? Chips?

Chips   Signs. With writing on. Can anyone read them?
(*He encourages the audience to read them out.*)

Audience   'Burglar Alarm'; 'Keep Out'; 'Beware of the
Guard Dog'; 'Trespassers Will Be Prosecuted'.

Mr Fisher   'Burglar Alarm'; 'Keep Out'; 'Beware of the Guard Dog'; 'Trespassers Will Be Prosecuted'? Mr Wheeler, we can't possibly risk going in there – just to get some Doggy Dins.

Mr Wheeler   But Chips *needs* it . . . what's this place called again?

Chips   An Adventure Playground.

Mr Wheeler   Well, this is a real adventure playground adventure!

Chips   OK, *I'll* come.

Mr Wheeler   Mr Fisher?

Silence. Then . . .

SONG: **A Real Adventure Playground Adventure**

During the song, **Baby Duck** *tends to side with* **Mr Fisher***, who gets in quite a state; they both point out the signs as* **Mr Fisher** *mentions them.*

Mr Wheeler	Let's go in
Mr Fisher	It says 'Keep Out'
Chips	But think of all that food
Mr Fisher	'Beware of the Guard Dog'
Mr Wheeler	He won't bite if we're not rude
Mr Fisher	'Burglar Alarm'
Mr Wheeler ⎫ **Chips** ⎭	Mr Fisher, please keep calm!
Mr Fisher	'Trespassers Will Be Prosecuted'
Mr Wheeler ⎫ **Chips** ⎭	We're not doing any harm.
	It's a real adventure playground adventure Don't you see?
Mr Fisher	But I really don't think we ought
Mr Wheeler	It's a quest to help a friend

Chips	Who happens to be me
Mr Fisher	But what happens if we all get caught?
Chips	Oh come on!
Mr Fisher	It says 'Keep Out'
Mr Wheeler	Well, you can stay out here
Mr Fisher	'Beware of the Guard Dog'
Chips	We'll be careful, never fear
Mr Fisher	'Burglar alarm'
Chips **Mr Wheeler**	If we set it off we run
Mr Fisher	'Trespassers Will Be Prosecuted'
Chips **Mr Wheeler**	We're not hurting anyone.
	It's a real adventure playground adventure
Mr Fisher	Yes, I know
	But I really do think it's wrong
	I'll stay here with Baby Duck
	Good luck
Chips **Mr Wheeler**	Right, off we go
	Now don't worry 'cos we won't be long.

Mr Fisher and **Baby Duck** *remain behind by the fence as gingerly* **Mr Wheeler** *and* **Chips** *crawl under the gate, and inside. The lighting focuses inside the Adventure Playground. Music echoes the tension.*

During the following action, **Mr Fisher** *unobtrusively sits, looking into the playground, and eventually goes to sleep.* **Baby Duck** *stays with him.*

Mr Wheeler *and* **Chips** *approach the kennel.* **Mr Wheeler** *motions* **Chips** *to hide behind the kennel.* **Mr Wheeler** *knocks on the kennel. No reaction. He knocks again. No reaction. He goes to knock again. As he does so,* **Securidog** *pops out, taking him by surprise.*

Securidog   Whadja name and whadja game?

Mr Wheeler   I beg your pardon?

Securidog   Whadja name and whadja game? Whadja doing here?

Mr Wheeler   I . . .

Securidog   I'll tell you whadja doing here. You're trespassing, and trespassers will be prosecuted so prosecuted you will be. Forthwith, straightway and without further ado. Whadja name? (*He takes out a notebook and pencil.*)

Mr Wheeler   Listen . . .

Securidog   I don't listen. My ears are trained not to listen.

Mr Wheeler   But look . . .

Securidog   I don't look. My eyes are trained not to look.

Mr Wheeler   You don't listen. You don't look. That's a bit stupid, don't you think?

Securidog   I don't think. My brain is trained not to think.

Mr Wheeler   You're not trained to do anything, by the sound of it.

Securidog   Oh yes I am. I am a trained trapper of trespassers. So there.

Mr Wheeler   Well, I'm not a trespasser. I've come to ask you a question. Are you trained to answer questions?

Securidog   Is it an easy question or a hard question?

Mr Wheeler   Easy.

Securidog   All right, then, I'll have a go. (*He concentrates.*)

Mr Wheeler   It's to do with your Doggy Dins. (*He points to the bowl.*)

Securidog   Yes?

Mr Wheeler   I have a friend, a cat, who is extremely hungry.

Securidog   Yes?

Mr Wheeler   Who is very partial to Doggy Dins.

Securidog   Yes?

Mr Wheeler   The question is, could you spare some?

Securidog   Yes.

Mr Wheeler   Oh thank you, I'll just . . . (*He goes to load some on his wheelbarrow.*)

Securidog   Stop! I said yes, I *could* spare some; I didn't say I was *going* to spare some. And I'm not. For a cat! I hate cats. And I hate friends of cats. So clear off before . . .

Mr Wheeler   But he's starving . . .

Securidog   Good. I'm glad. Clear off . . .

Mr Wheeler   Please . . .

Securidog   Or I'll throw you against the fence and make the alarm bell ring and then the Big Ones'll come and sort you out. Clear off. (*He stomps back inside his kennel.*)

Music. **Mr Wheeler** *takes his wheelbarrow and turns to go. He sees* **Chips**, *downcast, appear from behind the kennel. He stops.* **Mr Wheeler** *looks at the bowl of food, back to* **Chips**, *then to the kennel – there is no sign of* **Securidog**. **Mr Wheeler** *turns to the audience.*

Mr Wheeler (*in a stage whisper*)   Shall I take some?

Audience (*encouraged not to shout, but whisper back*)   Yes.

Mr Wheeler (*in a whisper*)   Chips.

He beckons **Chips** *over, and quickly mimes taking some food. Very gingerly* **Mr Wheeler** *takes a chunk of dog food, and passes it to* **Chips** *who loads it into the wheelbarrow. And another chunk. And another. Suddenly* **Securidog** *bursts out of the kennel.* **Mr**

Wheeler and **Chips** *naturally scatter to avoid capture or rough handling.*

Securidog   Right. You asked for it and you're going to get it. (*Seeing* **Chips**.) And you, you mangy moggy. Thieves with be prosecuted, and prosecuted you will be. Forthwith, straightway and without further ado.

Mr Wheeler *and his wheelbarrow back away, then head gingerly for the gate.* **Chips** *leaps into the suspended tyre and crouches, swinging.* **Securidog** *has come out further than we have seen him before. We now see he is tethered to the kennel and cannot chase the others any further.*

(*Seeing and grabbing the wheelbarrow.*) Right. For a start I'm confiscating this. This will be Exhibit A.

Mr Wheeler   Not my wheelbarrow, please.

Securidog   It contains stolen property. Kidnapped Doggy Dins. Exhibit B. Now you two, come here. You'll be Exhibits C and – and – four.

Chips   Hey. Look, Mr Wheeler. He's tied to the kennel. He can't chase us, let alone catch us. (*Taunting.*) Cooee, Securidog, come and catch me! Cooee! (*He leans down provocatively from the tyre.*)

Securidog   You cheeky cat, you'll regret that . . . (*He charges, but can't get far enough, because his tether won't stretch any more. He growls with frustration.*)

Chips   Oh, he's cross. Look. My, my. Like he's at the end of his tether! (*He laughs.*)

Mr Wheeler (*approaching*)   Now, Chips. Don't tease the poor fellow. After all, it can't be much fun being tied up.

Securidog   It's not. I hate it.

Mr Wheeler   The Big Ones, I bet?

Securidog   What?

Mr Wheeler   I bet it was the Big Ones tied you up?

Securidog   Yes. Said I might not do my job if I wasn't tied up. Said I might run away.

Mr Wheeler   Might you?

Securidog   Maybe.

Mr Wheeler (*deliberately buttering him up*)   You don't enjoy being nasty to people, do you?

Securidog   I'm only doing my job.

Mr Wheeler   You're quite friendly really, aren't you? (*He strokes him.*)

Securidog   I *would* be, but I haven't got any friends. Mm, that's nice!

Mr Wheeler   Be my friend.

Securidog   Mm. That's lovely. How?

Mr Wheeler   Give me back my wheelbarrow.

Securidog   What? (*Snapping out of his trance.*) You're just trying to get round me, aren't you? All that stroking. If I give you back your wheelbarrow I'll never see you again. Fine friend you'd be.

Mr Wheeler   But I need my wheelbarrow. If I go home without it, the Big Ones where I live will notice it's gone.

Securidog   Oh, that's all right, then.

Mr Wheeler   I beg your pardon?

Securidog   Because you're not going home. You're Exhibit C.

Mr Wheeler   But you're forgetting. You can't stop me going home.

Securidog   Why not?

Mr Wheeler   Because you're tied to your kennel.

Pause. This sinks in.

Securidog   Tell you what.

Mr Wheeler   What?

Securidog   I'll give you back your wheelbarrow . . .

Mr Wheeler   Thank you.

Securidog   And a few chunks of Doggy Dins . . .

Mr Wheeler   Oh, thank you.

He moves forward. But **Securidog** *still holds the wheelbarrow.*

Securidog   Wait for it! If . . .

Mr Wheeler   Yes?

Securidog   And only if . . .

Mr Wheeler   What?

Securidog   You untie me.

Mr Wheeler   Ah . . . I untie you?

Securidog   That's fair. Whadja say? (*He smiles innocently.*)

Mr Wheeler   Well . . .

Chips (*who has been listening from the tyre*)   Don't trust him, Mr Wheeler. It's a trick.

Mr Wheeler   But I must get my wheelbarrow back.

Securidog   Untie me and it's yours.

Chips   He'll double-cross you. He's just said he might run away.

Mr Wheeler   But you need some Doggy Dins.

Chips   But if we let him go I might not be around long enough to eat them.

Mr Wheeler   Oh dear . . . (*Idea – he turns to the audience.*) What do *you* think we should do? Untie him? Yes? No?

If the majority shout 'Yes', **Mr Wheeler** *says 'All right'. If the majority shout 'No', he says 'But I really think I must.' Tension music as he approaches* **Securidog**, *who smiles, looking as good as gold.* **Mr Wheeler** *unties his tether and puts the rope down by the kennel.* **Securidog** *politely hands over the wheelbarrow. He puts some chunks of Doggy Dins in it.* **Mr Wheeler** *wheels it away towards* **Chips**, *who leaps down to meet it. Just as we think the exchange has gone well . . .*

Securidog   Ha, ha, ha. I'm free. I'm free. I'll get you. I'll get you!

He charges at the retreating pair, who react horrified. Exciting music echoes the ensuing chase sequence. **Chips** *dashes to the tyre again.* **Securidog** *makes for* **Mr Wheeler***. The wheelbarrow is between them. They play a cat and mouse game round it – both side-stepping left, right, then left again. Then* **Securidog** *chases* **Mr Wheeler** *round the barrow. Once. Twice. On the third round,* **Securidog** *waits, and trips up* **Mr Wheeler** *as he comes round.* **Mr Wheeler** *falls on the ground.* **Securidog** *grabs the barrow, and wheels it back towards the kennel, passing* **Chips** *in the tyre, who lashes out at him, but can't reach.* **Securidog** *wheels the barrow into his kennel.* **Chips** *jumps down and goes to look at the prostrate* **Mr Wheeler***.* **Securidog** *emerges from the kennel, having left the barrow inside. He sees* **Chips***, facing away from him, and advances.*

The audience will probably shout a warning.

Chips *turns in the nick of time, and runs to the tyre.* **Securidog** *follows. A short chase round the tyre, then* **Chips** *nimbly leaps through it.* **Securidog** *tries to follow, but gets stuck half-way through.* **Chips** *gives him a couple of kicks up the backside. If possible* **Chips** *climbs on to the top of the tyre, above* **Securidog***.* **Securidog** *suddenly spots* **Mr Wheeler** *getting up and heading for the kennel to retrieve his barrow. He extricates himself from the tyre, giving it a good swing, making* **Chips** *hang on grimly.* **Securidog** *cuts off* **Mr Wheeler***'s progress to the kennel. He makes a grab for him, but* **Mr Wheeler** *ducks and nimbly darts through* **Securidog***'s legs, and runs towards the pipe.* **Mr Wheeler** *enters the pipe.* **Securidog** *follows him through and 'flushes' him out of the*

other end. **Mr Wheeler** *runs round and into the pipe again.*
Securidog *follows. Another flushing.*

But by now, **Baby Duck**, *outside the playground, has been watching in alarm, and woken* **Mr Fisher**, *who, seeing his chance, leaving his fishing-rod behind, crawls under the gate. Just as* **Mr Wheeler** *enters the pipe a third time,* **Mr Fisher** *calls out. The music stops momentarily so that we can hear him.*

Mr Fisher   Coo-ee!

Securidog *turns and sees* **Mr Fisher**. *He is confused, because the* **Gnomes** *look so similar. He looks back at the pipe, scratching his head.*

Securidog   Eh? Howdja get over there?

He makes towards **Mr Fisher**, *who runs between his legs, inside the pipe.* **Securidog** *leaps on top of the pipe, hoping to grab Mr Fisher as he comes out. Suddenly* **Mr Wheeler** *pops his head out of the other end.*

Mr Wheeler   Coo-ee!

Securidog *stops in his tracks – how did the gnome get through the pipe so quickly? He dashes to* **Mr Wheeler**'s *end.* **Mr Wheeler** *pops back in. Simultaneously* **Mr Fisher** *pops out again at his end.*

Mr Fisher   Coo-ee!

Securidog *turns back, totally mystified. He starts back to* **Mr Fisher**'s *end. Simultaneously,* **Mr Fisher** *disappears and* **Mr Wheeler** *pops his head out.*

Mr Wheeler   Coo-ee!

Securidog *stands on the centre of the pipe in confusion. He looks back to* **Mr Fisher**'s *end. Two legs appear.* **Securidog** *now sees what appears to be a very long gnome –* **Mr Wheeler**'s *head and* **Mr Fisher**'s *legs poking out.*

Securidog (*facing front*)   Aaaaaaaaaaah!

Now the **Gnomes** *both turn round – i.e.* **Mr Fisher***'s head and* **Mr Wheeler***'s legs are visible.* **Securidog** *looks again. He reacts.*

(*Facing front.*)   Aaaaaaaaaaah!

Now **Mr Wheeler** *stays as he is and* **Mr Fisher** *changes position – so four legs poke out.* **Securidog** *looks again. He reacts.*

(*Facing front.*)   Aaaaaaaaaaah!

The final coup! Both **Gnomes** *change positions – so two heads pop out.* **Securidog** *rubs his eyes in disbelief, then turns again. He reacts.*

Aaaaaaaaaaaaaaaaaah!

Chips *sees his chance. He jumps down from the tyre, and dashes into the kennel to retrieve* **Mr Wheeler***'s barrow.* **Securidog** *sees him and follows, into the kennel. Terrible sounds of a fight emerge from inside the kennel. Eventually* **Chips** *dashes out – with the barrow – and hides – maybe behind the pipe. The* **Gnomes** *hide inside the pipe.* **Securidog** *emerges, raging, from the kennel. He can see nothing.*

Then, suddenly, outside the fence, **Baby Duck** *starts strutting up and down.* **Securidog** *registers this with surprise.* **Baby Duck** *looks at him through the fence. He looks at* **Baby Duck***.* **Securidog** *barks ferociously.* **Baby Duck** *doesn't move, but quacks.* **Securidog** *jumps back, terrified. He barks again;* **Baby Duck** *quacks; he jumps back again. Then* **Securidog** *charges like a bull towards* **Baby Duck***. He crashes into the wire fence.* **Baby Duck** *retreats into the shadows.*

Immediately all hell is let loose. First the loud clanging of the burglar alarm, then police sirens, flashing blue lights. A car arrives. Doors slam. Voices boom from above.

Voice 1   Who's there? What's going on?

Voice 2   Come on out, whoever you are.

A searchlight (a police torch) swings around and comes to rest on **Securidog** *cowering by the fence.*

Voice 1   Hey look, it's only Securidog. He's escaped. Set the alarm off.

Voice 2   Get back in your kennel, you stupid animal.

Voice 1   Wasting our time.

Securidog, *tail between his legs as it were, meekly returns to his kennel, looking at the **Big Ones** above.*

Voice 2   And you can stay in there till the morning. We don't want any more false alarms.

Securidog *gets in the kennel.*

The searchlight goes out. The car doors slam and the car drives off. The lighting returns to normal.

*The **Gnomes** emerge from the pipe, and **Chips**, plus barrow. **Baby Duck** comes to meet them. They all shake hands, then start going under the gate. **Chips** stops, turns back, goes towards the kennel, and takes a few more chunks of dog food from the bowl and returns to the others, outside the gate. **Mr Wheeler** takes back his barrow. **Chips** takes a chunk of dog food and starts to eat it.*

Chips   Thank you, Gnomes; thank you, Baby Duck. Maybe holidays aren't so bad after all! Now . . .

SONG: **Holiday Island** (*reprise*)

Chips	Let's find your holiday island
Mr Wheeler ⎫ **Mr Fisher** ⎭	Our holiday do or die land
All	Where there's nothing to do But enjoy doing nothing Where there's nothing to do But have fun Let's find our holiday yours and my land Pie in the sky land Do or die land Island in the sun.

They start to exit, perhaps through the auditorium. **Baby Duck** *collects* **Mr Fisher**'s *fishing-rod for him.*

> Let's find our holiday island
> Yours and my land
> Pie in the sky land
> Do or die land
> Island in the sun.
>
> (*Optional repeat.*)
> Let's find our holiday island
> Yours and my land
> Pie in the sky land
> Do or die land
> Island in the sun.

They exit.

Curtain.

Act Two

Scene One

The Street.

We see the edge of the kerb of a pavement; the pavement is a rostrum, behind which there could be a backing of doors, shopfronts or a wall. There is a drain at road level, with the usual grating effect. Immediately in front of the kerb, there is a patch of wet tar, with a notice to inform us of the fact, surrounded by a few red and white cones and maybe a warning lantern.

To the other side, there is a road works section, with a barrier, a sign and some more red and white cones.

Wacker, *the pneumatic bouncer, is standing or lying horizontally on the pavement behind the tar. He remains lifeless until started up, and should not be lit too visibly yet.*

It is still night-time, but street-lighting effects should make the pavement and drain side of the stage clearly, though atmospherically, visible. The road works side should be fairly dark. Perhaps we hear a clock chime two a.m.

Music as **Chips** *enters energetically, turns and looks off, then beckons. He jumps off the pavement, between the drain and the road works.*

Baby Duck *enters.*

Chips *helps him down from the pavement, then exits.*

Baby Duck *starts to exit, then sees the wet tar. He spots the 'WET TAR' notice. He scratches his head, unable to read the sign. He looks at the audience and quacks a request for them to read the sign. Hopefully they read out 'Wet Tar'.* **Baby Duck** *goes to the tar and starts to dip his foot in, looking at the audience as if to say 'Shall I?' The audience should warn him not to. He repeats this.*

Chips *dashes on and pulls* **Baby Duck** *away from the tar.*

Chips   Hey, Duck. Come away. Like that's wet tar.

Baby Duck *quacks that he knows that – the audience told him. He* *returns to the tar and starts to put his foot in it.* **Chips** *grabs him* *again.*

NO! It's what the Big Ones use to mend the road. It's very sticky. If you tread in it you might never get out.

Baby Duck *quacks, alarmed.*

SONG: **Stuck Duck**

(*Singing.*)
> Don't put
> Your foot
> In the muck, Duck
> This black tacky
> Tarmacky
> Muck, Duck
> If you put
> Your foot
> In the muck, Duck
> You can bet
> Your luck
> You'll get
> Stuck, Duck.
>
> It's icky and ucky
> As ucky as can be
> So sticky and yucky
> You won't get free.

Suddenly **Baby Duck** *runs down.* **Chips** *rewinds him.* **Baby** **Duck** *cheekily comes to life again and heads for the tar.* **Chips** *restrains him.*

> Don't put
> Your foot
> In the muck, Duck
> This black tacky
> Tarmacky
> Muck, Duck
> If you put
> Your foot

> In the muck, Duck
> You can bet
> Your luck
> Lor' luv a duck
> You can bet
> Your luck
> You'll get
> Stuck, Duck.

(*Speaking.*) Right?

Baby Duck *quacks.*

We hear **Mr Fisher** *groan off-stage.*

Chips *looks off. He beckons.*

(*Calling.*) Come on, you two, keep up.

Mr Fisher *enters carrying his fishing-rod. He is tired.*

Mr Fisher   Ohhh. Keep up, he says; I can't even keep awake.

Chips *helps him down from the pavement.*

Chips   Well, you didn't expect your holiday island to be round the next corner, did you?

Mr Fisher *yawns and stops, virtually nodding off on the spot.*

Come on, Mr Wheeler.

Mr Wheeler *enters, pushing his wheelbarrow.* **Chips** *helps him down.*

Mr Wheeler   Coming, Chips. (*He sees litter.*) Oh no, look at this.

Mr Fisher   Look at what?

Mr Wheeler   This! Big Ones' rubbish, Mr Fisher. Scattered everywhere. What a mess!

Chips   Like it's the same all over the city, Mr Wheeler.

Mr Fisher   *Our* Big Ones put their rubbish in their dustbin.

Mr Wheeler (*seeing a litter bin*)   There's a sort of dustbin, Mr. Fisher. Come along. To work!

Mr Fisher   Oh no, Mr Wheeler.

Mr Wheeler   It's our duty, Mr Fisher. The Code of the Gnomes.

Mr Fisher   Our duty, Mr Wheeler, (*Giving in.*) the Code of the Gnomes.

SONG: **Big Ones, Are You List'ning?**

During the song, the **Gnomes**, *helped by* **Chips** *and* **Baby Duck**, *clear the rubbish into the litter bin.*

> Big Ones are you list'ning?
> You're a messy lot
> Clogging up the gutter
> With your garbage and your
>   grot
> Leave your rubbish
> In some other place
> Big Ones are you list'ning?
> You're a disgrace
>
> Half-sucked oranges
> Squashed fizzy drink cans
> Pizza boxes, lolly sticks
> Littering the street
> Bus tickets, apple cores
> Cheese and onion crisp bags
> Screwed up chewy
> Sweet wrappers
> Sticking to our feet.
>
> Big Ones are you list'ning?
> You're a messy crowd
> Really such untidiness
> Ought not to be allowed
> Leave your rubbish
> In some other place

Big Ones are you list'ning?
You're a disgrace

Please won't you stop it
Please don't just drop it
Find a litter bin
And throw the litter in.

Greasy newspaper
Some still with chips in
Rubber bands,
Old shopping lists
Torn up magazines
Matches, banana skins
Dirty paper tissues
Empty plastic bottles all
Smashed to smithereens.

Big Ones are you list'ning?
You're a messy bunch
Dropping on the pavement
The left-overs of your lunch
Leave your rubbish
In some other place
Bigs Ones are you list'ning?
You're a disgrace.

Big Ones are you list'ning?
You're a disgrace.

At the end of the song, **Mr Fisher** *collapses into the wheelbarrow and goes to sleep.*

Chips *winds up* **Baby Duck**.

Chips   Right then. Holiday Island here we come.

Mr Wheeler   How much further is it, Chips? My legs are dropping off.

Chips   Mr Fisher's dropped off already.

Mr Wheeler   Chips, I think we all need a rest.

Baby Duck *quacks indignantly, waddling vigorously.*

Chips   *He* doesn't. I've just wound him up.

Mr Wheeler   Well, Mr Fisher and I do. We're just not used to all this energetic exercise.

Chips   OK. We'll have a quick kip.

Mr Wheeler   Thank you.

He sits on his wheelbarrow and starts to settle to sleep.

Fluffy Duck, you too.

Baby Duck *quacks and shakes his head.*

What? You don't want to sleep?

Baby Duck *quacks 'no'.*

Chips   Like I told you. I just wound him up.

Mr Wheeler   Oh dear. That means he's full of beans; he'll never sleep. (*To* **Baby Duck**.) Well, stay here, then. Don't wander off. Exploring.

Baby Duck *quacks, a little defiantly.*

Mr Fisher   Don't worry, Mr Wheeler. (*Yawning.*) He can look after himself. (*He settles to sleep.*)

Mr Wheeler   But he's only a baby duck.

Chips   Listen, I'll stay awake and make sure he doesn't get into danger.

Mr Wheeler   Would you? Thank you. I'd hate anything to happen to him.

Chips   No problem. (*He yawns.*) You have a kip, and I'll stay awake. (*He yawns again.*)

Mr Wheeler (*not sure*)   Mm. Good-night.

Chips   Night.

Mr Wheeler   Good-night, Mr Fisher.

Mr Fisher *snores loudly.*

Good-night, Fluffy Duck.

Baby Duck *quacks.* **Mr Wheeler** *goes to sleep.* **Chips**
remains awake.

Music – sleepy music.

Chips *yawns and nods off to sleep. Straightaway he snaps out of it.*

Chips   Brrrrrr (*A keeping-awake noise.*) Must keep awake.

Music.

Chips *yawns and nods off again. Straightaway he snaps out of it.*

Brrrrr. Must keep awake. (*He perhaps does a quick exercise, or hits
himself.*)

Music. **Chips** *nods off, fast asleep.*

After a pause, **Baby Duck** *stirs, gets up, and waddles off. The
audience may well shout out a warning, but* **Baby Duck** *tries to
keep them quiet, taking them into his confidence as he explores.
Whatever happens he goes over to the road works side, avoids the tar
and investigates the road works sign, cones, etc. Then he wanders round
behind. If necessary he climbs up on to the pavement rostrum. He finds
the inert* **Wacker** *and quacks, fascinated. He looks along the length
of it, then prods it. Seeing a button or lever, he presses it.*

Wacker *roars into life. A sound effect of a pneumatic engine starting
up could be used.* **Wacker** *bounces happily, though menacingly, into
full view. The startled* **Baby Duck** *gets out of vision of* **Wacker**,
who bounces about singing.

SONG: **I'm Wacker**

Wacker   Whack, whack,
                                    Whacketty whack.
                                    Whack, whack,
                                    Whacketty whack.

                                    I'm Wacker
                                    I'm Wacker

And I pack a
Punch
Whacking the tar
With a crack and a
Crunch
I jump
And I bump
With a stamp and a pat
Smacking, attacking it
Whacking it
Flat.

Whack,
Whacketty whack.
Whack, whack
Whacketty whack.

I whack here
I whack there
I whack any old where
I'm a wacker of no fixed abode
Nothing can stop
My hoppity hop
Unless you want whacking get
    out of me road.

I'm Wacker
I'm Wacker
And I pack a
Punch
Whacking away
With a crack and a
Crunch
I jump
And I bump
With a stamp and a pat
Smacking, attacking it
Whacking it
Flat.

>   Whack,
>   Whacketty whack.
>   Whack, whack,
>   Whacketty whack!

Baby Duck, *intrigued, emerges from the shadows to introduce himself. He quacks a greeting.* **Wacker** *is at first uncertain how to react, but then starts to show aggression.*

(*Speaking.*) Whack you flat! Whack you flat! Whack you flat!

Music as he bounces after **Baby Duck**, *chasing him along the pavement and back again.* **Baby Duck** *goes to jump off the pavement – into the wet tar area – but stops, just in time, and manages to jump safely avoiding the tar. But at this moment his clockwork starts to run down. He is paralysed – in an ideal place for* **Wacker** *to jump down on him.*

Ha! Ha! Whack you flat! Whack you flat!

Wacker *prepares to jump. His engine revs up to a frightening crescendo. The audience will probably have been shouting. In any event, the* **Gnomes** *wake up, size up the situation, and dash to the rescue. They pull* **Baby Duck** *clear in the nick of time.* **Wacker** *jumps down, landing painfully on the road.*

Ow! (*He rubs his whacking leg.*)

Meanwhile, **Mr Wheeler** *shelters* **Baby Duck**.

Mr Fisher   We should never have gone to sleep, Mr Wheeler.

Mr Wheeler   Chips said he'd stay awake. (*Calling.*) Chips!

No reaction. **Mr Wheeler** *manages to give* **Baby Duck** *two winds – ratchet noises.*

Mr Fisher (*dashing to* **Chips**)   Chips!

Wacker (*moaning*)   Ow!

Mr Wheeler *leaves* **Baby Duck**, *and he and* **Mr Fisher** *go over to* **Wacker**.

Mr Wheeler   What do you think you're doing?

Wacker   I'm rubbing my whacking plate, aren't I?

Mr Wheeler   I beg your pardon?

Wacker   Rubbing my whacking plate. I think I've sprained a sprocket.

Mr Fisher   What does that mean?

Wacker   It means my whacking days may be limited. And a wacker that can't whack is worse than worthless. I'll be a whackless wacker! (*He bursts into tears.*)

Mr Fisher   Now, now. Don't get in a state.

Wacker   I'm sorry. I'm not usually like this. I'm a happy wacker, really. A bouncy wacker. (*He tries a bounce.*) Ow.

Mr Wheeler   Calm down. Stand up straight.

Wacker (*doing so*)   Ow.

Mr Wheeler   Take his other side, Mr Fisher.

They support him.

Just stand still for a while.

Wacker   I can't stand still. When I get turned on, I have to whack. (*He bounces a little.*)

Mr Fisher   Why?

Wacker   Because I'm a wacker. I was born to wack. Whacking's my whole life.

Mr Wheeler   What do you whack?

Wacker   Anything. Everything. Tar on roads mostly. But given the chance I'll whack anything. Everything. (*He tries a few bounces.*) Hey, that feels better. Thank you.

Mr Wheeler   Don't mention it.

Wacker (*bouncing, testing himself*)   I'm Wacker, I'm Wacker, and I pack a punch . . .

His bounces are now taking the **Gnomes** *up in the air with him. They react with little 'Ohs'.*

Whack! Whack! Whack!

He bounces around with the **Gnomes** *hanging on.*

Mr Fisher   Whoa! Whoa! I'm feeling giddy!

Wacker   Whack! Whack! Whack!

Mr Wheeler   Let go of him, Mr Fisher.

They both let go. They fall to the ground.

Are you feeling better?

Wacker (*in rhythm*)   Whack! Whack! I'm feeling fine! Thank you, you've been very kind! Whack! Whack! (*His bounces are getting bigger and wilder. He gets very near the* **Gnomes**.)

Mr Fisher   Look out! You nearly whacked us!

Wacker   Sorry. I can't help it. It's my life! Whack you flat! Whack you flat! (*Back to normal, he approaches the* **Gnomes** *again.*)

Tension music.

Mr Wheeler   Look out, Mr Fisher!

Wacker   Whack you flat! Whack you flat!

The **Gnomes** *struggle up and bump into each other trying to escape.* **Wacker** *chases them round, then up on to the pavement.*

Whack you flat! Whack you flat!

The only place the **Gnomes** *can jump down to is the wet tar area.*

Into the tar! Into the tar!

Mr Fisher   No, no!

Mr Wheeler   Help, help!

They land in the tar. Their feet make contact, and they struggle to pull them out. The sticky mess of the tar makes this difficult.

Wacker   Here I come! Whack you flat! (*He prepares to jump.*)

Mr Wheeler   You'll sprain your whacking plate! Stop!

Wacker   I can't! I'm born to whack, whack you flat!

Mr Fisher   But we helped you! You can't whack *us*!

Wacker   I'm sorry. Nothing personal. It's only Wacker nature. Whack you flat! (*His engine revs up to a frightening crescendo.*)

Mr Fisher   Help! Help!

Baby Duck, *who has been resting since being rescued, suddenly notices what is going on and, quacking, wakes up* **Chips**, *pointing out the plight of the* **Gnomes**. *He pushes* **Chips** *over to the* **Gnomes***; then his clockwork starts to run down. This is hardly noticeable, because there is so much action going on elsewhere, but this helps later on.* **Baby Duck** *stops, by the drain, immobile, facing front, or lying on his side.*

Chips, *having sized up the situation, springs to the rescue. He leaps on to the pavement and turns off* **Wacker***'s switch or lever.* **Wacker** *judders to a standstill, trying to turn himself on again.*

Wacker   Whack . . . you . . . flat! . . . I'll . . . get . . . you! . . . Whack . . . you . . . flat! . . . Whack . . . (*He is still.*)

Chips *struggles to pull the* **Gnomes** *free of the tar.*

Mr Fisher   You said you'd stay awake.

Chips   Sorry, man. I was whacked.

Mr Fisher   *You* were whacked. We nearly got whacked to smithereens.

Mr Wheeler   Yes. Well, there's no time for arguments.

Chips *pulls them free.*

Thank you, Chips. Now, please get us out of here before Wacker attacks again.

Chips   It's OK. He's off now.

Mr Wheeler   Well, I think *we* should be off now too. This was meant to be a dream holiday, not a nightmare holiday.

The **Gnomes** *retrieve their wheelbarrow and fishing-rod.*

Come on, Fluffy Duck. Time to go.

Baby Duck *utters a plaintive quack. All turn. He quacks again. Worried, they go to him.*

Mr Fisher (*seeing* **Baby Duck** *motionless*)   I thinks he's gone to sleep.

Chips   He looks a bit off colour to me.

No reaction.

Mr Wheeler   No, no. He's run down.

Mr Fisher   So am I. I've never felt so run down in my life.

Mr Wheeler   No, no, Mr Fisher. His clockwork's run down. Help me stand him up.

They stand **Baby Duck** *up, and turn him round.* **Mr Wheeler** *goes to wind his key. The key has vanished.*

Mr Wheeler (*suddenly realizing, after winding an imaginary key for a moment*)   Where's it gone?

Mr Fisher   Where's what gone?

Mr Wheeler   His key? It's disappeared. Chips, where's his key?

Chips   Search me.

Mr Wheeler   We must search everywhere. Without his key, Fluffy Duck will never work again.

They look around on the ground. The audience may shout out 'Down the drain'. In any event . . .

Chips (*after a pause*)   I've got it!

Mr Wheeler   Thank goodness. Give it here.

Chips   No – I don't mean I've got it, I mean I've got it, get it?

Mr Wheeler   No.

Chips   An idea. Like where was he lying?

Mr Fisher   There.

Chips   Right, it's fallen down there.

Mr Wheeler   Where?

Chips   There. The drain.

Mr Fisher   Drain? What's a drain?

Chips (*showing them*)   This. It's where the rainwater goes. The key must have dropped through.

Mr Wheeler   There's water down there?

Chips   And a key, I bet.

Mr Fisher (*pulling at the drain*)   We'll never get it back from down there, Mr Wheeler.

Mr Wheeler (*idea*)   Yes, we will. That is to say, *you* will, Mr Fisher.

Mr Fisher   I will?

Mr Wheeler   This is your moment, Mr Fisher. Fetch your fishing-rod!

Mr Fisher   My . . . (*Realizing.*) Of course! My fishing-rod.

Music starts as he takes his rod, sits cross-legged on the kerb, and dangles the line down the drain. The others watch eagerly.

SONG: **Sitting Fishing**

(*Singing.*)   Sitting
                                                    Fishing
                                                    Dangling my line

Sitting
Thinking
Nothing's so fine
Sitting
Fishing
Rod in my hand
Sitting
Fishing
Nothing's so grand.

Sitting
Fishing
Hope for a bite
Sitting
Thinking
Life is all right
Sitting
Fishing
That's how I find
Perfect
Pleasure
Pure peace of mind.

I may not be fishing for fishes
But that doesn't matter to me
I'm not fishing for fishes
Or wishing for fishes
My wish is
To fish for a key.

As **Mr Fisher** *sings the last verse, the others join in, singing in harmony or to 'Ah'.*

Sitting
Fishing
Dangling my line
Sitting
Thinking
Nothing's so fine
Sitting

> Fishing
> Rod in my hand
> Sitting
> Fishing
> Nothing's so grand.

(*Speaking.*) A bite! A bite! Heave-ho, my beauty!

Tension music as he slowly pulls up the key. **Mr Fisher** *is radiant. All are delighted. The music continues as* **Mr Wheeler** *takes the key off the hook, and winds up* **Baby Duck***. Ratchet noises.* **Baby Duck** *quacks happily back into action, then bows a thank you. All cheer and applaud.* **Chips** *is standing quite near the immobile* **Wacker***. He throws his arms wide, expressing delight, and, by mistake, his paw hits* **Wacker***'s 'on' button.* **Wacker** *starts juddering into life.*

Wacker   Aaaaaaaaaaaaaaaaaaaah!

All turn to see **Wacker** *starting to jump.*

I'm Wacker, I'm Wacker, and I pack a punch! I'll get you, I'll get you. Whack you flat! Whack you flat!

All panic and, collecting their things, start to scuttle off.

Wacker *chases* **Mr Fisher** *and* **Chips** *off stage.*

Mr Wheeler *and* **Baby Duck** *beat a hasty retreat and exit the other side.*

Mr Fisher *and* **Chips** *return, breathless.* **Wacker** *is still heard in pursuit.*

Chips *pushes* **Mr Fisher** *towards the side* **Mr Wheeler** *and* **Baby Duck** *exited.*

Mr Fisher *exits to safety.*

Chips *thinks quickly what to do. He indicates to the audience that his plan is to lure* **Wacker** *into the wet tar. Then he positions himself behind it.*

Wacker *enters. He stops.*

(*To the audience.*) Where are they?

Audience   There!

Wacker   Where?

Audience   There!

Wacker *turns and sees* **Chips**, *who makes rude faces at him.*

Wacker   Whack you flat! Whack you flat! I'll get you! (*He jumps towards* **Chips**, *and lands in the tar. He struggles unsuccessfully to get out.*)

Chips *runs off, laughing and thanking the audience.*

Wacker *makes a big effort to follow, but loses his balance and falls headlong into the wet tar. He lies there, helpless.*

Aaaaaaaaaaaaaaaaaah! I'm stuck!

The lights fade to a black-out as he squirms like a stranded whale.

Scene Two

The Island.

In order to cover the scene change, it is suggested that immediately after the end of Scene One, **Chips** *is discovered in a follow-spot, beckoning to the others to escape. He leads them off-stage – into the auditorium.* **Chips**, **Mr Fisher**, **Mr Wheeler** (*plus wheelbarrow*) *and* **Baby Duck** *hurry through the audience, escaping from the possibly-pursuing* **Wacker**.

Meanwhile, a front-cloth or tabs fly in to cover the scene change. This is completed by the time the characters return to the stage.

The scene opens on an empty stage. Dawn.

Chips *and the others remain at one side of the stage, breathless, having a quick rest.* **Baby Duck** *quacks, worried, looking back in the direction from which they have come.*

Mr Wheeler   It's all right, Fluffy Duck, I don't think Wacker's following us.

Chips   Still wallowing in the tar, I reckon.

Mr Fisher   Serve him right, trying to whack us.

Mr Wheeler   Oh, Mr Fisher, that's unfair, he didn't *want* to whack us, but whacking's all he knows about, poor fellow.

Mr Fisher   Chips was right. This concrete jungle, as he calls it, isn't safe to explore on your own. Wackers, Securidogs, crossing the road . . .

Chips   Talking of which here's another road to cross right now . . .

Mr Fisher   Oh dear . . .

Chips   Don't get in a sweat, Mr Fisher. Last one.

Mr Wheeler   Last one? You mean . . .

Chips   Island here we come. Over this road and you're there.

All react excitedly.

Mr Fisher   Jumping toadstools. What are we waiting for? (*He steps forward.*)

Immediately there is the loud roar of a car passing, plus the strong beam of headlights. **Chips** *grabs* **Mr Fisher** *back.*

Chips   Easy, Mr Fisher, easy. You've forgotten the song, haven't you?

Mr Fisher *looks uneasy.*

Mr Wheeler?

Mr Wheeler *shakes his head.*

(*To the audience.*) Come on, everyone, let's remind them. Everybody up!

The audience is encouraged to stand up. The house lights come up.

One, two, three . . .

SONG: **Use Your Eyes and Ears** (*reprise*)

Chips ⎫	Use your eyes and ears
Audience ⎭	Before you use your feet
	Look and listen
	Before you cross the street
	Double check and when
	you're satisfied
	Walk don't run
	To the other side.

Chips (*to the audience*)   Thank you!

He looks at the **Gnomes***, who are still uncertain.*

Just one more time; then they'll *never* forget. One, two,
three . . .

Chip ⎫	Use your eyes and ears
Audience ⎭	Before you use your feet
	Look and listen
	Before you cross the street
	Double check and when
	you're satisfied
	Walk don't run
	To the other side.

Chips   Thanks very much, everyone. You can sit down
now.

The house lights fade.

(*To the* **Gnomes**.) Mr Fisher, Mr Wheeler. You're on your
own.

Mr Fisher *and* **Mr Wheeler** *nervously sing.*

Mr Fisher ⎫	Use your eyes and ears
Mr Wheeler ⎭	Before you use your feet
	Look and listen
	Before you cross the street

Pause as they look and listen.

Double check

Pause as they double check.

> And when you're satisfied
> Walk don't run to the other
> side.

Chips   You've got it!

The music continues as all four 'cross the road' – perhaps walking on the spot.

The music builds to the entrance of the 'island'. A traffic island. This is hopefully on a truck, and comes to meet them. It has a flashing Belisha beacon and two bollards.

*All except **Mr Fisher** jump on when it arrives in position. **Chips** sits on a bollard.*

Mr Fisher (*disappointed*)   Is this it?

Chips   This is it.

Mr Fisher   This is an island?

Chips   Like it's the only island I know. A traffic island.

Mr Fisher   I see.

Mr Wheeler   Cheer up, Mr Fisher.

Mr Fisher   Well, I'm sorry. I'm very grateful to Chips for bringing us here. But I must admit it's not quite what I'd expected.

Mr Wheeler   How do you mean?

Mr Fisher   Well, I can't really imagine the Big Ones coming *here* for their holidays. As I understand it, they go to an island to get away from all the problems of living in a city.

Chips   Right on! Say no more! This traffic island's where *I* come to get away from all the problems of living in a city.

Mr Fisher   Really?

Chips   Of course! Here I'm safe. No traffic. No Securidogs. No Wacker. Out of sight!

Mr Wheeler   He's right, Mr Fisher. Out of sight! (*He looks around.*) I'm beginning to enjoy myself already.

Mr Fisher   But where's the sun? Islands always have the sun.

After a pause, **Baby Duck** *points up at the Belisha beacon.*

Chips   That's right, Duck! This island has its own personal built-in sun. What's more, it never gets hidden behind a cloud.

Mr Wheeler   He's right, Mr Fisher. And look, here's your very own seat.

He shows him a bollard. **Mr Fisher** *clambers up.*

Mr Fisher   Mmm. Yes. Well. I certainly feel I could relax here.

Mr Wheeler   Exactly. It's perfect, Chips. Thank you.

Chips   My pleasure, Mr Wheeler.

Mr Fisher   It's perfect, but for one thing . . .

Chips   What's that, Mr Fisher? Do my best to oblige.

Mr Fisher   Water. No water. Islands are always surrounded by water.

Chips   Ah. Water. (*He considers.*)

There is a sudden clap of thunder. The lighting on the cyclorama darkens.

Baby Duck *quacks and points upwards. We hear rain beginning to fall, and perhaps see a rain effect on the cyclorama, or even projected on the island.*

Here you are! *Rain*water!

Mr Fisher (*radiant*)   Now it *is* perfect. Thank you, Chips.

Chips   My pleasure, Mr Fisher.

SONG: **Holiday Island** (*reprise*)

Mr Fisher ⎫ **Mr Wheeler** ⎭	Now We've found our holiday island Our holiday yours and my land Where there's nothing to do But enjoy doing nothing Where there's nothing to do But have fun We've found our holiday yours and my land Island in the sun.

They indicate the Belisha beacon. **Chips** *joins in the song.*

Mr Fisher ⎫ **Mr Wheeler** ⎬ **Chips** ⎭	Yes We've found our holiday island Our holiday pie in the sky land If we're feeling too warm We can splash in the water

They enjoy the rain.

> Then get dry in the sun's
> Golden beams
> We've found our holiday
>   yours and my land
> Pie in the sky land
> Do or die land
> Island of our dreams.

At the end of the song, the general lighting increases. It is early morning. The rain stops.

Mr Wheeler   This is the best holiday we've ever had, Mr Fisher.

Mr Fisher   This is the *only* holiday we've ever had, Mr Wheeler.

Baby Duck *quacks, a little dejected.*

What? What's the matter?

Baby Duck *mimes he didn't like the rain.*

Mr Wheeler   Didn't you like the rain?

Mr Fisher   We're used to rain. We're outside in all weathers.

Mr Wheeler   We'd better watch you don't get all rusty. What about you, Chips? Do you mind the rain?

Chips   Don't have any choice, Mr Wheeler. When you haven't got a home, a drop of rain's the least of your worries.

Mr Wheeler   Of course, I'm sorry. I forgot you haven't a home.

Chips   I've forgotten what it's like *having* a home.

Pause.

Mr Fisher   Well, talking of home, it's morning.

Mr Wheeler   You're right, Mr Fisher. Our Big Ones may well be home from Granny's soon. We'd better be on our way. Come on, Fluffy Duck.

They gather their things, rather forgetting **Chips**.

Mr Fisher   Now, cross the road; look and listen – all clear. Follow me. Home. Back to my toadstool.

The **Gnomes** *and* **Baby Duck** *check the road and 'cross'. Music, as* **Baby Duck** *notices* **Chips** *still on the island. He quacks.*

Mr Wheeler   What? (*Getting the message from* **Baby Duck**.) Chips! (*Calling.*) Chips! Aren't you coming?

Chips   No hurry. No point in hurrying when you've no place to hurry to.

Pause.

Mr Fisher   Mr Wheeler.

Mr Wheeler   Yes, Mr Fisher?

Mr Fisher   Why don't we take Chips home with us?

Mr Wheeler   Why not indeed? Chips. Come with us.

Chips   Well . . .

Mr Wheeler   There's a shed in our back yard. The Big
Ones never go in it except at weekends. You could sleep
there.

Chips   Does it have a roof?

Mr Wheeler   Of course.

Chips   A roof over my head again? Hey, I don't know,
I'm so used to being free – like no ties.

Mr Fisher   You'd still be free. Free to come and go over
the wall whenever you like.

Mr Wheeler   Please come. It's the least we can do to
thank you for our exciting holiday.

Mr Fisher   Please . . .

Baby Duck *quacks imploringly.*

Chips   Well, OK, I'll try anything once!

He jumps down. Pleased, the others start to go.

And besides –

They stop and turn.

– you're going the wrong way!

He checks the road and crosses. The others join him.

Mr Wheeler   Come on then. As the Big Ones say, after
a holiday, however perfect, there's nothing like going
home!

The music starts.

SONG: **Back Home**

Mr Wheeler ⎱ **Mr Fisher** ⎰	Back home To our back yard Back home It's time to go Back home Where we belong Back home To the world we know
Mr Wheeler	Back to the dustbin, the hose and the tap
Mr Fisher	Back to my toadstool and get a good nap
Mr Wheeler ⎱ **Mr Fisher** ⎰	Back to the life of a garden gnome Back to back In our back yard Back home.
Mr Wheeler ⎱ **Mr Fisher** ⎰ **Chips**	Holidays can't last for ever All good things must end they say Now our weekend trip is over So we must wend our way.

They start off.

All	Back home
Mr Wheeler ⎱ **Mr Fisher** ⎰	To our back yard
All	Back home
Chips	It's time to blow
All	Back home
Mr Wheeler **Mr Fisher**	Where we belong
All	Back home
Mr Wheeler ⎱ **Mr Fisher** ⎰	To the world we know Back to the Big Ones, the shed and the wall

> Back as though nothing had
>   happened at all
> Back to the life of a garden
>   gnome

All (**Chips** *referring it to the* **Gnomes**)

> Back to back
> In our back yard
> Back home.

It is suggested that the characters proceed on their journey home by going down into the auditorium, with the house lights up; this also takes the focus off the stage to accommodate the scene change. The following two verses should be sufficient for the journey through the auditorium.

> Back home
> To our back yard
> Back home
> It's time to go
> Back home
> Where we belong
> Back home
> To the world we know
> Back to the dustbin, the hose
>   and the tap
> Back to the toadstool and get
>   a good nap
> Back to the life of a garden
>   gnome
> Back to back
> In our back yard
> Back home.

> Back home
> To our back yard
> Back home
> It's time to blow
> Back home
> Where we belong
> Back home

To the world we know
Back to the Big Ones, the
shed and the wall
Back as though nothing had
happened at all
Back to the life of a garden
gnome
Back to back
In our back yard
Back home.

The characters reach the stage, on which the back yard set is now ready. The lights go up just downstage. The house lights fade.

All cross the stage singing the following verse, and exit the other side.

Back home
To our back yard
Back home
It's time to go
Back home
Where we belong
Back home
To the world we know
Back to the dustbin, the hose
and the tap
Back to the toadstool and get
a good nap
Back to the life of a garden
gnome
Back to back
In our back yard
Back home.

The heads of **Mr Wheeler** *and* **Mr Fisher** *appear over the wall. They start climbing down, lowering the wheelbarrow, and helping* **Baby Duck** *down.* **Chips** *watches from the top of the wall.*

As they sing the lights very gradually increase.

Back home
To our back yard

Back home
It's time to blow
Back home
Where we belong
Back home
To the world we know

The next section is sung out of tempo, to accommodate action.

Back where we started, climb
over the wall
Mind how we go now, take
care not to fall
Back to the life of a garden
gnome
Back to back
In our back yard
Back home.

Back to the dustbin, the hose
and the tap
Back to the toadstool and get
a good nap
Back to the life of a garden
gnome
Back to back
In our back yard
Back home.

During the final lines, **Mr Fisher** *runs happily to his toadstool and climbs up. The* **Gnomes** *are back to back in their usual positions.* **Baby Duck** *watches;* **Chips** *stays up on the wall. It is now daylight.*

Mr Wheeler ⎫
Mr Fisher ⎭

Back to back
In our back yard
Back home.

Scene Three

The Back Yard. Morning.

Mr Wheeler   Absence makes the heart grow fonder, Mr Fisher.

Mr Fisher   Indeed, Mr Wheeler.

Mr Wheeler (*seeing* **Chips** *still on the wall*)   Chips. Come down and see the shed.

Chips (*shy at invading their territory*)   It's OK, Mr Wheeler, I'll just sus things out from up here.

Mr Wheeler   As you wish. Fancy a drop of water?

He starts to arrange the hose, giving **Chips** *the end.* **Baby Duck** *is subdued, wandering around. He stops at the dustbin. He quacks.*

Mr Fisher (*going to him*)   It's all right, Fluffy Duck, we won't let the Big Ones throw you in there again. Come and see the shed. You can shelter there too . . .

They start towards the shed off-stage. **Mr Wheeler** *goes to turn on the tap.*

Sudden noise stops everyone in their tracks. The **Big Ones**' *car drives up. After a final rev. of the engine, it stops. Car doors slam.*

The shadows of the **Big Ones** *give a lighting change to heighten the tension.*

The **Gnomes** *hurry to their original opening positions. If necessary, Mr Wheeler helps* **Mr Fisher** *up on to his toadstool, then returns to his wheelbarrow. They adopt their frozen positions.* **Baby Duck** *runs round, then stops behind the dustbins, hiding.* **Chips** – *not understanding what is going on* – *stands on the wall rooted to the spot.*

We hear the voices of the **Big Ones**, *on their way to the back door.*

Mr Big One   Unpack later. Let's have a nice cup of tea first.

Miss Big One   Can I turn the telly on, Mum?

Mrs Big One   All right, love.

There is the sound of the back door being unlocked.

(*With a sigh.*) It's always nice to get home.

Miss Big One   Hey, Mum, look. On the wall.

Chips *reacts.*

Mrs Big One   Hello, puss. We haven't seen you before.
Are you lost?

Mr Big One   Looks a bit thin to me.

Miss Big One   Can we give him some milk?

Mrs Big One   Why not?

Miss Big One   Come on. Puss, puss, puss. Want some milk?

Chips *hesitates.*

It's all right, we won't hurt you.

Chips *starts climbing down, using the hose if necessary.*

Good boy. Come on.

Chips *goes towards the back door.*

Oh, Mum. He looks ever so hungry. Can we keep him?

Mrs Big One   Well . . .

Mr Big One   Tell you what. We'll stick a note on the gate.
And if nobody claims him, he can stay and live with us.

Chips *looks happy. He turns to the* **Gnomes***, who beam with
pleasure, and maybe even nod encouragement.*

Chips *exits.*

Baby Duck *creeps out from behind the dustbin to see what is going
on.*

Mrs Big One   What's that by the dustbin?

Miss Big One   It's my baby duck.

Mr Big One   The one that didn't work? I thought you'd
thrown it away.

Mrs Big One   I *did* throw it away.

Mr Big One   You must have missed. I'll pop it back in.

The **Gnomes** *and* **Baby Duck** *look alarmed. In fright,* **Baby Duck** *scuttles out, waddling perfectly.*

Miss Big One   Look! He's working again. He's all right!

Mrs Big One   Well, I never.

Mr Big One   You can't throw him away now.

Miss Big One   I never wanted to in the first place! Come on, Baby Duck, come and meet our new pussycat.

Baby Duck *smiles happily, looks at the* **Gnomes** *and waves. They smile back.*

Baby Duck *exits.*

Mrs Big One   Hello, Gnomes!

The **Gnomes** *react.*

Mr Big One   Dear old Gnomes. Brightening up the back yard as usual.

Mrs Big One   I always like coming home because I know they'll be waiting to welcome us.

Mr Big One   Funny. They're only stone, but they're really part of the family. Wouldn't be the same without them. I really must get that fish pond built for them, with some real fish in it.

Mrs Big One   Come on, love, let's get the kettle on.

The door slams. The lights return to normal.

The **Gnomes** *look much moved.*

Mr Fisher (*after a pause*)   You know, Mr Wheeler?

Mr Wheeler   What, Mr Fisher?

Mr Fisher   The Big Ones aren't so bad, really.

Mr Wheeler   They're only human, Mr Fisher.

Mr Fisher   Real fish in a real fishpond!

Mr Wheeler   I bet *their* holiday wasn't as exciting as ours.

Mr Fisher   We found our island.

Mr Wheeler   We nearly got whacked.

Mr Fisher   I did some real fishing.

Mr Wheeler   Even my wheelbarrow came in handy.
Doggy Dins. Fluffy Duck.

Mr Fisher   And we managed to help two friends in distress.

Mr Wheeler   The Code of the Gnomes!

Mr Fisher   My life, Mr Wheeler, is not a wasted life after
all.

SONG: **The Code Of The Gnomes** (*reprise*)

Mr Fisher ⎫	If ever you're in danger or
Mr Wheeler ⎬	need a friend
	Be sure that we'll stick by you
	until the bitter end.
Mr Wheeler	It's up to us
Mr Fisher	It's up to us
Mr Wheeler	It's up to us
Mr Fisher	It's up to us
Both	We won't wait
	Or hesitate
	Just put us to the test
Mr Wheeler	It's up to us
Mr Fisher	It's up to us
Mr Wheeler	It's up to us
Mr Fisher	It's up to us
Both	The Code of the Gnomes
	We do our best.

As the song ends, the two **Gnomes**, *nodding asleep, freeze into the
positions in which they opened the play. The lights fade to a black-out
as the curtain falls.*

Mother Goose's Golden Christmas

With sincere thanks to
John Hole
for whom this is my tenth
commissioned play, and without
whose confidence, help and
encouragement I might have
given up after the first.

Mother Goose's Golden Christmas was first presented at the Queen's Theatre, Hornchurch, on 19 December 1977, with the following cast:

Mother Goose	Brian Hewlett
Little Jack Horner	David Brenchley
Little Bo Peep	Deirdre Dee
Little Miss Muffet	Nicolette Marvin
Little Tommy Tucker	Lennox Greaves
Little Polly Flinders	Patience Tomlinson
Big Bad Wolf	Jack Chissick
Bigger Badder Wolf	Mike Maynard
Fairy Lethargia	Penny Jones
The Goose	Isobil Nisbet
The Giant	Tim Pearce
The Spider	Caroline Swift
The Monster of the Moat	Caroline Swift
Humpty Dumpty	Caroline Swift

Directed by Paul Tomlinson
Settings by David Knapman
Musical direction by David Carter

Characters

Mother Goose, *the purveyor of nursery rhymes, probably the 'dame' part, lovable old lady, looking after her nursery rhyme 'family'.*

Little Bo Peep, *weepy girl (because she is always losing her sheep!). Dressed in red (for reasons which will become apparent).*

Little Tommy Tucker, *fat, usually hungry boy – sings for his supper.*

Little Miss Muffet, *the most imaginative of the 'family' – her stories of meeting fearsome spiders are taken with a pinch of salt by the others.*

Little Jack Horner, *the nearest we get to a 'Simple Simon' or 'Idle Jack' part. Limited intelligence because his sole purpose in life is sitting in corners putting his thumb in and pulling plums out.*

Little Polly Flinders, *grubby, skinny girl dressed in rags – the skivvy who cooks and cleans; but not looked down on or even discontented with her lot – this is her role in life and she enjoys it. Very shy – whispers a lot.*

The Goose, *lovable, mute bird, must be capable of pathos, but humour as well; mimes to convey her thoughts, often interpreted by the audience.*

The Big Bad Wolf, *a small, rather nervous villain.*

The Bigger Badder Wolf, *a larger, rather confident villain.*

Giant Bossyboots, *the Wolves' employer. Ruthless, unsuccessful alchemist whose only aim is to make gold.*

The Spider, *frightening frightener.*

Fairy Lethargia, *a lumpy, sleepy, reluctant fairy, who only emerges at Christmas time to sit on the Christmas tree. She can do magic spells, but only under pressure.*

The Monster of the Moat, *a non-speaking monster, the guardian of the Giant's Castle. Probably similar to the Loch Ness Monster and in segments, which divide.*

Humpty Dumpty, *a last-minute appearance – preferably played by a child.*

As the play is based upon the well-known collection of Nursery Rhymes called 'Mother Goose's Nursery Rhymes', the ideal period in which to set it is Victorian, with all the settings and costumes resembling a beautiful Victorian children's book.

Act One

Scene One

The Book. Home of the Nursery Rhyme characters. Dawn, Christmas Eve.

This is their equivalent of a house; indeed it has a door, and maybe windows. It is suggested that the Book is three-quarters open, the covers facing the audience. On the front cover is the title – 'Mother Goose's Golden Christmas Annual', with perhaps a picture representing Mother Goose flying on a Goose, accompanied by several young people. As perhaps the ideal time in which to set the play is Victorian, the design of the cover could well be in the style of one of the famous children's book illustrations of the period – e.g. Arthur Rackham or Kate Greenaway. It may be considered a good idea to start with the tabs already out, so that the audience can see the Book and its title before the house lights go down. Alternatively, a painting of the book on a gauze front cloth would give the magical possibility of 'mixing through' to the real Book.

Music, as the lights come up on the Book.

The door of the Book opens and, surreptitiously, **Little Miss Muffet** *creeps out, yawns and stretches, and looks both ways to see if anyone is coming. She beckons, and* **Little Jack Horner** *tiptoes out. They greet each other with excitement but no noise. Then* **Little Polly Flinders** *emerges, sweeping with a broom. The others shush her with a finger to their mouths and take away the broom, leaning it against the Book. As the three huddle together, as though discussing a secret plan,* **Little Tommy Tucker** *comes out, eating a large sausage or a piece of pie, and not looking where he is going. He bumps into the group, who turn on him and shush him. Finally,* **Little Bo Peep**, *with her shepherdess's crook, comes out, ignoring the others but looking into the early morning light – in the hope of seeing her lost sheep. She shrugs her disappointment as* **Little Jack Horner** *takes away her crook and leads her to the others. This section should not take long. The idea is not to set up the individual characters, but rather to convey the fact that these five people live in the Book, and, early this morning, having just woken up, are up to something secret.*

Little Miss Muffet *shuts the door, and in fairly soft voices they sing.*

SONG: **We Wish You a Merry Christmas**

During the song the children bring forward a Christmas tree and, setting it to one side of the stage, start to decorate it with tinsel and baubles, etc., which they take from a largish box labelled 'Decorations', and which they wheel on for the purpose. Occasionally someone checks that no one is coming out of the door — the idea being, as we shall soon discover, that the children are doing this as a surprise for **Mother Goose**.

Little Miss Muffet
Little Jack Horner
Little Bo Peep   *(singing)*
Little Tommy Tucker
Little Polly Flinders

> We wish you a Merry Christmas
> We wish you a Merry Christmas
> We wish you a Merry Christmas
> And a Happy New Year.
>
> Good tidings we bring
> To you and your kin
> We wish you a Merry Christmas
> And a Happy New Year.
>
> Now bring us some figgy pudding
> Now bring us some figgy pudding
> Now bring us some figgy pudding
> And bring some out here.
>
> We wish you a Merry Christmas
> We wish you a Merry Christmas

At this point the Christmas tree lights go on and the **Children** *react happily.*

> We wish you a Merry Christmas

Little Tommy Tucker *is pushed forward. He gives a good tug on the bell-rope. The bell rings.*

> And a Happy New Year.

Giggling with excitement, the **Children** *hide to wait for the reaction.*

After a short pause, we hear **Mother Goose**'*s voice as she comes to answer the door, hurriedly putting on a dressing-gown.*

Mother Goose Who on earth can that be at this unearthly hour? (*She opens the door and steps out, and sees the lit-up tree. She gasps.*) Ah . . . ! Look what's grown in the night. An electric light tree. Someone must have planted a bulb!

The **Children** *pop out from hiding, making* **Mother Goose** *jump. They gather round.*

Children Tara! Surprise, surprise! Happy Christmas, Mother Goose, etc.

Mother Goose Oh, little ones. All I can say is . . . (*Suddenly.*) Aaaaaah!

All jump.

Little Tommy Tucker What's the matter, Mother Goose?

Mother Goose You're standing on my foot, Tommy dear.

Little Tommy Tucker Oh, sorry. (*He moves.*)

Mother Goose Thank you, dear, and thank you, all of you, for such a lovely seasonal surprise. But haven't you forgotten something?

Little Miss Muffet What?

Mother Goose I'm not sure. But somehow it doesn't look complete . . .

The **Children** *all think hard.* **Mother Goose** *suddenly sees the audience.*

Oh . . . ! (*To the audience.*) Good morning. Hallo. Look, little ones, visitors. You're jolly early. I'm not even dressed yet. I don't usually open the door in my dressing-gown.

Little Jack Horner   I didn't know you *had* a door in your dressing-gown. Tara!

Mother Goose   Thank you, Jack. Anyway – (*To the audience.*) – now you're here, I'm Mother Goose and I look after all the nursery rhyme children and we all live in this big Book, and I know there's something missing off that Christmas tree. Can *you* spot it?

The audience is encouraged to shout out that there is no fairy on the Christmas tree.

Of course. That's it. They're right! The fairy. Where is she?

Little Bo Peep   She only works at Christmas. Sleeps the rest of the year.

Mother Goose   What a lazy fairy! Hibernating like a hedgehog. Anyone remember her name?

Little Polly Flinders *raises her hand.*

Well, Polly?

Little Polly Flinders *whispers in* **Mother Goose**'*s ear, then smiles shyly.*

That's right. Fairy Lethargia. We'd better give her an alarm call and wake her up. After three. One, two, three.

All (*calling*)   Fairy Lethargia.

No reaction.

Mother Goose   One, two, three.

All (*calling*)   Fairy Lethargia.

No reaction.

Mother Goose   We need a few more decibels, I reckon. (*To the audience.*) How about all joining in? Would you do that? Thank you. One, two, three.

All (*including the audience*)   Fairy Lethargia.

Mother Goose   And again. One, two, three.

All   Fairy Lethargia.

Suddenly, a large yawn, accompanied perhaps by a drum roll, heralds the awakening of **Fairy Lethargia**. *She crawls, unfairylike and anything but dainty, out of the decorations box. She holds a wand, complete with star on the end. She cannot stop yawning. This could possibly be accompanied by pretty, tinkling fairy music to point up the irony.*

Fairy Lethargia   Oh no, it's not Christmas time again already, is it? (*She gives a huge yawn.*)

Mother Goose   Yes. And you're late, Fairy Lethargia.

Fairy Lethargia   I'm sorry, I – ooh. (*Suddenly she sees the audience and makes an attempt to do a fairy balletic-type movement as she goes into rhyming couplets.*)

Hallo, hallo, 'tis Christmas Eve and I am Fairy Lethargia,
My wand and spells and magic powers are here to watch
    and guardjya
Throughout the festive season my eyes on you I'll keep
    (*Yawning.*)
Except when they start shutting, 'cos I need my beauty
    sleep. (*She falls asleep on her feet.*)

Mother Goose   One, two, three.

All (*calling*)   Fairy Lethargia.

Fairy Lethargia *jumps awake.*

Fairy Lethargia   Oh no, it's not Christmas time again already, is it? (*She gives a huge yawn.*)

Mother Goose   Yes, it is.

Little Miss Muffet   And you're meant to be on the tree.

Fairy Lethargia   I'm not sitting on that tree. It's all prickly. And I might drop off.

Little Jack Horner   That's your trouble – you're *always* dropping off. Tara!

Fairy Lethargia   Cheek. Tell you what; we'll compromise. (*She waves her wand.*)
My magic wand looks like a star, I'll stick it on the tree
And like a beacon burning bright, it'll make you think of
   me.

She arranges her wand on the tree.

Return I shall for turkey, for Christmas pud and booze
Till then I think I'll say ta ta and have a little snooze.

She nips back into the decorations box, yawns and vanishes from sight. N.B. *It may well be advisable for the box to extend a little into the wings, so that* **Fairy Lethargia** *can escape through one side to the wings between appearances.*

Mother Goose   Charming. Daintiness personified. She works too hard, that's her trouble. A twelve-hour year. She's the same every Christmas. Do you remember, little ones, when . . . (*She breaks off, then turns to the audience.*) Oh, I'm sorry. How rude. I haven't even introduced my family to you, have I? Tell you what, let's see if you can guess who they all are – because . . .

SONG: **Once Upon A Time**

Little Bo Peep	It
	Really won't surprise us
Little Jack Horner	If you recognize us
All the Children	From a nursery rhyme
Mother Goose	And I'm sure you've heard them
	Or even learnt them
	Once upon a time.

The **Children** *act out each other's story as appropriate. First,*
Little Bo Peep *comes forward.*

Mother Goose	Here's a girl all pale and wan
	And she's crying, so something's
	wrong
Little Bo Peep	I can't help but weep
	I've lost all my sheep
	And don't know where they've
	gone.

The music continues.

Mother Goose (*speaking to the audience*)   Who is she?

The audience may give her an answer. She ad libs her thanks.

All	She's
	Little Bo Peep
	Little Bo Peep
	From the nursery rhyme
	Little Bo Peep
	You must have learnt it
	Once upon a time.
Little Jack Horner	I was eating Christmas pie
	In the corner, then – who knows
	why?
Mother Goose	He put in his thumb
	And pulled out a plum –
Little Jack Horner	What a good boy am 1!

Again **Mother Goose** *asks the audience who he is.*

All	He's
	Little Jack Horner
	Little Jack Horner
	From the nursery rhyme
	Little Jack Horner
	You must have learnt it
	Once upon a time.

Mother Goose	Here's a girl you'll know, I s'pose
	In the cinders she warmed her toes
All (*except* **Mother**	Her mother then caught her
Goose *and* **Little**	And told off her daughter
Polly Flinders)	For spoiling her new clothes.

The audience shout out who it is.

All	She's
	Little Polly Flinders
	Little Polly Flinders
	From the nursery rhyme
	Little Polly Flinders
	You must have learnt it
	Once upon a time.

Little Tommy Tucker	Now bring me some figgy pudding
	Please bring me some figgy
	pudding –
	I am singing for my supper
Mother Goose	What shall we give him?

All (*except* **Little**	
Tommy Tucker)	White bread and butter
Little Tommy Tucker	It's no wonder
	I get fat
Mother Goose	Who can tell me . . .
	Who is that?

The audience shout out the answer.

All	He's
	Little Tommy Tucker
	Little Tommy Tucker
	From the nursery rhyme
	Little Tommy Tucker
	I'm sure you learnt it
	Once upon a time.

Little Miss Muffet	In the forest yesterday
	I was eating my curds and whey

Mother Goose	Along came a spider
	Who sat down beside her
Little Miss Muffet	And frightened me away.

The audience call out her name.

All	She's
	Little Miss Muffet
	Little Miss Muffet
	From the nursery rhyme
	Little Miss Muffet
	I'm sure you learnt it
	Once upon a . . .
	Little Miss Muffet
	Little Tommy Tucker
	Little Polly Flinders
	Little Jack Horner
	Little Bo Peep
	I'm sure you learnt them
Girls	Once upon a time
Boys	Once upon a time
Girls	Once upon a time
Boys	Once upon a time
All	Once upon a time.

Mother Goose   There you are, I told you you knew them all already! Right, little ones, breakfast time. (*She calls loudly.*) Polly!

Little Polly Flinders *comes forward shyly.*

Little Polly Flinders (*whispering*)   Yes, Mother Goose.

Mother Goose   Put the kettle on.

Music, as the **Children** *revolve the Book, to reveal a room the other side. It is a kitchen with a large dining-table and a hearth complete with cinders, hob and traditional-style kettle. The Christmas tree and decorations box remain at the side of the stage. N.B. The revolve of the Book* could *take place during the last chorus of the song.* **Little Polly Flinders** *puts the kettle on.* **Mother Goose** *and the* *others sit at the table.* **Mother Goose** *pours herself some cereal from a packet or jar, and passes it down the line. First* **Little Jack Horner***, then* **Little Miss Muffet** *pour themselves some; then* **Little Tommy Tucker** *pours all the remaining cereal on to his plate. The music stops as* **Little Bo Peep** *– on the end – bursts into tears. N.B. This section should be played at a fair speed.*

Little Jack Horner   Oh, stop being weedy, Bo Peep.

Little Bo Peep   I'm not being weedy. Tommy's taken all the cereal, the selfish pig.

Little Tommy Tucker   I'm a growing boy.

Little Bo Peep   Growing? Huh. If you grow any more you'll burst. Like a fat balloon.

Mother Goose   Stop arguing, you two. Bo Peep, there's more cereal in the cupboard. So stop crying. Tommy, go and fetch her some.

Little Tommy Tucker *does so.*

Little Miss Muffet   She's always crying.

Little Bo Peep   So would you if you kept losing your sheep. (*She starts sobbing again.*)

Little Miss Muffet   That's nothing compared with having to fight off great monster spiders every day.

Little Jack Horner   So you say.

Little Miss Muffet   What's that meant to mean?

Little Jack Horner   Well, *we* never see these giant spiders of yours. *No one* sees them except you.

Little Miss Muffet   Are you suggesting I invent them?

Little Jack Horner   No. I'm just saying I've never seen one.

Little Bo Peep   That's because he sits at home all day putting in his thumb and pulling out plums. What a waste of time.

Little Tommy Tucker   No, it's not. They're very nice plums.

Little Bo Peep   Well, we all know you're a greedy hog who never stops stuffing his face.

Little Tommy Tucker   I'd rather be a greedy hog who never stops stuffing his face than one of your miserable stupid sheep who keep wandering off . . .

Little Bo Peep *is about to retaliate.* **Mother Goose** *interrupts.*

Mother Goose   Ting-a-ling-a-ling-a-ling. End of Round One. That's enough. It's Christmas, time of good cheer. Now, what's the matter, little ones?

All the **Children** *start to react angrily to the phrase 'little ones'. Then they think better of it. Silence.*

Eh?

Little Polly Flinders *brings everyone a mug of tea.*

Thank you, Little Polly.

All the **Children** *look at one another as if to say – 'there you are'.* **Little Polly Flinders** *sits.*

What have I said now?

Little Polly Flinders (*whispering*)   Little.

Mother Goose   Little?

Little Jack Horner   Sorry, Mother Goose, but we're all getting a bit fed up with being 'Little'. *Little* Jack Horner.

Little Miss Muffet   *Little* Miss Muffet.

Little Bo Peep   We're all 'Little'.

Little Tommy Tucker   And we always have to do the same old 'little' things.

Little Jack Horner   Day after day after day.

Little Polly Flinders (*whispering*)   That's why we argue sometimes. It gives us something else to think about.

The others nod.

Mother Goose   I see. But, children, your nursery rhymes are so popular. Everyone knows them. You can't just stop doing what you do in them and start doing something else. People expect nursery rhymes to carry on for ever.

Little Jack Horner   But I'm fed up with sitting in corners pulling out plums. There must be something more to life than that.

Little Bo Peep   And I don't *enjoy* losing my sheep all the time. (*She starts to cry.*)

Little Polly Flinders (*whispering*)   I'd like to get away from my dirty old cinders sometimes. Not for always. Just sometimes.

Little Tommy Tucker   All I do is sing for my supper. That's child's play. I'd like a challenge. An adventure.

Little Miss Muffet   And I'm tired of being terrified by fierce spiders which nobody really believes I see anyway.

Little Jack Horner   In short, Mother Goose, we're bored. Bored with being 'Little' people of 'little' consequence.

Pause.

Mother Goose (*having an idea*)   I tell you what. I was wondering what I could give you all as a Christmas present. And now I know. I'll think up a brand new nursery rhyme story with all of you in it.

The **Children** *look interested.*

An adventure story. Excitement. Danger. A story in which each one of you does great things, each one of you has his or her big moment. How about it?

Children   Yes, please; thank you, Mother Goose; how does it start? Let's hear it now; etc.

Mother Goose (*laughing*)   Hold on! Quiet! Give me a chance to cogitate. (*She has an idea.*) Magic. Every good story needs a bit of magic. Where can we find some magic?

They all wait a moment – to allow the audience to come up with the solution if they want to.

Little Polly Flinders (*whispering, pointing to the decorations box*)   Fairy Lethargia.

Mother Goose   Of course. Lethargia. We'd better wake her up. She can do something useful for once. One, two, three.

All (*calling*)   Fairy Lethargia.

Fairy Lethargia (*crawling from the box*)   What is it now? (*She yawns.*)

Little Miss Muffet   Will you come and be in our story?

Fairy Lethargia   No, I'm too tired for stories.

Little Bo Peep   Please. All we want is some of your magic.

Fairy Lethargia (*indignantly*)   What?

Little Jack Horner   Just a little.

Little Tommy Tucker   To make it a really special story.

Fairy Lethargia (*flattered*)   Oh, very well. If it's a special story, count me in. Let's see. (*She collects her wand from the tree and waves it.*)

　To make your story special, to give it extra zip,
　Three magic spells I'll let you have, and now I'll have a
　　kip.

She replaces the wand and, yawning, returns to the decorations box.

Mother Goose   Thank you, Fairy Lethargia. Three
spells. Mmm. We must only use them for emergencies and
crisisises. Now, gather round, little ones . . . I'm sorry,
gather round, everybody, and I'll begin the story. Now, let's
see.

Music, as the **Children** *listen to* **Mother Goose** *improvising
the story. A lighting change here – narrowing to the 'family' group –
would help the atmosphere.*

Once upon a time, not very far away from here, at the other
side of the forest, loomed a vast, mysterious, impenetrable
stone castle. It was surrounded by a deep, inky-black moat
in which lived a savage Monster who kept guard over the
owner of the castle – the terrifying Giant Bossyboots. The
Giant had only one interest in life – gold. Not that he had
any, but he dreamed of possessing more gold than anyone
else on earth. So he consulted all the old tomes about
alchemy, trying to discover the secret of how to make gold.
Then one day, as Mother Goose and her nursery rhyme
children were sitting down to breakfast . . .

*From now on, the story takes over. The lighting changes and the music
continues.*

The **Goose** *enters, perhaps in a follow spot. The* **Goose** *is tired
and frightened. With wings flapping she breathes heavily to suggest she
has been running or flying. She takes a short rest, looking off stage to
check she is not being followed. Suddenly she sees the Book, rushes to it,
searches till she finds the bell-rope and pulls it.*

Inside, the **Children** *and* **Mother Goose** *react to the bell. This
is really a two-level reaction – in one sense it's a natural reaction to
hearing a doorbell, and in another sense it is excited anticipation,
because the* **Children** *know this is part of* **Mother Goose***'s
story.*

Little Bo Peep   Maybe my sheep have come home!

They jump up; dash to the door, open it and cluster round the **Goose***,
leading it, confused by all the fuss, downstage.* **Mother Goose**

watches, not getting too involved; she wants the **Children** *to experience the excitement of this new story.*

Little Miss Muffet   Hallo, who are you?

Little Jack Horner   It's a duck! Hallo, ducky!

Little Bo Peep   No, it's not a duck. It's a goose. You're ignorant.

Little Jack Horner   Not as ignorant as your sheep. Baaaaah!

Little Bo Peep *bursts into tears again. The* **Goose** *reacts frightened, flapping its wings.*

Little Tommy Tucker   It's all right. Don't get in a flap. We're not going to hurt you.

Little Miss Muffet   Who are you? Where have you come from?

Little Polly Flinders *suddenly comes into her own, almost taking herself by surprise.*

Little Polly Flinders   Quiet! Sorry, but I think the Goose is frightened. (*To the* **Goose**.) It's all right; you can tell us.

The **Goose** *points to her beak and shakes her head.*

What's the matter?

The audience will possibly shout out that the **Goose** *cannot speak.*

You *can't* tell us? Oh, you can't speak?

The **Goose** *nods.*

Well, that doesn't matter. You can show us what you're trying to say and we'll all guess. (*Taking in the audience.*) Won't we? Now, are you lost?

The **Goose** *nods, then points off.*

Little Jack Horner   She's pointing to the forest.

The **Goose** *indicates 'beyond the forest'.*

Little Polly Flinders   What? Through the forest? The other side of the forest?

The **Goose** *nods.*

(*Asking the others.*) What's the other side of the forest?

The audience may shout out 'The Giant's Castle'. If not, **Little Polly Flinders** *gets the answer herself – or from one of the others.*

The Giant's Castle?

The **Goose** *nods nervously.*

Little Tommy Tucker   You want to go to the Giant's Castle?

The **Goose** *immediately flaps her wings in panic, and shakes her head.*

Little Polly Flinders   No? What then?

The audience may suggest that the **Goose** *has come from the Giant's Castle.*

Oh. You've *come* from the Giant's Castle? Through the forest?

The **Goose** *nods.*

Little Bo Peep   You didn't see any lost sheep, did you?

The **Goose** *shakes her head.*

The Others   Shhh. Bo Peep, shut up, etc.

Little Polly Flinders   What were you doing in the Castle?

The **Goose** *does a Marcel Marceau-type mime, using her hands/wings to suggest being locked in – showing imaginary walls.*

Little Jack Horner   Playing Blind Man's Buff?

Little Miss Muffet   Looking for a secret panel?

The **Goose** *shakes her head at each of these suggestions. The audience may help.*

Little Polly Flinders   You were locked in?

The **Goose** *nods.*

Little Miss Muffet   In a dungeon?

The **Goose** *shakes her head and mimes pacing up and down. Again, the audience should help.*

Little Polly Flinders   In a cage?

The **Goose** *nods.*

What were you doing in a cage?

The **Goose** *mimes laying eggs; sitting down then up. The audience are encouraged to help again.*

Little Jack Horner   Sitting in a hot bath.

Little Polly Flinders   No. Laying eggs?

The **Goose** *nods.*

And why should the Giant lock you in a cage laying eggs?

The audience should be encouraged to reach the answer, using the following logical stages. If required, **Little Polly Flinders** *can find the solution herself:*

(1) What does the **Giant** *desire most? Gold.*

(2) What could eggs have to do with gold? They could be golden eggs.

(3) Perhaps the **Giant** *thought that this goose was the* **Goose** *that laid the Golden Egg?*

(4) Therefore he locked her in a cage, so that she couldn't escape, in the hope that she'd eventually lay a golden egg.

But you never laid a Golden Egg?

The **Goose** *shakes her head.*

So you escaped. And now you're homeless?

The **Goose** *nods.*

Little Miss Muffet You can live with us if you like, can't she, Mother Goose?

Mother Goose *'re-enters' the scene.*

Mother Goose Well . . .

All look at her, pleading . . .

With a name like mine, how can I refuse?

The **Goose** *reacts happily. All cheer.*

What's your name, Goosey?

The **Goose** *shrugs her shoulders.*

That's a funny name.

The audience may shout out that she has not got a name.

You haven't got a name?

The **Goose** *shakes her head.*

Well, that's terrible. We can't adopt you if we don't know what to call you. What are we to do?

Little Tommy Tucker Let's think of a good goosey name for her.

Mother Goose Good idea, Tommy. Any ideas?

The **Children** *cannot think of anything.*

No? (*To the audience.*) Can *anyone* think of a good goosey name?

The audience shout out ideas, some of which are put to the **Goose***, who selects one – a different name for each performance. In the script let us call her Gertie.*

Gertie? She likes Gertie? I know. Tommy. Sing a song for her.

Little Tommy Tucker   All right. It'll make a change from singing for my supper!

SONG: **The Song of the Goose** (*Part 1*)

Little Tommy Tucker   Gertie!
                                                  You needn't flap
                                                  Gertie!
                                                  Don't fly away
                                                  Gertie!
                                                  We'll take you under our wing
                                                  So
                                                  Gertie!
                                                  Please stay.

Hey, I've got an idea. Why doesn't everyone (*Taking in the audience.*) join in whenever I sing the word Gertie? Would you do that? Then Gertie will see how many friends she's got to protect her from the Giant.

Little Bo Peep   Shall I give a signal with my crook? – Every time I lift it like this, we all shout 'GERTIE'. All right? Let's have a practice. (*She raises her crook.*)

All (*including the audience*)   Gertie!

Little Bo Peep   And again. (*She raises her crook.*)

All (*including the audience*)   Gertie!

Little Bo Peep   Lovely!

SONG: **The Song of the Goose** (*Part 2*)

All (*with audience*)	Gertie!
Little Tommy Tucker	You needn't flap
All (*with audience*)	Gertie!
Little Tommy Tucker	Don't fly away
All (*with audience*)	Gertie!
Little Tommy Tucker	We'll take you under our wing
	So
All (*with audience*)	Gertie!

Little Tommy Tucker   Please stay.

All	Who escaped from the Castle?
All (*with audience*)	Gertie!
All	Who escaped from the cage?
All (*with audience*)	Gertie!
All	Who escaped from the Giant?
All (*with audience*)	Gertie!
All	And left him in a rage?
	Well it was

Optional chorus

All (*with audience*)	Gertie!
All	You needn't flap
All (*with audience*)	Gertie!
All	Don't fly away
All (*with audience*)	Gertie!
All	We'll take you under our wing
	So
All (*with audience*)	Gertie!
All	Please stay,
	Yes, it was

Final Chorus

All (*with audience*)	Gertie!
All	You needn't flap
All (*with audience*)	Gertie!
All	Don't fly away
All (*with audience*)	Gertie!
All	We'll take you under our wing
	So
All (*with audience*)	Gertie!
All	Please stay.
All (*with audience*)	Gertie!

During the song the **Goose** *gets happier and happier, dancing energetically.*

Mother Goose   Well done, everybody. Now, come on, all of you. Jobs. Jack – you can make the beds. Polly –

washing up. I need someone to help me make the figgy
pudding.

Little Tommy Tucker   I will!

Mother Goose   All right. But fingers off my figgies. And
someone to search for some holly to decorate the Book. Bo
Peep?

Little Bo Peep   I'd rather stay here in case my sheep
come home.

Little Miss Muffet   I'll go holly-hunting. Gertie can
come too.

Gertie *nods.*

Mother Goose   Don't be long. (*She gives* **Little Miss
Muffet** *a basket.*)

Little Miss Muffet (*as she and* **Gertie** *set off*)   No. It's not
far to the forest. There's lots of holly there.

Gertie *stops abruptly at the mention of the word 'forest'. She
trembles. Music echoes the danger.*

What's the matter, Gertie? The forest? Don't worry.
(*Indicating the audience.*) We'll make sure you're safe, won't we?

All   Yes.

Little Miss Muffet   'Bye.

Music.

Little Miss Muffet *and* **Gertie** *set off, perhaps through the
auditorium, towards the forest.*

The others wave.

The Others   'Bye.

Mother Goose   Come on, children, to work.

*They all revolve the Book back to its original position; then they enter
the Book. Meanwhile, and after they are all in, the scene change takes
place. If this needs a few extra seconds, it may be an idea to have a*

*…o spot on **Little Miss Muffet** and **Gertie** as they progress …gh the auditorium, waving to the audience.*

Scene Two

*The Forest/**Spider**'s Lair.*

*This set should not be too complex. It could consist of several cut-out trees and/or borders, if possible reminiscent of a potentially sinister Arthur Rackham-style forest. Intertwining branches, interesting shapes. Incorporated into this is a holly bush or two, plus a raised 'Tuffet' in front of the **Spider**'s Lair – this could be a gnarled old tree trunk: but it should not be designed in such a way that the audience will spot straight away that something nasty is going to pop out – the entrance of the **Spider** should be a surprise.*

Sinister music as the lighting comes up on the rather spooky forest. Dramatic shadows made by the trees: perhaps some sinister noises – an owl hooting, a bat screeching.

*The **Big Bad Wolf** enters, sniffing the ground ahead of him, searching for tracks. He moves stealthily, stopping every few steps and sniffing – using his nose like a metal detector. Suddenly he finds a scent.*

Big Bad Wolf   Aha . . . (*He scurries along, following it, head down, body bent over. After a few paces he bangs straight into a tree trunk.*) Ow! (*A sound like a wolf's howl. He rubs his head.*) I don't like this creepy forest. I'm going home. (*He stands upright, banging his head on an overhead branch.*) Ow! (*A bigger howl. He rubs his head.*) Oh, I can feel one of my turns coming on. Tranquillizer, quick. (*He fumbles for a very large bottle of pills.*) Oh, my nerves, my nerves they're in tags and ratters, raggers and tatty, tatties and rags, oh, they're in shreds, they really are. (*He pops a huge gob-stopper pill in his mouth. With his mouth full.*) That's bett . . . (*Suddenly he sees the audience. He reacts with violent surprise, spitting out the pill, and half-retreating behind the tree. To the audience.*) Wh-wh-who are you? D-don't answer. I d-d-don't want to know. You didn't see that, do you understand, me t-taking that t-t-tranquillizer. I didn't take it.

'Cos I don't need t-t-tranquillizers. I'm f-f-fearless, n-nerveless, n-nothing frightens me. I'm the B-b-big B-b-bad W-w-wolf. No kid. And I'm strong, buff as old toots, I mean t-t-tough as old boots. So there. Ya boo! And that reminds me. Boo. I mean, that's what I'm here for. Looking, for a boo. Boo? Boo who? No, not boo-hoo, I mean, not looking for a boo, I mean looking for who you shouldn't say boo – to. Oh dear. (*He has an idea.*) Maybe you could help. You see, I jerk for the Wyant, I mean work for the Giant in the castle, and he has a sweet little pet, a snowy-white Goose we all love, and who loves us too. But today, horror of horrors, she's esca . . . she's disappeared, lost without trace, and the Giant is in tears, he's so worried about what awful fate may have befallen his little feathered friend. Now, all you kind animal lovers, hear my plea for a dumb creature in danger – and tell me, have you seen the Giant's Goose?

The audience should shout out 'no' – they will realize the **Big Bad Wolf** *is up to no good.*

Are you sure?

Audience   Yes.

Big Bad Wolf   Thank you. In that case I'd better go on searching. (*He puts his head down and starts sniffing again. Calling.*) Goosey, Goosey, Goosey. (*He starts to exit.*)

The **Bigger Badder Wolf** *enters suddenly.*

The **Big Bad Wolf** *bumps into him and jumps.*

Ooh! Oh, it's you. (*He takes out another tranquillizer, and pops it in his mouth – in fact 'palming' it.*)

Bigger Badder Wolf   Of course it's me. Pull yourself together. And stop taking those tranquillizers.

He bangs the **Big Bad Wolf** *on the back, but instead of making him spit it out, it in fact makes him swallow it. He reacts wide-eyed.*

Have you found the Goose?

Big Bad Wolf   N-n-no. I was just asking these kind
people . . .

Bigger Badder Wolf   Yes, I heard. Huh. (*He turns on the
audience.*) Now listen, you lot. I don't know who you are or
why you're here, but something tells me you're all lying
through your well-brushed teeth. You may think you can
bamboozle the Big Bad Wolf with your devious tricks, but
(*He cackles evilly.*) I'm the *Bigger Badder* Wolf and no one, but
no one, fools me.

Big Bad Wolf   Hear, hear.

Bigger Badder Wolf   I am the greatest.

Big Bad Wolf   Hear, hear. And I am the second greatest.

Bigger Badder Wolf   Hear, hear.

Big Bad Wolf   ⎫ And nobody stands in our way.
Bigger Badder Wolf   ⎬ Hear, hear.

*Both confidently turn inwards as though to move off, and bump into
each other. Both jump and scream. The* **Big Bad Wolf** *reacts
nervously, the* **Bigger Badder Wolf** *reacts angrily.*

SONG: **With a Huff and a Puff**

*The 'huh, huh' noise suggested is a combination of exhaled breath and
a sinister laugh.*

The Wolves	Huh huh huh huh huh huh huh
	With a huff and a puff
	We're rough and we're tough
	If you're climbing a tree, then
	We'll knock down your ladder.
	To make you feel sad
	Will make us feel glad
Big Bad Wolf	'Cos I'm big and bad
Bigger Badder Wolf	He's big and bad
	And I
Both	Huh huh huh huh huh

Bigger Badder Wolf	Am bigger and badder!
Both	Huh huh huh huh huh huh huh
	With a huff and a puff
	We're rough and we're tough
	And we do dirty deeds for
	A reas'nable figure,
	And if people twig
	We don't care a fig
Big Bad Wolf	'Cos I'm bad and big
Bigger Badder Wolf	He's bad and big
	And I
Both	Huh huh huh huh huh
Bigger Badder Wolf	Am badder and bigger!

Both	If you're on your way home
	On your own in the night
	We'll be waiting in lurk
	To give you a fright.
	Huh huh huh huh huh huh huh
	We'll creep up behind,
	Then one leap in the dark
	And you'll find
	That our bite is far worse than
	our bark.

	Huh huh huh huh huh huh huh
	With a huff and a puff
	We're rough and we're tough
	We would rob our old granny
	And not reimburse 'er;
	It's not just a fad –
	We've *always* been mad! –
Big Bad Wolf	'Cos I'm big and bad
Bigger Badder Wolf	He's big and bad
	And I
Both	Huh huh huh huh huh
Bigger Badder Wolf	Am bigger and worser!

Both	So watch out and don't cross our path
	It's years since we last had a bath
	Yes, we're dirty and vicious
	And highly suspicious
	With venom as vile as an adder –
	Two wolves at the door
	Means trouble in store
	One big and bad
	And one
	Huh huh huh huh huh
	Bigger and badder!
	Huh huh huh huh huh huh huh
	Huh!

At the end of the song, the music continues.

The **Big Bad Wolf** *and the* **Bigger Badder Wolf** *exit downstage, one each side, sniffing for the* **Goose**'s *tracks. The* **Big Bad Wolf** *exits L, the* **Bigger Badder Wolf** *exits R.*

Simultaneously, from up R, **Little Miss Muffet** *and* **Gertie** *enter, collecting holly in their basket.*

The music continues. They are unaware of any danger, in spite of possible audience reaction. They advance down L to another holly bush.

The **Big Bad Wolf**, *nose to the ground, enters up L and starts to cross the stage.*

The audience shout a warning, whereupon **Gertie** *turns and sees the* **Big Bad Wolf**. *She gets in a flap, and desperately tries to mime to* **Little Miss Muffet** *that they are in danger.*

In the nick of time, sizing up the situation, **Little Miss Muffet** *pulls* **Gertie** *off down L: in their panic they both drop their holly.*

At the same time, the **Big Bad Wolf** *picks up the* **Goose**'s *scent up RC and triumphantly follows it downstage. The music stops.*

Big Bad Wolf   She's near. She's near. I can smack her trells – smell her tracks. Oh! Goosey, Goosey, Goosey! (*To the audience.*) I'm getting warm, aren't I?

Audience   No.

Big Bad Wolf   Oh, yes I am.

Audience   Oh, no you're not.

Big Bad Wolf   Oh, yes I am.

Audience   Oh, no you're not.

Big Bad Wolf   Oooooh – no I'm not. (*Sniffing.*) I've lost the scent again. Grrrr. Now listen, *please*, please help me or I'll get into trouble with the Bigger Badder Wolf. Which way did she go, eh? Did she go that way? (*He points off R.*)

Audience (*lying*)   Yes.

Big Bad Wolf (*pointing off L*)   This way?

Audience   No.

Big Bad Wolf (*pointing off R*)   That way?

Audience   Yes.

Big Bad Wolf   You're sure?

Audience   Yes.

Big Bad Wolf   You're not having me on?

Audience   No.

Big Bad Wolf   Thank you. (*He starts to exit down R.*)

The **Bigger Badder Wolf** *enters suddenly down R.*

The **Big Bad Wolf** *bumps into him, and jumps with fright.*

Bigger Badder Wolf   You useless, wittering, witless wolf. You're not the second greatest, not the third greatest, you're the three thousand, two hundred and forty-fourth greatest. Just. And (*To the audience.*) as for you lot – I was watching all the time. You're nothing but a mass of mamby-pamby flamboyantly fickle, feckless fibbers. The Goose went *that* way, and she had a girl with her and they were collecting holly.

Big Bad Wolf   Golly.

Bigger Badder Wolf   No, holly.

Big Bad Wolf   Ooh, you rotten lot. I trusted you.

Bigger Badder Wolf   Ha, ha, ha. Try fooling someone your own size next time. You can't fool the greatest.

Big Bad Wolf   And you can't fool the three thousand, two hundred and forty-fourth greatest. Just. Not a second time, anyway.

Bigger Badder Wolf (*to the audience*)   So, watch out.

Big Bad Wolf (*taking his pocket-watch out*)   Half-past eleven.

Bigger Badder Wolf   What?

Big Bad Wolf   Half-past eleven. You said 'watch out'.

Bigger Badder Wolf (*hitting him*)   Idiot. Come on.

They start to exit.

(*To the audience.*) Watch your step.

Big Bad Wolf (*watching his feet*)   If I watch my step, I can't see where I'm going. (*He bumps into the* **Bigger Badder Wolf**.)

Bigger Badder Wolf   Oh, for wickedness' sake . . . (*Hitting him.*) I'm telling *them* to watch *their* step.

They start to move off.

Big Bad Wolf   Ah. Yes. (*To the audience, as evilly as he can.*) Tread very, very carefully, or you'll put your foot in it.

They growl – then both howl (OW!): they have each put their foot in the holly dropped by **Gertie** *and* **Little Miss Muffet**. *If possible, we can see it sticking to their feet. Then they overbalance and sit in the holly.*

Eventually the **Big Bad Wolf** *and* **Bigger Badder Wolf** *run off screaming and shaking their paws in revenge at the audience.*

Immediately, from up L, **Little Miss Muffet** *and* **Gertie** *enter nervously: they edge down C, then across R, looking warily about them.*

The two **Wolves** *enter up L on tiptoe.*

The **Wolves** *spot* **Little Miss Muffet** *and* **Gertie** *and, trying to 'shush' the audience, advance upon them. Hearing the audience's warning,* **Little Miss Muffet** *and* **Gertie** *see the* **Wolves** *and a short chase starts – possibly through the auditorium and back on to the stage. N.B. This chase should not be too long or involved. Back on stage, all chase round a tree.*

After one revolution of the tree **Little Miss Muffet** *and* **Gertie** *escape off R.*

The **Wolves** *are left chasing each other round the tree. Eventually they bump into each other and fall over.*

Furious, the **Wolves** *look wildly about them, then exit down L. Immediately* **Little Miss Muffet** *and* **Gertie** *enter up R and dash down C.*

Little Miss Muffet   Quick, Gertie, run home to the Book.

Gertie *wavers.*

Don't worry about me. I'll see you later.

Gertie *speeds off down R.*

Little Miss Muffet*, out of breath, sits down on the tuffet, and brings her curds and whey out of her basket. She begins to tuck in, hungrily and nervously.*

Suddenly finish music to sinister music, as, from his lair, the large, furry, frightening **Spider** *enters slowly. He sees* **Little Miss Muffet***, exults, and advances towards her.*

The audience scream a warning. The **Spider** *arrives beside* **Little Miss Muffet***. Sensing danger she slowly turns her head – in the wrong direction. Her head comes forward again; the* **Spider** *crosses* *behind her to the other side. She looks round again – in the other direction, thus missing the **Spider** again. Her head comes forward. She cannot understand the audience's concern. The **Spider** sits down beside her. Suddenly she 'feels' his presence and, with a slow burn, turns her head to face him. She sees him and screams. She leaps up and runs in a panic down R, then turns and runs across towards down L.*

*Meanwhile, the **Spider** retreats back into his lair, and the **Wolves** enter suddenly down L.*

Little Miss Muffet *runs straight into the arms of the **Wolves**. They hold on to her firmly.*

Bigger Badder Wolf   Got you. Ha, ha, ha. Now, little girl, where is she, eh?

Big Bad Wolf   Where's Goosey Goosey?

Little Miss Muffet   I don't know. Let me go, you're hurting.

Bigger Badder Wolf   Not until you help us find that scraggy bird.

*Suddenly there is a dramatic lighting change. Everything is black but for a small spotlight on **Little Miss Muffet**'s face. The action freezes.*

SONG: **My Big Moment**

Little Miss Muffet   This must be my big moment
My moment of glory
In the story
This will be my closest shave
This must be my big moment
This is my time to be brave.

*At the end of the song the lights return to normal and the action starts again, the **Wolves** hanging on to the struggling **Little Miss Muffet**.*

All right, all right. I'll tell you. I'll tell you all I know.

Bigger Badder Wolf   Sensible. Right, where is she?

Big Bad Wolf   Where's Goosey Goosey?

Little Miss Muffet   But only if you stop hurting my arms.

Bigger Badder Wolf   All right.

They release their grip.

Now, where is she?

Little Miss Muffet   Come and sit down and I'll tell you.

She sits to one side to the tuffet. The **Big Bad Wolf** *moves towards her.*

Bigger Badder Wolf   Stop. (*To* **Little Miss Muffet**.) No trickery now.

Little Miss Muffet   Of course not. (*Sweetly.*) How could I ever trick two such clever wolves as you?

Big Bad Wolf (*flattered*)   Hey, she's right, B.B.W. We're the greatest.

Bigger Badder Wolf   Well, all right. But we've got our eyes on you.

They sit down on the tuffet, the **Big Bad Wolf** *next to* **Little Miss Muffet**, *and the* **Bigger Badder Wolf** *next to him.*

Little Miss Muffet   Are you hungry?

Big Bad Wolf   Starving. Didn't have any breakfast.

Little Miss Muffet   You can share my elevenses if you like. (*She offers her curds and whey.*)

Big Bad Wolf   Ooh, thanks. What is it?

Little Miss Muffet   Curds and whey.

Big Bad Wolf   Ughhh. Sounds horrible.

Little Miss Muffet   Try some.

Bigger Badder Wolf   Hold it. (*He sniffs the bowl.*) Could be poison.

Little Miss Muffet   Don't be silly. (*She takes some on her finger and eats it.*)

Big Bad Wolf   Yes. Don't be silly, B.B.W. (*He takes a spoonful.*) Mmm. Very tasty. Try some.

The **Bigger Badder Wolf***, after a moment's hesitation, tries some.*

Bigger Badder Wolf   Mmmmm.

Little Miss Muffet*, in preparation for what is to happen, shuts her eyes tight.*

Music, as the **Spider** *emerges stealthily from his lair, and advances upon the* **Wolves***.*

The **Bigger Badder Wolf** *is holding the bowl, tucking in greedily. The* **Spider***, in pantomime fashion, taps the* **Bigger Badder Wolf** *on the shoulder. He thinks it is the* **Big Bad Wolf***.*

Get off.

Big Bad Wolf   What?

Bigger Badder Wolf   You've had your turn. Don't be greedy.

The **Spider** *again taps the* **Bigger Badder Wolf** *on the shoulder.*

I said get off.

Big Bad Wolf   I don't know what you're talking about.

The **Spider** *sits down beside the* **Big Bad Wolf***.*

Bigger Badder Wolf   Stop bashing me.

Big Bad Wolf   I didn't bash you. (*Turning to the* **Spider***.*) Did I?

The **Spider** *shakes his head. The* **Big Bad Wolf***'s head returns front.*

No. Cheek. I never touched you.

The **Big Bad Wolf** *does an enormous double take, sees the* **Spider** *again, and, terrified, exits.*

The **Bigger Badder Wolf***, who is still tucking in, does not see the* **Big Bad Wolf** *go. The* **Spider** *moves along the tuffet, bringing himself next to the* **Bigger Badder Wolf***. He digs him in the ribs.*

Bigger Badder Wolf   I've told you, don't do that. You've had your share.

The **Spider** *taps his knee.*

And don't tickle my leg either.

The **Spider** *does it again.*

I'm warning you . . .

The **Bigger Badder Wolf** *taps the* **Spider***'s 'knee'. The* **Spider** *shakes with laughter. The* **Bigger Badder Wolf** *suddenly does a double 'thinks' look, and gingerly reaches out and touches the* **Spider***'s knee – it clearly does not feel like the* **Big Bad Wolf***'s knee. He runs his hand up and down the* **Spider***'s leg/legs, gradually getting panic-stricken.*

Finally, the **Bigger Badder Wolf** *looks round, sees the* **Spider***, screams and dashes off, throwing down the bowl and spoon.*

Hearing the scream, **Little Miss Muffet** *opens her eyes and, summoning up all her courage, turns to see the* **Spider***. The* **Spider** *cheekily and endearingly waves a leg or two.* **Little Miss Muffet** *tentatively waves back, then stretches across and shakes hands with the* **Spider***. They share a moment of triumph over the* **Wolves***. She gives him a kiss and waves goodbye. He waves back with all his legs.*

Little Miss Muffet *exits towards home, i.e. down R.*

The **Spider** *picks up the bowl of curds and whey and starts to gobble it up. The lights fade.*

Scene Three

Back at the Book.

Music. **Mother Goose**, **Little Jack Horner**, **Little Tommy Tucker**, **Little Bo Peep** and **Little Polly Flinders** *enter.*

During the song they could well be effecting the scene change back to the Book, revolving it to display the inside, then decorating it, etc., and preparing the table and props for the cookery scene that follows.

SONG: Getting Ready for Christmas

Mother Goose
Little Jack Horner
Little Bo Peep   *(singing)*
Little Tommy Tucker
Little Polly Flinders

> We're getting ready for
>   Christmas
> We're getting ready for
>   Christmas Day
> Building a snowman
> From cotton-wool snow
> Hanging up the holly
> And the mistletoe
> We're getting ready
> Getting ready for Christmas
> Ready,
> Steady –
>
> We're getting ready for
>   Christmas
> We're getting ready for
>   Christmas Day
> Filling the stockings
> As full as can be
> Wrapping up the presents
> For the Christmas tree

We're getting ready
Getting ready for Christmas
Ready,
Steady –

It's nearly time for the
    celebrations
Fun and festivity lie in store
It's time to put up the
    decorations
With a welcoming Christmas
    wreath upon the door

We're getting ready for
    Christmas
We're getting ready for
    Christmas Day
Roasting the chestnuts
And chopping the wood
Blowing up balloons and
Helping stir the pud
We're getting ready
Getting ready for Christmas
Ready,
Steady –
Go!

Suggested instrumental verse for dance.

We're getting ready for
    Christmas
We're getting ready for
    Christmas Day
Shining a candle
From each window pane
Making paper hats and
Miles of paper chain
We're getting ready
Getting ready for Christmas
Ready,

> Steady –
>
> It's nearly time for the
>   celebrations
> Fun and festivity lie in store
> It's time to put up the
>   decorations
> With a welcoming Christmas
>   wreath upon the door.
>
> We're getting ready for
>   Christmas
> We're getting ready for
>   Christmas Day
> Stuffing the turkey
> And scrubbing the floors
> Sweeping out the chimney
> For old Santa Claus
> We're getting ready
> Getting ready for Christmas
> Ready,
> Steady –
> Go, go, go –
> Christmas
> Hallo.

Little Jack Horner, **Little Bo Peep** *and* **Little Polly Flinders** *exit to do more decorating on the 'outside' of the Book.*

Mother Goose *and* **Little Tommy Tucker** *remain behind to prepare the figgy pudding. The following slapstick-style scene could be embellished further into a 'speciality' if it is felt that not enough scope is given here: but it should not last too long, as, however funny it may be, it does hold up the plot.*

Mother Goose (*putting on an overall and chef's hat*)   Now, Tommy, time to make the figgy pudding.

Little Tommy Tucker   Now bring me some figgy
  (*singing*)   pudding,
                      Now bring me . . .

Mother Goose   Yes, all right, dear. Be a good boy and fetch me the dough.

Little Tommy Tucker   Dough?

Mother Goose   Dough. D.O. Dough.

Little Tommy Tucker   Oh. Dough. Right ho. (*He goes to the back of the set, singing as he works.*) Do, ray, me, fah, so, la, te (*Coming forward with the tray of dough.*) DO!

Mother Goose (*busy doing something else, e.g. weighing out currants, so not looking.*)   Hurry up, dear.

Little Tommy Tucker *staggers under the weight of the dough, and puts it down, on the floor in front of the table. He has to crouch to do this, so is temporarily out of* **Mother Goose**'s *vision.*

(*Looking up and not seeing him.*) Tommy!

Little Tommy Tucker *stands up. She sees him.*

Stop playing, dear (*Coming round to the front of the table.*) and (*One step per word.*) go-fetch-the-dough. (*On the word 'dough' she steps in the dough.*) Ohhhh!

Together they pull it off her boot.

Little Tommy Tucker   Oh. You've put your foot in it!

Mother Goose   Now concentrate, Tommy. (*Returning behind the table.*) Place the dough *here*. (*Patting the end of the table, then returning to counting her currants.*)

Little Tommy Tucker *struggles with the dough, which should be rather pliable and elastic.*

Here. (*She gives another pat.*)

Little Tommy Tucker *manages to put the dough down where* **Mother Goose** *wants it.*

Here. (*This time her hand crashes into the dough.*) Ughhhh!

Little Tommy Tucker   You've put your hand in it now.

Mother Goose   Tommy, a little con-cen-tra-tion if you please.

Little Tommy Tucker   Con-cen-tra-tion.

Mother Goose *kneads the dough into a large ball. A rolling-pin is visible on the table.*

Mother Goose   Take the dough (*She hands it to him.*) and roll it.

Little Tommy Tucker   Eh?

Mother Goose (*back with her currants*)   Roll it. Hurry up.

Little Tommy Tucker *shrugs his shoulders and rolls the ball of dough along the floor.*

Little Tommy Tucker   Wheeee!

Mother Goose (*seeing this*)   No, no, no, Tommy. Use the rolling-pin. (*She hands him the rolling-pin.*) This. (*She returns to her currants.*)

Little Tommy Tucker *takes the rolling-pin, and after a moment's hesitation, uses it as a bat to roll the dough further along the floor.*

(*Seeing this.*) No, no, no, Tommy. (*Deliberately.*) Roll it with the rolling-pin, thus. (*She mimes the movement.*)

Little Tommy Tucker (*echoing the movement*)   Thus.

Mother Goose   Thus.

Little Tommy Tucker   Thus.

It now becomes a rhythmic movement, complete with knees bend, etc. Both enjoy it.

Mother Goose   Thus.

Little Tommy Tucker   Thus.

As they continue, **Mother Goose** *gets carried away.*

Mother Goose (*suddenly*)   Stop it! Now get on with it, Tommy, and con-cen-trate.

Little Tommy Tucker *mouths the word 'con-cen-trate' with her. He starts rolling the dough correctly, except that he is still doing it on the floor.*

(*Seeing this.*) No, no, no, Tommy. Not on the floor. On the table. On the table.

Little Tommy Tucker *immediately jumps on the table, giving* **Mother Goose** *a fright.*

Aaaaah! Not you, the dough.

Little Tommy Tucker   Oh. (*He collects the dough, puts it on the table and starts rolling it with the rolling-pin. If possible, as the dough gets flatter and bigger, it spreads on to* **Mother Goose***'s outstretched hand and arm, so that they get rolled too. In rolling rhythm.*) Thus. Thus. Thus.

He eventually notices the bump, investigates, and, looking for where the bump leads, traces it up the arm to find **Mother Goose***'s long-suffering face staring at him. She slowly lifts her hand, letting the dough hang.*

Mother Goose
Little Tommy Tucker } Con-cen-trate.

Mother Goose   Now, fetch the baking tin.

Little Tommy Tucker *goes to the back of the set.* **Mother Goose** *scatters the currants over the dough and wraps it over, 'folding in the ends'.* **Little Tommy Tucker** *brings forward a tin, then suddenly screams, and drops the tin like a hot brick, with a clatter.*

Mother Goose (*with a jump*)   What was that?

Little Tommy Tucker   The baking tin. It's baking! Tara!

Mother Goose (*dividing the dough in two*)   Don't be silly. Now, we'll make one family-size figgy pudding (*She places half the dough in the tin, and scatters dusting powder on it.*) and a dozen small ones. (*She starts dividing the other half into smaller tennis-ball-size sections.*)

Suddenly **Little Tommy Tucker**'s *attention is drawn to the baking tin, where the pudding is 'rising' rapidly. In fact this is done with a balloon blowing up beneath the dough. N.B. This may have to be in a different tin, switched for the original one. This could have a thin layer of dough over the balloon, which pushes it up when blown up. As the pudding gets bigger and bigger,* **Little Tommy Tucker** *grabs* **Mother Goose**'s *attention. They both look at it, then* **Mother Goose** *prods it with a wooden spoon (with a pin attached). It bursts, spraying dough or dusting powder over their faces.*

Mother Goose   Self-raising flour! (*Returning to the small ones.*) Right, Tommy. Into the oven.

The oven could be 'under the table' or in another part of the set. **Tommy** *starts to get in it.*

Not you. The figgy puddings.

Tommy *gets out of the oven. To music,* **Mother Goose** *starts throwing the balls of dough to* **Little Tommy Tucker***, the idea being that he should transfer them to the oven. If the actor playing* **Little Tommy Tucker** *can juggle, he could go into a short routine here. Eventually, he has too many to hold and* **Mother Goose** *is throwing more, without looking at him.*

At this point, **Little Jack Horner***,* **Little Bo Peep** *and* **Little Polly Flinders** *enter.*

Little Tommy Tucker *throws the 'balls' to them; they spread out and catch the 'balls' in a circular chain. The last one returns the 'balls' to the table for* **Mother Goose** *to pick up and throw at* **Little Tommy Tucker** *again. She is unaware that this is going on, of course. The catching game, to music, continues for a short while. Then* **Mother Goose** *notices what is going on. Her immediate reaction is one of annoyance, but this changes to amusement and enjoyment. She suddenly picks up a frying pan or similar object and, as the 'balls' come back to her, whacks them, cricket or tennis-style. The first few she hits stay on the stage. Then* **Little Tommy Tucker** *starts throwing into the 'chain', 'balls' from another source. These are* *cotton-wool balls, and are clouted fair and square by* **Mother Goose** *into the audience. N.B. This fairly traditional panto routine could be omitted; the cookery scene could end on the line 'Self-raising flour', at which point the others enter.*

Suddenly, as the fun with the audience is in full flood, **Gertie** *enters from the forest and runs to the door and pulls the bell-rope.*

The 'game' freezes at the sound of the bell.

Little Bo Peep   Is that my sheep?

Mother Goose   No, it's Little Miss Muffet and Gertie back from holly hunting, I expect.

Little Jack Horner *opens the door; in rushes* **Gertie** *in a flurry, flapping her wings. They all cluster round her.*

Little Jack Horner	⟩ What is it?
Little Tommy Tucker	⟩ What's the matter? etc.
Little Bo Peep	⟩ What's happened, Gertie? etc.

Gertie *is confused.*

Mother Goose   Quiet. You can see she's in a state. Polly. Come and do your stuff.

Little Polly Flinders *comes forward.*

Little Polly Flinders   What is it, Gertie? Did you meet somebody?

Gertie *nods, and does a wolf impersonation. The audience will probably help interpret.*

What? A monster? The Giant? A wolf?

Gertie *nods, and mimes 'two'.*

Two wolves?

Little Bo Peep (*freezing with terror*)   Wolves?

Little Polly Flinders   Did they chase you?

Gertie *nods.*

Mother Goose   Where's Little Miss Muffet?

Gertie *mimes a boxing match.*

Little Polly Flinders   She's fighting them?

Gertie *nods.*

Mother Goose   Ooh. (*She swallows hard.*) I hope she's careful. (*Trying not to appear too worried.*) She had a clean apron on this morning. (*She blinks away a tear.*)

Little Tommy Tucker   She'll be all right, Mother.

Little Bo Peep   Wolves! (*She bursts into tears.*)

Little Jack Horner   Don't cry, Bo Peep; Little Miss Muffet will be back soon.

Little Bo Peep   I'm not worried about her, I'm worried about my poor little sheep. Alone in the forest. Surrounded by wolves. Wolves like nothing better than sheep – to eat! I'll never see them again.

The others look at one another and shrug their shoulders, as she dashes out of the door, to 'outside' the Book, which then revolves to reveal the outside cover again. **Little Bo Peep** *looks out in all directions, hoping for a glimpse of her sheep.*

SONG: **Sheep, Sheep**

Little Bo Peep

Sheep, sheep
This is Bo Peep
Oh can you hear
What I say?
Or have you strayed
Too far?

Sheep, sheep
I'm losing sleep
Oh don't you know
How I care
Please tell me where
You are.

One by one, the others, **Little Jack Horner**, **Little Tommy Tucker** *and* **Little Polly Flinders** *– put their heads over or round the Book.*

Little Jack Horner (*speaking*)   Baaaaaaaa!

Little Tommy Tucker (*speaking*)   Baaaaaaaa!

Little Polly Flinders (*speaking*)   Baaaaaaaa!

All three (*speaking*)   Baaaaaaaa!

Little Bo Peep *swings round, thinking her sheep have been found. When she sees it is the others sending her up, she is cross, but tries to preserve her dignity.*

Little Bo Peep (*speaking*)   Oh, it's you.

The other three sing with a sheep-like wobble in their voices.

Little Polly Flinders
Little Tommy Tucker } (*singing together*)
Little Jack Horner

> Baaaaaa! Baaaaaa!
> We've not strayed far
> And we'll return
> Very soon
> This afternoon
> You'll see.
>
> Baaaaaa! Baaaaaa!
> Daft things we are!
> But if you leave
> Us alone
> We'll hurry home
> For tea.

Little Bo Peep *tries to take no notice.*

Little Bo Peep

> Sheep, sheep
> This is Bo Peep
> Oh tell me why
> Must you go?

Why are you so
Unkind?

Little Polly Flinders ⎫
Little Tommy Tucker ⎬ (*singing together*)
Little Jack Horner ⎭

Baaaaaa! Baaaaaa!
Stupid we are
But we'll come back
Without fail
Bringing our tails
Behind.

Little Bo Peep   Sheep, sheep

Little Polly Flinders ⎫
Little Tommy Tucker ⎬ Baaaaaa! Baaaaaa!
Little Jack Horner ⎭

Dabbing her eyes, **Little Bo Peep** *has a final look, shakes her head and goes back in the Book.*

Little Polly Flinders ⎫
Little Tommy Tucker ⎬ Baaaaaa! Baaaaaa!
Little Jack Horner ⎭

Little Bo Peep   Sheep, sheep.

Their heads disappear from view.

Sinister chord as the **Bigger Badder Wolf** *enters, rubbing his hands in glee; he has seen* **Little Bo Peep** *go in. He is followed by the* **Big Bad Wolf***, head down sniffing the tracks. The* **Bigger Badder Wolf** *stops.* **The Big Bad Wolf** *bumps into him. The* **Bigger Badder Wolf** *hits him.*

Big Bad Wolf   Sorry, B.B.W. (*Nervously he takes out a tranquillizer.*)

Bigger Badder Wolf (*imitating*)   Sorry, B.B.W. (*Crossly.*)
And stop taking tranquillizers.

He knocks it out of the **Big Bad Wolf**'s *hand, making it bounce high in the air. The* **Bigger Badder Wolf** *catches it under his hat. Alternatively it is allowed to bounce out into the auditorium.*

Big Bad Wolf   Sorry, B.B.W.

Bigger Badder Wolf   And stop saying 'Sorry, B.B.W.' It gets on my nerves.

Big Bad Wolf   Sorry, B.B.W. (*He realizes too late, and clamps his hand over his mouth.*)

Bigger Badder Wolf   Now, listen. Tracks end here, right?

Big Bad Wolf   Right here, right.

Bigger Badder Wolf (*pointing to the Book*)   Goose in there, therefore, right?

Big Bad Wolf   Right there, therefore, right.

Bigger Badder Wolf   Problem: to get inside, right? And not to be left outside, right?

Big Bad Wolf   Ah! Right. Not left outside, but right inside, right! Not outside left but inside right to centre forward and shoot and it's a goal! Hooray! (*He jumps up and down.*)

The **Bigger Badder Wolf** *clamps his hand over the* **Big Bad Wolf**'s *mouth.*

Bigger Badder Wolf   Shhh. Solution: take off your coat.

Big Bad Wolf   What?

Bigger Badder Wolf   Take off your coat.

Big Bad Wolf   I'll catch cold.

Bigger Badder Wolf   You'll catch more than a cold if you don't. Now (*Helping him out of his coat.*) take it off and turn it inside out, right?

Big Bad Wolf   Inside out, right. Not outside in, left. Inside out . . .

Bigger Badder Wolf   And don't start all that again.

Big Bad Wolf   I didn't start it. You started it.

By this time, the **Big Bad Wolf***'s coat is back on – inside out, revealing the thick sheepskin lining.*

Bigger Badder Wolf   Now. Baaaa.

Big Bad Wolf   I beg your pardon?

Bigger Badder Wolf   Baaaa. Baaaaa! (*He encourages the* **Big Bad Wolf** *to copy the noise.*)

The **Big Bad Wolf** *has not a clue what he is on about.*

Big Bad Wolf   Baaaa?

Bigger Badder Wolf (*nodding*)   Baaaaa! (*Louder and more manic.*) Baaaaaa!

Big Bad Wolf   Do you want a tranquillizer?

Bigger Badder Wolf   Oh, give me strength!

Big Bad Wolf   No, but it'll calm you down.

Bigger Badder Wolf   You baaaa.

Big Bad Wolf   Me baaaa?

Bigger Badder Wolf   Yes, you baaaa. Look, didn't you hear that girl bleating on about her lost sheep?

The **Big Bad Wolf** *nods.*

(*Slowly and clearly.*) Well, *you* are now a wolf in sheep's clothing, right? And that means . . .

He is stopped by a shout off.

Little Miss Muffet   Mother Goose! Mother Goose!

Bigger Badder Wolf   Look out!

The **Bigger Badder Wolf** *drags the* **Big Bad Wolf** *off to hide. They exit the side opposite the one they entered — i.e. not the side established as leading to the forest.* **Little Miss Muffet** *rushes on from the forest: she rings frantically on the bell.*

Little Miss Muffet   Mother Goose! Quick.

The door opens and **Mother Goose**, **Gertie** *and the four other* **Children** *emerge, and cluster round her.* **Little Polly Flinders** *carries the kettle with her.*

All   She's back. Thank goodness you're safe. Are you all right? etc.

Little Miss Muffet (*breathless*)   Wolves. After Gertie. From the Giant's Castle. They're coming.

Little Bo Peep   What are we going to do?

Little Jack Horner   Shut ourselves in the Book.

All turn to go in the door.

Little Miss Muffet   No.

They stop.

They're strong. They'll smash the door down if they know Gertie's inside. (*She grabs* **Gertie**.) I'll hide with her in the forest.

Little Polly Flinders   Can I come?

Little Jack Horner   And me.

Little Tommy Tucker   Me too! I'll bring the figgy pud. All right, Mother Goose?

Mother Goose   I suppose so, dear. But do take care, all of you.

Little Tommy Tucker *rushes in and collects some figgy pudding.*

Little Bo Peep   I'd better stay here, in case my sheep turn up. (*She starts sniffing.*)

Mother Goose   Very well, dear.

Little Miss Muffet   Come on.

Little Miss Muffet *leads a nervous* **Gertie** *off. The others follow – they exit towards the forest,* **Mother Goose** *waving.*

Mother Goose   I'll see you off.

Mother Goose *exits.* **Little Bo Peep** *goes back in the Book and shuts the door. Immediately, music is heard as the* **Wolves** *enter from the other side.*

The **Bigger Badder Wolf** *pushes the disguised* **Big Bad Wolf** *to the door. The* **Big Bad Wolf** *rings the bell, then bends over to look more like a sheep.*

Big Bad Wolf   Baaaaa! Baaaaaa!

The door opens.

The **Bigger Badder Wolf** *backs away to avoid being seen, and in fact exits on the forest side, looking eagerly towards the Book. This is to prevent the audience thinking he is chasing after the others.*

Little Bo Peep *emerges.*

Baaaaaa!

Little Bo Peep (*yelling with delight*)   Little sheep! You've come home!

She falls upon the 'sheep', stroking and hugging him. By this time the audience may well be screaming a warning.

You're safe from the Wolves, now. Come in.

She takes him in and shuts the door behind them. Pause. Suddenly, a bloodcurdling scream is heard. The door opens again and **Little Bo Peep**, *screaming, tries to get out, but each time is seen to be pulled roughly back inside. Growling noises from the* **Big Bad Wolf**. *But* **Little Bo Peep** *has her crook with her and manages to stave off the* **Wolf** *with it. N.B. It may be possible to work out a short routine using the crook as a catching device.* **Little Bo Peep** *could emerge from the door a couple of times, but be suddenly caught round the neck*

with the crook and hauled in again. Then the situations could be reversed, with **Little Bo Peep** *catching the* **Big Bad Wolf** *by the neck trying to drag him inside so she can get out. Finally the door is shut, and we imagine the* **Big Bad Wolf** *is a little stunned inside.* **Little Bo Peep**, *screaming still, rushes down R, nearly exits, then, remembering that the others went in the other direction, turns round and starts to run off L.*

Mother Goose *enters down L.*

Little Bo Peep *is stopped in her tracks.*

Little Bo Peep Oh, Mother Goose, Mother Goose. (*She flings herself into* **Mother Goose***'s arms, pointing indoors to where the* **Big Bad Wolf** *is. Hysterically.*) A wolf, a wolf. Rang the bell and I thought it was one of my sheep and let him in and . . . ohhh! (*She sobs.*)

Mother Goose There, there, dear. You're safe now. Stop crying.

The sobbing lessens with the reassuring pats on the back.

Little Bo Peep I'm sorry. I can't help it. He was so horrible – and he's still in the Book!

Mother Goose There, there.

For the first time, **Little Bo Peep** *looks up, through tear-stained eyes, at* **Mother Goose**.

Little Bo Peep Oh, Mother Goose, how strong your arms are.

Mother Goose All the better to comfort you, my dear.

Music chord.

Little Bo Peep Oh, Mother Goose. (*A little uncomfortable.*) How big your eyes look today.

Mother Goose All the better to watch over you, my dear.

Music chord.

Little Bo Peep (*nervously*)   Oh, Mother Goose, how long and sharp your teeth look.

Mother Goose   All the better to *bite* you with, my dear.

*Music. Dramatic struggle, but not too long, in which 'Mother Goose' is revealed to be the **Bigger Badder Wolf** in disguise – in fact, wearing **Mother Goose**'s dress. N.B. This revelation should, if possible, come as a real surprise to the audience. The tussle ends with the **Big Bad Wolf** entering from the Book, rubbing his head; he is finishing off writing a note, which he speedily attaches to the door. Then he helps subdue the struggling, screaming **Little Bo Peep**. They lift her up and tuck her under their arms. Suddenly the lighting changes dramatically, to solely a follow spot on **Little Bo Peep**. Simultaneously the action freezes.*

SONG: **My Big Moment** (*reprise*)

Little Bo Peep (*singing*)   This must be my big moment
My moment of glory
In the story
This will be my closest shave
This must be my big moment
This is my time to be brave.

*At the end of the song, the lighting reverts and the action starts again, and the growling **Wolves** carry off the struggling **Little Bo Peep**. They exit down L towards the forest. Simultaneously, **Mother Goose** enters up L, in her undies, still spinning from the shock of being attacked by the **Bigger Badder Wolf**.*

*The audience may well shout out that **Little Bo Peep** has been caught, or that the **Wolves** have left a note. In any case, she staggers to the door, goes to open it, notices the note, rips it off the door and studies it.*

Mother Goose (*reading*)   'We, the Wolves of the Giant's Castle, wish to inform Mother Goose that Little Bo Peep is in our clutches. If you ever want to set eyes on her again you must bring the Giant's Goose into the Forest within the hour and we will do a swap. The Goose for Little Bo Peep.

Yours threateningly, The Big Bad Wolf and the Bigger Badder Wolf.' Oh, no. What's to be done? (*Calling.*) Children! (*Remembering.*) They've all gone. Poor Little Bo Peep. Poor Gertie. Now calm down, Mother Goose, calm down, don't panic, don't panic, don't panic. (*Pause. She takes a deep breath to calm down. Suddenly she shouts.*) HE — LP! Emergency, emergency. He — lp! (*She has an idea.*) Fairy Lethargia, of course. (*To the audience.*) Quick, let's wake her up. One, two, three.

Audience *and* **Mother Goose** (*calling together*)   Fairy Lethargia.

Mother Goose   Once more. One, two, three.

Audience *and* **Mother Goose** (*calling together*)   Fairy Lethargia

A yawning, stretching **Fairy Lethargia** *eases her way out of the decorations box.*

Fairy Lethargia   Cor dear, I'm up and down like a blinking yoyo . . . oh. (*She sees the audience as she climbs out, puts on her act again.*)

> Hallo, hallo, it's Christmas Eve, and I'm your Christmas Fairy
> My spells will get you out of spots and situations hairy . . .

(*Suddenly she sees* **Mother Goose**.) Ha, ha, ha, ha.

Mother Goose   What's the matter?

Fairy Lethargia   You look funny with your undies on.

Mother Goose   I look funnier with them off.

Fairy Lethargia   Ha, ha, ha, ha.

Mother Goose   Stop laughing. This looks serious.

Fairy Lethargia   It doesn't from where I'm standing. Ha, ha.

Mother Goose   I've been hijacked by a wolf. And Little Bo Peep's been kidnapped. Wolfnapped. I need the first of our three spells, please.

Fairy Lethargia   Oh.

Mother Goose   Oh what?

Fairy Lethargia   OK. (*Taking the wand off the tree.*) What's it to be?

Mother Goose   Er. (*She thinks.*) Miss Muffet and Polly and Tommy and Jack – oh, and Gertie – I need them here, so we can decide what to do.

Fairy Lethargia   Where are they now?

Mother Goose   If I knew that, I wouldn't ask for a spell to get them back, would I?

Fairy Lethargia   All right, all right, don't get your knickers in a twist. (*She looks at* **Mother Goose**'s *undies and giggles again.*)

Mother Goose   I'll go and find my dressing-gown.

Mother Goose *goes in the door.*

Fairy Lethargia *takes up a pose, holds up the wand, and starts the spell, accompanied by not-very-graceful movements.*

SONG: **Fairy Lethargia's Magic Spell**

Fairy Lethargia   Gertie and Little Miss Muffet
                             And Tommy and Polly and Jack
                             Abracadabra, hocus pocus
                             Magic the lot of them back.

At the end of the spell, the four **Children** *and* **Gertie** *return 'by magic'. This could be achieved by use of trap doors, flash boxes, a swift black-out, etc. At any event, all five return, and are surprised to find themselves transported back to the Book.* **Little Tommy Tucker** *carries a substantially reduced figgy pudding;* **Little Polly Flinders** *carries her kettle.*

Fairy Lethargia *curtsies to acknowledge possible audience applause – depending on how well the magical appearances were done!*

Little Jack Horner (*waking up*)   What's happened?

Fairy Lethargia   Spell Number One's happened, that's what. Pretty spectacular, eh? (*She blows her fingernails, or does some other self-congratulatory movement.*)

Little Tommy Tucker   We're back.

Little Miss Muffet   But why?

Mother Goose *enters from the Book; she wears her dressing-gown.*

Mother Goose   Oh, thank goodness. Well done, Lethargia. Have a rest, dear. Children, listen.

The **Children** *and* **Gertie**, *still 'waking up', gather round* **Mother Goose**.

Little Bo Peep has been wolfnapped. By the kids . . . I mean, kidnapped by the Wolves.

This jerks them into life.

Children   What? How? Where have they taken her? etc.

Mother Goose   Shhh. Listen. They left a note saying that if we ever want to see her again, we must meet them in the forest.

Gertie *involuntarily flaps her wings.*

Then they will give us back Little Bo Peep on condition that we – that we – well, children, that we – in exchange as it were – give them back – (*She can hardly bring herself to say it.*) – Gertie.

Music. **Gertie** *slowly turns away from the group, and, head down, sadly waddles down-stage. She is obviously crying. N.B. This must not be overdone – it is a very tender moment. The others watch her.*

Gertie, dear. I wouldn't have had this happen for all the world, you know that, don't you?

Gertie *nods.*

But what can I do? Eh? I must save Little Bo Peep. I'm sorry.

Gertie *nods and, resigned, starts moving off towards the forest. The music builds as the others all set off too. A sad procession, which* **Fairy Lethargia** *joins.* **Little Polly Flinders** *still has her kettle. The lights fade.*

Scene Four

The Forest – without the **Spider***'s Lair.*

The music continues as the scene changes. The following sequence is all done in mime to music. If desirable, a forest front cloth could fly in to cover the scene change. The two snarling **Wolves** *enter, carrying a distressed* **Little Bo Peep***. They pause for a few moments to shake their fists at the audience, who should be booing them. The* **Bigger Badder Wolf** *removes* **Mother Goose***'s dress, while the* **Big Bad Wolf** *retains a grip on* **Little Bo Peep***. The dress is thrown roughly on the ground, and maybe stamped on. Then they exit, or, if a front cloth is not being used – it may be possible, for example, for them to enter through the auditorium and reach the stage just as the scene change has been effected, taking the dress off on the way – they hide behind a tree.*

The music continues, playing a sad version of the **Goose***'s song, as* **Gertie***, with the* **Children***,* **Mother Goose** *and* **Fairy Lethargia***, enter the forest. They, too, could come through the auditorium, or go across the front cloth, or simply arrive in the forest. They find* **Mother Goose***'s dress on the ground, and know they are on the right route.* **Mother Goose** *takes the dress with her. The* **Children** *surround* **Gertie** *protectively.*

Suddenly, the **Wolves** *and* **Bo Peep** *emerge. The two sides confront each other.* **Little Bo Peep** *outstretches her arms for help.* **Mother Goose***, firmly but sympathetically, forces the* **Children** *to let* **Gertie** *go. Each one kisses her goodbye.* **Mother Goose** *takes her by the wing and advances to 'no-man's land' in the centre.*

The **Wolves** *bring* **Little Bo Peep** *forward. The exchange is made.* **Little Bo Peep** *embraces* **Mother Goose**, *who leads her back to the 'family'.*

Meanwhile, the **Wolves** *grab* **Gertie** *and perhaps put a rope round her neck, before roughly forcing her to go with them towards the Giant's Castle. The others watch them disappear, with obviously conflicting emotions – relief for* **Little Bo Peep**'s *safety and sadness at* **Gertie**'s *disappearance.*

The music stops.

Little Bo Peep   Where's Gertie going?

Mother Goose   Back to the Giant's Castle. It was either her or you, dear.

Little Bo Peep   But we can't just let her be locked up in a cage again. (*To the others.*) Can we?

Little Miss Muffet   She's right.

Little Tommy Tucker   But what else can we do? Mother Goose?

Mother Goose   It's up to you, children. Remember, this is *your* story, *your* adventure . . .

Pause. **Fairy Lethargia** *falls asleep on her feet.*

Little Jack Horner   We'll rescue Gertie.

All   Hear, hear; hooray, etc.

Little Polly Flinders (*plucking up courage*)   And – and – and teach that stinking old Giant Bossyboots a lesson he'll never forget.

All   Hear, hear; hooray, etc.

Mother Goose   But don't forget it'll be dangerous – we'll have to face the forest and the castle and the Wolves and the Giant, not to mention the Monster of the Moat.

Little Tommy Tucker   They'll help make it a real adventure.

Little Miss Muffet   And we've still got two of Fairy Lethargia's spells left. Haven't we?

Fairy Lethargia *is still asleep on her feet. All turn to see her. She snores.*

Little Bo Peep   She's nodded off again.

Mother Goose   Come on, then, everybody. One, two, three.

All   Fairy Lethargia.

Fairy Lethargia (*suddenly waking with a start*)   Oooh! (*Lifting her wand, and putting on her act.*)

Hallo, hallo, 'tis Christmas Eve, and I'm . . .

All (*shouting her down*)   No! Quiet! Shh! etc.

Fairy Lethargia   What's going on?

SONG: **Off to the Rescue**

They all sing except **Fairy Lethargia**, *who joins in at an appropriate moment.*

Off through the forest
Off to the castle
Off to the rescue we race;
Summon up courage
Tackle the Monster
Challenge the Giant and put
   those two Wolves in their place;
We must find her
We can't be that far behind her
We'll follow the track
And bring our Goose back
Leave no stone unturned
Till we have returned
With her found
Safe and sound.

Off through the forest

Off to the castle
Off to the rescue we race;
Nothing can stop us
We won't be beaten
We'll do our best for our quest
    must be no wild goose chase;
When we see her
Somehow we'll force them to free
    her
We know that it's right
We'll stand up and fight
Then back to the Book
By hook or by crook
We'll vamoose
With our Goose!
Off to the rescue
Off to the rescue . . .

Suddenly **Little Jack Horner** *trips over something and falls over. He shouts out. The music stops, all except a tremolo rumble of excitement.*

Little Miss Muffet   Enjoy your trip?

Little Jack Horner (*getting up*)   There's something there – in that patch of grass.

They look. Suddenly **Little Polly Flinders** *finds something.*

Little Polly Flinders   Look.

Little Miss Muffet   An egg.

Mother Goose   A *golden* egg. It's beautiful.

Little Tommy Tucker   Gertie must have laid it . . .

Little Bo Peep   So she *is* the Goose that laid the Golden Egg.

Fairy Lethargia (*taking control*)   That's right. She was so grateful to you all for showing her kindness that she laid it for you.

Into couplets — but not sent up.

> Throughout your quest, this egg will be your lucky charm
> As long as you don't lose it, you can come to no harm.

Little Bo Peep   Thank you, Gertie.

Little Tommy Tucker   We'll pay you back.

Little Polly Flinders⎫
Little Miss Muffet   ⎬ We're on our way!
Little Jack Horner ⎭

SONG: **Off to the Rescue** (*continued*)

All   Off to the rescue
                                 Off to the rescue
                                 This Golden Egg will protect us
                                     from danger we know
                                 So
                                 Off to the rescue
                                 We go.

As the song ends, the 'Quest' exits.

Fairy Lethargia *waves farewell. Then she replaces her wand on the Christmas tree, yawns and stretches and gets back into the decorations box. The music swells as the lighting narrows down to the star on the wand. Then it fades to a black-out.*

The Christmas tree, with the wand on it as a star, remains in view throughout the Interval.

Act Two

Scene One

N.B. This scene is optional. Its function is to re-establish the plot, but this may be felt to be unnecessary.

The Edge of the Forest (front cloth), with the Giant's Castle visible in the distance.

The entr'acte music becomes sinister as the house lights go down.

The **Wolves** *enter, dragging* **Gertie** *behind them. She still has the sack over her head. The* **Wolves** *savagely push and pull her, playing up to the audience reaction against them. Finally they exit the other side. The music changes, and from off we hear singing. The 'Quest' then enters continuing the song.* **Little Polly Flinders** *still carries her kettle.* **Mother Goose** *has put on her dress and carries her dressing-gown.*

SONG: **Off to the Rescue** (*reprise*)

Mother Goose
Little Miss Muffet
Little Jack Horner ⎫
Little Bo Peep ⎬ (*singing together*)
Little Tommy Tucker ⎭
Little Polly Flinders

> Off through the forest
> Off to the castle
> Off to the rescue we race
> Summon up courage
> Tackle the Monster
> Challenge the Giant and put
>   those two Wolves in their place;
> We must find her
> We can't be that far behind
>   her . . .

The music continues under the following dialogue.

Little Miss Muffet (*excited*)   There's the castle. It's not far.

Little Bo Peep   Looks really spooky. (*Wanting reassurance.*) Where's the Golden Egg?

Little Jack Horner   Tommy's eaten it.

Little Tommy Tucker   I haven't.

Mother Goose   Here it is. (*She takes it from her pocket.*)

Little Polly Flinders (*whispering in amazement*)   It's bigger.

Mother Goose   What, dear?

Little Polly Flinders   The egg's grown. It's bigger.

Mother Goose   So it is.

Little Jack Horner   How eggstraordinary! Tara!

All groan at the pun.

SONG: **Off to the Rescue** (*reprise, continued*)

All   Off to the rescue
                            Off to the rescue
                            Our Golden Egg will protect us
                                from danger we know
                            So
                            Off to the rescue
                            We go.

As the song ends, they all exit towards the Castle.

The lights fade to a black-out.

Scene Two

*The Entrance to the **Giant**'s Castle.*

Huge studded double doors dominate the scene upstage – giving an idea of the gigantic scale of the Castle. In front of the doors is a raised drawbridge. A sign says 'BEWARE OF THE MONSTER OF THE MOAT', and downstage is a bank, to suggest the moat between it and the doors. Perhaps a lighting effect could suggest water reflections from the moat. On the bank is a bell-push or bell-rope; if it is the latter, it could extend up into the flies, as though going up to a bell tower. Another sign says 'RING THE BELL AND UTTER THE PASSWORD'.

The **Wolves** *enter dragging* **Gertie**.

Bigger Badder Wolf   Ring the bell.

Big Bad Wolf   What?

Bigger Badder Wolf   Ring the bell.

Big Bad Wolf (*nervously*)   I'd rather not.

Bigger Badder Wolf   What do you mean (*Imitating.*) 'I'd rather not'? We can't get inside unless we ring the bell.

Big Bad Wolf   You ring it, then.

Bigger Badder Wolf   Why me?

Big Bad Wolf   You're more musical than I am.

Bigger Badder Wolf   Don't be so stupid. What's the matter with you? Why won't you ring the bell?

Big Bad Wolf   It m-m-means m-m-moving towards the m-m-moat and the M-m-m-monster.

Bigger Badder Wolf   The Monster isn't worried about you.

Big Bad Wolf   No, but I'm a little worried about *him*.

Bigger Badder Wolf   Oh, for wickedness' sake – hold this horrible bird.

The **Big Bad Wolf** *does so. The* **Bigger Badder Wolf** *strides confidently up to the bell-rope and pulls it. He returns.*

There you are. Nothing to it.

The very loud boom of the deep, ominous, clanging bell makes them both jump. From high up in the flies we hear the sound of a sash window being raised. The **Wolves** *look up.*

Giant's Voice (*booming down from the flies*)   Password.

Bigger Badder Wolf   Password.

Bigger Badder Wolf ⎫
Big Bad Wolf   ⎬ (*chanting together*)
                        ⎭
  Copper and silver leave us cold
  What we want is lots of gold.

Giant's Voice   Again.

Bigger Badder Wolf   Why? Don't you believe us?

Giant's Voice   Yes. But I enjoy hearing it.

Bigger Badder Wolf ⎫
Big Bad Wolf   ⎬ (*chanting together*)
                        ⎭
  Copper and silver leave us cold
  What we want is lots of gold

Giant's Voice   You may enter.

Bigger Badder Wolf   Thanks, Boss. We've got the Goose.

Giant's Voice   Splendid. (*He laughs – a hollow, evil, booming laugh.*)

With a sinister creaking sound, the drawbridge lowers, and clanks on to the bank. Music, as the **Wolves** *and* **Gertie** *start to go across. The* **Big Bad Wolf** *is nervous, and surreptitiously takes out a tranquillizer and pops it in his mouth. The* **Bigger Badder Wolf** *catches him at it, and slaps him on the back. The gob-stopper-size tranquillizer pops out – into the moat. The* **Wolves** *react worried, and even more so when they hear the sound of the* **Monster**, *underwater, being woken up, hit by the flying gob-stopper – a sort of 'ow' sound, followed by a roar of anger. The* **Wolves** *cling on to each other as well as* **Gertie**, *as, suddenly, an enormous head – rather like the head of the Loch Ness Monster – rears us from the moat, and* *advances towards them, snapping its jaws and uttering frightening sounds.*

The **Wolves** *manage to edge their way along the drawbridge, pushing* **Gertie** *ahead of them. They reach the doors, enter the castle — more sinister creaking sounds — and close the doors.*

The drawbridge raises itself, perhaps hitting the **Monster** *on the 'chin' as it does so. The* **Monster**, *disappointed, returns under the water with a dissatisfied moan. The music continues.*

Little Miss Muffet *enters downstage, and beckons on* **Mother Goose** *and the other* **Children**. *They enter on tiptoe.* **Mother Goose** *still carries her dressing-gown — she puts it down in a suitable place during the following scene.*

Little Jack Horner (*loudly*)   Cor, it's gigantic!

All   Shhhh!

They all huddle downstage, organized by **Mother Goose**, *and start to whisper tactics. They are stopped by the booming sound of the* **Giant***'s voice.*

Giant's Voice (*from the flies above*)   Hallo, Goosey. Welcome home. Ha, ha, ha. Into your cage, there's a good bird.

There is the clank of a cage door closing and a key turning.

Now, back on the job. I want a Golden Egg, do you hear? A Golden Egg. And if you don't lay it soon, you'll be shut in a dungeon without food or water till you rot. So lay, blast you, lay.

Giant footsteps are heard retreating. **Mother Goose** *and the* **Children** *react to the speech, shaking their fists up towards the flies.*

Little Jack Horner (*loudly, incensed*)   Mother Goose . . .

All   Shh.

Little Jack Horner (*whispering*)   Mother Goose, let me rescue Gertie from that big bully Bossyboots. Let Little Jack Horner be Jack the Giant-killer.

Mother Goose   It's your story, dear; so good luck.

All   Good luck, Jack. Take care, etc.

Mother Goose   Don't forget the Golden Egg. (*She hands it to him.*)

* * * * *

The following three speeches should be inserted if Act Two, Scene One has been omitted.

Little Polly Flinders   The egg's grown. It's bigger.

Mother Goose   So it is.

Little Jack Horner   How eggstraordinary. Tara!

* * * * *

Little Bo Peep   How are you going to get in the Castle?

Little Jack Horner   I'll swim across the moat.

Little Tommy Tucker   But look (*He points to the sign – 'BEWARE OF THE MONSTER OF THE MOAT'.*) 'Beware of the Monster of the Moat.'

Little Jack Horner   I'm not frightened of a Monster – I've got the Golden Egg.

*Dramatic rumble music as **Little Jack Horner** approaches the moat. The others huddle together, watching. **Little Jack Horner** stands on the edge of the bank and flexes his legs and arms as if to dive into the moat. As an afterthought, he turns back and waves to the 'family'. As he does so, the **Monster**'s head rears up, unseen by him, but visible to the others and to the audience. All try to warn him. He smiles disbelievingly, and turns back to find himself virtually nose to nose with the **Monster**. He screams and jumps impulsively, and in his panic to escape, throws his arms in the air, allowing the Golden Egg to fly from his hand and fall into the watery depths of the moat. A splash sound effect could enhance this. The **Monster** disappears again, the 'threat' having gone.*

Little Miss Muffet   Now look what you've done.

Little Jack Horner (*hardly able to believe it*)   I'm sorry. I jumped.

Little Tommy Tucker   So did the Golden Egg. Right into the moat.

Little Bo Peep (*on the verge of tears*)   We'll never rescue Gertie now.

Little Miss Muffet   What can we do? Mother Goose?

Mother Goose   Is it an emergency?

Little Bo Peep (*emotionally*)   Of course it is. We must get the Golden Egg back.

Mother Goose   If it's an emergency, there's only one thing to do –

Pause, during which the audience may call out, 'Get Fairy Lethargia' –

Little Polly Flinders (*eventually, whispering*)   Call Lethargia.

Mother Goose   What, dear?

Little Polly Flinders (*louder*)   Call Fairy Lethargia.

Mother Goose   Bullseye! Come on, everyone! (*Looking at the castle.*) But not too loudly. One, two, three.

All (*including* **audience***; calling together*)   Fairy Lethargia.

They look towards the decorations box – still in position at the side of the stage.

A loud yawn heralds **Fairy Lethargia**'s *arrival from the box.*

Fairy Lethargia   Up, down, up, down, up, down. I'm not a flipping Jack-in-the-Box, you know.

Mother Goose   It's an emergency.

Fairy Lethargia   It always is. (*Suddenly noticing the castle.*) Oo-er. Where are we? I'll say this much. Your story's very moving.

Little Tommy Tucker   Moving?

Fairy Lethargia   Yes – it's never in the same place twice. Just as well I don't get travel-sick. Whose is this humble abode, eh?

Little Miss Muffet   The Giant's.

Fairy Lethargia   Ooh, I don't like giants.

Little Miss Muffet   Why not?

Fairy Lethargia   They always look down on people! Right, come on. (*She yawns.*) I can't hang around all afternoon. I thought this was an emergency.

Little Bo Peep (*crossly*)   It is. But you won't let us get a word in edgeways.

Fairy Lethargia   Ooooh! Hark at her. Fairies have feelings, you know. I know when I'm not wanted. (*She yawns.*) Night, night. (*She starts to climb back into the box.*)

Mother Goose   You've offended her now. Fairy Lethargia, please, you must help.

Fairy Lethargia   Why? You're all right. You've got the Golden Egg. Night.

Little Jack Horner   But that's the whole point. We haven't.

Fairy Lethargia   Eh? (*She stops.*)

Little Jack Horner (*sheepishly, pointing to the moat*)   I dropped the egg in the water.

Fairy Lethargia (*after a pause to take in the news*)   You dropped the egg in the water? Knowing you, I'm surprised you didn't add a pinch of salt, turn the gas on and boil it for three minutes. All right, I'll help. You'll have to dredge the bed of the moat. Like looking for buried treasure.

Little Miss Muffet   We *are* looking for buried treasure.

Mother Goose   What can we use to try and scoop it up?

The audience may shout solutions.

Little Polly Flinders (*eventually*)   We could try my kettle!
(*She holds it up.*) And I've got some string . . . (*She produces the
string and starts to tie it on the handle.*)

Little Tommy Tucker   No, Polly, that'll never work.
Anyway, I've made my mind up. *I'm* going to find it – like a
pearl diver.

Mother Goose   You're most certainly not, Tommy dear.
Not with Daughter of Dracula in there gnashing her mashers.

Little Tommy Tucker   If Jack can grapple with the
Giant, I can mix it with a Monster.

Fairy Lethargia   Fighting words, Little Tommy T. But
why not use Polly's kettle too?

Little Tommy Tucker   How?

Fairy Lethargia   Stand there and I'll show you! (*She
positions him.*) Right. A bit of a hush, please. A bit of
atmosphere.

SONG: **Fairy Lethargia's Magic Spell** (*reprise*)

Fairy Lethargia   Spell number two is on Tommy
                             Him with the little fat tum . . .

Little Tommy Tucker (*speaking*)   Here! No need to be
personal.

The Others   Shhh.

Fairy Lethargia   Don't be so touchy. The magic has to
know who to work on . . .

Little Tommy Tucker   It's all very well . . .

Fairy Lethargia   Oh, all right. I'll start again. (*She sings.*)
                             Spell Number Two is on Tommy
                             Another young Tom he'll become;
                             Abracadabra, hocus pocus
                             Magic him into Tom Thumb

As the spell ends, there is a flash and a bang, and magically **Little Tommy Tucker** *disappears. Perhaps a trap could be used for this, in conjunction with a flash box, or a very short black-out would effect it. In his place there is a similarly dressed doll about nine inches high. The music continues.*

Mother Goose   Oo-er! Tommy! He's gone.

Fairy Lethargia   No, he hasn't. Look.

Mother Goose *sees the doll.*

Mother Goose   Oh, Tommy, I know I kept saying you ought to diet, but I didn't mean it, dear, I didn't mean it!

Fairy Lethargia   Shh. Polly, put Tom Thumb in your kettle.

Very gently, **Polly** *does so.*

Now, lower the kettle into the moat . . .

Mother Goose   Take care, dear, Tommy's in your hands.

Gingerly, **Little Polly Flinders** *picks up the kettle, holding it by the string. Suddenly the lighting snaps to black-out, all except for a follow spot on* **Little Polly Flinders**. *The action freezes as she sings.*

SONG: **My Big Moment** (*reprise*)

Little Polly Flinders   This must be my big moment
My moment of glory
In the story
This will be my closest shave
This must be my big moment
This is my time to be brave.

Little Polly Flinders *turns and makes her way towards the moat. The lights fade to a black-out, and the scene changes very rapidly. N.B. It may be possible to start the scene change during the song — perhaps by bringing in black tabs behind* **Little Polly Flinders**.

Scene Three

In the moat.

The following sequence, which takes place underwater, is all mimed and moved to music. It could possibly be done in U.V. lighting, or using 'black art', or it could be done using projection or lighting effects, depending on the scale of the production and the facilities available. It should take place downstage of the 'entrance to the Giant's Castle' set, because the change back, as well as the change into the underwater sequence, should be very quick. The sequence is 'magnified', so that 'Tom Thumb' can be played by the normal-sized **Little Tommy Tucker**. *Therefore, in due course, the kettle, the* **Monster** *and the Golden Egg should all be 'blown-up' versions. N.B. The* **Monster** *cannot realistically be expected to be to scale. The overall effect of the sequence, apart from the exciting nature of* **Little Tommy Tucker**'s *venture underwater, could be one of pure magic – using all the best 'tricks' the theatre can offer.*

The scene underwater could be enhanced by rocks and waving weeds. To start with there could be a 'ballet' of fishes of different shapes and sizes. With a large cast, these could be actors, but the effect could be gained in U.V. lighting with cut-outs on rods operated by puppeteers dressed in black; or, perhaps projection or large 'mobiles' operated from the flies could achieve this. Then the huge kettle arrives, as though let down by **Little Polly Flinders** *on the string. Ideally it floats in gently from the flies and comes to rest on the bed of the moat, scattering the fishes. If this is impractical, the scene could start with the kettle already in position. The kettle will most probably be a cut-out – an enlargement of the normal-sized one.*

'Tom Thumb' *clambers out of the kettle. The actor can enter between the tabs after the kettle has flown in, and climb over the cut-out. He looks warily about, then starts searching for the Golden Egg – behind rocks, weeds, etc. When he is out of sight, the* **Monster** *of the moat enters; played by four or more actors, each one a 'segment'. It is long like a centipede, all the legs moving in unison. It is not unlike the Loch Ness Monster, perhaps, but the head looks frightening, its jaws snapping as it stomps along. Clearly from the audience point of view, it should look amusing as well as frightening. Suddenly, after a 'dance'* *around, it sees the kettle and reacts startled – a jolt going from segment to segment, accompanied by the relevant feet jumping back in surprise.*

The **Monster** *goes to examine the kettle more carefully. Perhaps the head peeps behind it, or perhaps the whole body investigates the back of it. At the same time '***Tom Thumb***' struggles back with the 'blown-up' Golden Egg – about his own height. A cut-out is more practical than a shaped object. He starts struggling to put the Golden Egg inside the kettle. With a great effort he manages it, but, just before it disappears from view, the* **Monster** *re-emerges and sees it – and '***Tom Thumb***'. Stamping its feet in fury, it backs away ready to 'charge'. '***Tom Thumb***', still at ground level, sees the* **Monster***, reacts with fear; then the action freezes, the lighting dramatically changes to a follow spot on '***Tom Thumb***' and the music goes into 'My Big Moment', which '***Tom Thumb***' mimes. It could be amusing to have a garbled underwater singing voice off. Then the lighting and the action revert to their former states.*

*Now follows an exciting moved/choreographed section during which the Monster 'charges' '***Tom Thumb***', who has to nip sharply out of the way. Perhaps he could acrobatically 'leapfrog', in stages from segment to segment. At least twice he manages to escape the 'charge'. Then the* **Monster** *adopts a subtler approach and attempts to 'surround' '***Tom Thumb***' with itself – the head and the tail meeting. He escapes between the feet. Then, surrounding him again, the* **Monster** *does its 'coup' – it divides into individual segments, as many as the actors inside, each of which has its own face, and, ideally, snapping jaws. This can be incorporated effectively into a visually exciting pattern, as '***Tom Thumb***' weaves his way in and out of the little Monsters.*

Finally he tricks them, perhaps by encouraging them to advance on him like a rugby scrum, then escaping, leaving them heads together in a circle, revolving. He climbs back up into the kettle, not forgetting to give two big tugs on the string. He disappears inside.

The kettle rises up, as if pulled by **Little Polly Flinders***. The* **Monster** *or Monsters, frustrated, watch it go. The lights fade to a black-out.*

Scene Four

The Entrance to the **Giant**'*s Castle.*

The scene changes back, as speedily as possible, to the position at the end of Scene Two. **Little Polly Flinders** *is pulling the kettle up from the bed of the moat, watched by the other* **Children** *and* **Mother Goose**, *with* **Fairy Lethargia**, *who has nodded off again.* **Little Polly Flinders** *carefully brings the kettle downstage. The others cluster round.*

Little Bo Peep   Well?

Little Polly Flinders (*producing the egg*)   He's done it! Look.

Little Miss Muffet (*gasping*)   It's grown again. It's twice the size!

Indeed it has grown.

Little Jack Horner   How eggsciting! Tara!

All groan.

Mother Goose   Children, less levity, more gravity. Where's our Little Tommy?

Little Polly Flinders (*taking out the doll*)   Here he is.

Mother Goose (*taking it*)   I do believe he's even smaller. He's shrunk in the wash! Lethargia!

Fairy Lethargia (*waking quickly*)   Hallo, hallo, 'tis Christmas time . . . (*Realizing.*) Oh. Beg pardon. Did it work?

Mother Goose   Yes, thank you. But we'd like our Tommy back to scale, please.

Fairy Lethargia   Spell Three. Right.

Mother Goose   Spell Three? Wrong. Spell Two, part two. You can't leave him like that. We might tread on him.

Fairy Lethargia   Oh, all right. I'll do Spell Two in reverse. That ought to work. Put him over there.

Mother Goose *positions the doll on the ground, holding it with one hand, standing it on her other hand.* **Fairy Lethargia** *concentrates, using her fingers to 'count' through the tricky reversed spell.*

SONG: **Fairy Lethargia's Magic Spell** (*reprise*)

Fairy Lethargia   Thumb Tom into him magic
Pocus hocus, Arbadacarba
Become he'll Tom young another
Tommy on is Two Number spell.

There is a sudden flash and/or black-out.

Magically, **Little Tommy Tucker** *returns, taking the place of the doll.* **Mother Goose** *is still crouched on the ground holding an ankle now.*

All   Hooray; well done, Lethargia; hallo, Tommy, etc.

Little Tommy Tucker (*blinking, getting his bearings*)   Hallo. Thanks.

Fairy Lethargia   Everyone all right?

Mother Goose   Aaaaaaah!

Little Tommy Tucker (*looking down*)   Hallo, Mother Goose. What are you doing down there?

Mother Goose   You're standing on my hand, Tommy dear.

Little Tommy Tucker   Oh, sorry. (*He steps off.*)

Mother Goose *gets up, rubbing her hand.*

Fairy Lethargia *goes back to the decorations box and climbs inside, yawning.*

Thanks for holding the string, Polly.

Little Polly Flinders   Did you see the Monster?

Little Tommy Tucker   Yes, he was vast, and he divided . . .

He is interrupted by the booming roar of the **Giant**'s *voice and footsteps from above. All react, and draw back, listening.*

Giant's Voice   Goosey, Goosey. I'm coming. Is my Golden Egg ready? (*Pause.*) Grrrrh. Nothing. (*A roar of anger, with fists beating on a table.*) Lay, blast you, lay, or you'll be my Christmas dinner. Roasted alive.

Giant footsteps are heard receding.

Mother Goose   Save your memoirs for another day, Tommy. This one could be Gertie's last.

Little Jack Horner   Right. My turn. Give me the Golden Egg.

Little Bo Peep   How are you going to get in the castle?

Little Miss Muffet   You can't swim the moat.

Little Jack Horner (*heroically*)   I'm going to ring the bell and order them to lower the drawbridge.

Mother Goose   But look, dear, the sign says 'Utter the password'. We don't know the password.

The audience should shout out that they know it, because they heard the **Wolves** *use it.*

(*To the audience.*) *You* know it? Can you tell us what it was, please? (*She pieces it together and then repeats it.*)

Copper and silver leave us cold
What we want is lots of gold.

Got it, Jack? Off you go, dear, and good luck.

The others whisper good luck, as they draw back to watch. Music, as **Little Jack Horner** *strides to the bell and rings it. The very loud, deep clang sends a shudder through everyone. From above, the* **Giant**'s *footsteps approach the window.*

Giant's Voice   Password.

Little Jack Horner
Copper and silver leave us cold
What we want is lots of gold.

Giant's Voice   You may enter.

With a sinister creaking sound, the drawbridge lowers, and clanks on to the bank.

Summoning up his courage, **Little Jack Horner** *strides into the castle. The drawbridge stays down.*

The four **Children** *gather round* **Mother Goose**. *They look worried.*

Mother Goose (*sensing the reason for their long faces*)   He'll be all right, children. And there's nothing we can do to help by worrying. We just have – to try and concentrate on something else. Listen . . .

SONG: **When You're Feeling Worried**

It is suggested that during the song, tabs come in behind **Mother Goose** *and the* **Children**, *to accommodate the scene change. Ideally, the drawbridge would still be visible but this may well be impractical.*

This is a cumulative song, in the style of 'One Man Went to Mow'. The activities mentioned in each verse should each have a big action or gesture to accompany them every time they are sung. The recurring whistle should give some of them trouble.

Mother Goose   When you're feeling worried
                             And your skies are looking grey
                             Just whistle a tune
                             (*Whistle.*)
                             And very soon
                             Your worry will hurry away.

(*Speaking.*) Of course, you don't *have* to whistle a tune. Any ideas?

Little Miss Muffet   When you're feeling worried
                             And your skies are looking grey
                             Try physical jerks
                             It always works.

Little Miss Muffet
Mother Goose Just whistle a tune
(*Whistle.*)
And very soon
Your worry will hurry away.

Little Tommy Tucker When you're feeling worried
And your skies are looking grey
Eat treacly pud
And you'll feel good.

Little Tommy Tucker Try physical jerks
Little Miss Muffet It always works
Mother Goose Just whistle a tune
(*Whistle.*)
And very soon
Your worry will hurry away.

Little Bo Peep When you're feeling worried
And your skies are looking grey
Try bouncing a ball
Against a wall.

Little Bo Peep Eat treacly pud
Little Tommy Tucker And you'll feel good
Little Miss Muffet Try physical jerks
Mother Goose It always works
Just whistle a tune
(*Whistle.*)
And very soon
Your worry will hurry away.

Little Polly Flinders When you're feeling worried
And your skies are looking grey
Go pick up a broom
And sweep the room.

Little Polly Flinders Try bouncing a ball
Little Bo Peep Against a wall
Little Tommy Tucker Eat treacly pud
Little Miss Muffet And you'll feel good
Mother Goose Try physical jerks

It always works
Just whistle a tune
(*Whistle.*)
And very soon
Your worry will hurry away.

During the last chorus, **Fairy Lethargia** *is woken up by the noise, and pops out of the decorations box to see what is going on. She decides to join in.*

Fairy Lethargia	When you're feeling worried And your skies are looking grey Just have a good yawn And sleep till dawn

Fairy Lethargia **Little Polly Flinders** **Little Bo Peep** **Little Tommy Tucker** **Little Miss Muffet** **Mother Goose**	Go pick up a broom And sweep the room Try bouncing a ball Against a wall Eat treacly pud And you'll feel good Try physical jerks It always works Just whistle a tune (*Whistle.*) And very soon Your worry will hurry away.

All	When you're feeling worried And your skies are looking grey Start marching along And sing this song Just have a good yawn And sleep till dawn Go pick up a broom And sweep the room Try bouncing a ball Against a wall Eat treacly pud And you'll feel good

> Try physical jerks
> It always works
> Just whistle a tune
> (*Whistle.*)
> And very soon
> Your worry will hurry
> Your worry will hurry
> Your worry will hurry away
> (*Shouting.*)   Don't worry!

At the end of the song, all the **Children** *have cheered up.*

Mother Goose   There you are. Are you still worried about Jack?

Children   No.

Mother Goose   Good. Mother Goose was right, wasn't she?

Children   Yes.

Mother Goose *suddenly frowns and bites her nails and taps her foot nervously and scratches her neck, etc., then she starts whistling.*

Little Polly Flinders   What's the matter, Mother Goose?

Mother Goose   Oooh. I'm so worried I can't stand it. (*She calls.*) Jack. Jack. I'm coming to help you, dear.

Mother Goose *grabs her dressing-gown and runs off.*

(*As she goes.*) Go home, children. And don't worry!

Ideally, **Mother Goose** *would dash along the drawbridge into the castle, just before it closes: but perhaps she runs off and as the lights fade to a black-out we hear the clanking sound of the drawbridge rising, thus giving the impression that she has just made it in time.*

Scene Five

The **Giant**'s *Workshop.*

In this set, everything is magnified. There is a high window, open, and an overgrown chair and table, which stretches off, thus making the table-top accessible from the wings one side. The chair should be constructed in such a way that normal-sized people can use it as a stepping-stone to the table-top. On the table is a cage with a barred door; **Gertie** *is inside. Throughout the whole set there should be not a trace of the colour gold. On stage level are several steaming cauldrons, foaming beakers, test tubes, etc., and tomes piled high. To one side is a giant oven, with a dial marked 'OFF', 'ON', 'HOT', 'HOTTER', and 'OUCH'. On a shelf or side table are visible several large tins or jars, marked 'CUSTARD POWDER', 'MUSTARD POWDER', 'GUN POWDER', 'CHOWDER POWDER', 'ITCHING POWDER', 'TALCUM POWDER'. A vase of daffodils and a lighted candle are also visible. The large tomes are open, covers facing the audience: 'TEACH YOURSELF ALCHEMY' and 'GOLD-MAKING FOR BEGINNERS'.*

As the scene starts, the heads of the two **Wolves** *menacingly creep up over the books. They laugh nastily. The heads return to their reading. Suddenly* **Bigger Badder Wolf** *speaks.*

Bigger Badder Wolf   Aha! Here's an experiment we haven't tried.

Big Bad Wolf   Aha! (*He tries to imitate the* **Bigger Badder Wolf***, but it turns into a cough.*) Read it out, B.B.W.

Bigger Badder Wolf (*reading slowly and deliberately*)   How to make a bar of gold. (*He rubs his hands in anticipation.*)

Big Bad Wolf   A bar of gold!

Bigger Badder Wolf   Take one heavy brick.

Big Bad Wolf   One heavy brick. (*He finds one, and staggers with the weight.*)

Bigger Badder Wolf   Drop it . . .

Big Bad Wolf   Drop it. (*He drops it on the* **Bigger Badder Wolf**'s *foot*.)

Bigger Badder Wolf   Aaaaah! What did you do that for?

Big Bad Wolf   You said 'drop it'.

Bigger Badder Wolf   I hadn't finished. Drop it in a cauldron.

Big Bad Wolf   Ah. Drop it in a cauldron. (*He does so*.)

Bigger Badder Wolf   Add one yellow daffodil.

Big Bad Wolf   One yellow daffodil. (*He finds one, sniffs it, sneezes, and throws it in the cauldron*.)

Bigger Badder Wolf (*lyrically*)   Add the golden tones of the song of the yellow-hammer.

Big Bad Wolf   Eh?

Bigger Badder Wolf   The yellow-hammer.

Big Bad Wolf   Oh. (*He produces a large yellow hammer – the sort for banging in nails*.) Got one.

Bigger Badder Wolf (*not seeing, too busy reading the experiment*) Good. Make it sing.

The **Big Bad Wolf** *looks mystified, then looks at the hammer and encouragingly 'la las' a few notes. No reaction from the hammer.*

Big Bad Wolf   B.B.W.

Bigger Badder Wolf   Mm?

Big Bad Wolf   The yellow hammer doesn't want to sing.

Bigger Badder Wolf   Well, bash it on the head.

Big Bad Wolf   Eh?

Bigger Badder Wolf (*impatiently*)   Bash it on the head.

After a doubting pause, the **Big Bad Wolf** *smashes the hammer down on the* **Bigger Badder Wolf**'s *head.*

Ow! What are you doing? What's this?

Big Bad Wolf   A yellow hammer.

Bigger Badder Wolf   For wickedness' sake! I meant a bird, a yellow-hammer bird. Oh, never mind. Stir in a spoonful of custard powder.

The **Big Bad Wolf** *runs his hand along the jars or tins, calling them out as he goes.*

Big Bad Wolf   Talcum powder, itching powder, chowder powder, gun powder, mustard powder, custard powder.

He takes down the jar and pours some in. He replaces the jar.

Bigger Badder Wolf (*before the* **Big Bad Wolf** *has finished, making him hurry*)   And a pinch of mustard powder.

The **Big Bad Wolf** *dashes back, and, by mistake, takes down the gun powder. He pours some in. The audience must realize his mistake.*

Big Bad Wolf   Mustard powder. One pinch of. (*He replaces the jar.*)

Bigger Badder Wolf   Expose to the golden rays of the sun.

Big Bad Wolf   We can't. There's no sun today. (*Pointing out of the window.*) It's cloudy.

Bigger Badder Wolf   We'll have to find a substitute. (*He looks around.*) Ah. Try the golden rays of that candle instead.

Big Bad Wolf   Oh, right.

He takes the lighted candle and throws it in the cauldron. Immediately there is a loud explosion and smoke from the cauldron. The impact knocks the **Wolves** *over. As they recover, the* **Bigger Badder Wolf** *starts hitting the* **Big Bad Wolf***. Suddenly the* **Giant**'*s voice is heard.*

Giant's Voice (*off*)   Wolves! Wolves!

They spring to attention.

Bigger Badder Wolf   Yes, Boss?

Big Bad Wolf   Y-y-yes, B-b-boss?

Giant's Voice   Any Golden Eggs from that Goose yet?

Bigger Badder Wolf   Just checking, Boss. (*He deliberately takes the large key to the cage from inside his coat and hands it to the* **Big Bad Wolf**.) Cage. (*He glances to the cage on the table above.*)

Big Bad Wolf (*realizing the implication*)   Oh n-no, n-no, n-not m-me, p-please.

Bigger Badder Wolf   Why not you?

Big Bad Wolf   You know I can't stand heights. I'll get giddy. I'll have one of my turns. (*He reaches for a tranquillizer.*)

Bigger Badder Wolf   Oh, come on then.

Music, as he pushes the **Big Bad Wolf** *to the chair.*

A brief comic interlude as they climb up – the **Big Bad Wolf** *falling on or stepping on the* **Bigger Badder Wolf**, *who pushes him on ahead.*

Eventually they reach the cage, unlock the door and, pushing **Gertie** *aside, look inside. They shake their heads and close and lock the door. The music stops.*

Nothing. We'd better go and tell him.

Big Bad Wolf (*nervously*)   Ooh.

The music starts again as the **Wolves** *exit along the table into the wings – towards where the* **Giant** *is presumably sitting at the other end.*

After a pause, **Little Jack Horner** *enters from the opposite side. He takes in the huge furniture and creeps about checking nobody is around. He puts his finger to his mouth to make sure the audience remain quiet and don't give the game away.*

Little Jack Horner *spots* **Gertie** *in the cage; or it may be better for him to whisper 'Where's Gertie?' to the audience, and incorporate* *their help — not vocally, but pointing to the cage. He climbs up the chair and arrives on the table. He tiptoes to the cage.*

Little Jack Horner (*whispering*)   Gertie! Psst. It's me. Jack.

Gertie *rushes excitedly to the bars, flapping her wings.*

Shhh. I've come to rescue you. (*He tries the cage door.*) Where's the key?

Gertie *indicates the* **Wolves** *off, and the audience, not forgetting to whisper, interpret.*

The Wolves. Oh. (*He ponders what to do.*)

Mother Goose, *still carrying her dressing-gown, enters stealthily.*

Mother Goose (*whispering*)   Jack, Jack.

Little Jack Horner *jumps in surprise, then recovers and looks down from the table top, just as* **Mother Goose** *is passing below, so her back is now turned away from him.*

Little Jack Horner (*in a loud whisper*)   Mother Goose!

Mother Goose *nearly has a heart attack and ducks under the chair seat.* **Little Jack Horner** *slips from the table on to the chair seat. He kneels, then slowly slides his head over the edge; simultaneously* **Mother Goose** *slowly slides her head out from underneath. The heads meet, making* **Mother Goose** *and* **Little Jack Horner** *nearly jump out of their skins.*

Mother Goose (*recovering*)   Oh, it's you, dear. What a relief. I'm all of a quiver. Like a nervous jelly.

Little Jack Horner (*whispering*)   Shhh!

The sudden roar of the **Giant**'s *voice is heard, off.*

Giant's Voice (*off*)   What? Still no Golden Egg? Right, Goosey Goosey; you've had your last chance. Ha, ha, ha, ha.

The laughter approaches.

Little Jack Horner (*whispering*)   Quick, he's coming. Gertie's locked in the cage up here but the Wolves have the key.

Mother Goose (*after a pause, whispering*)   I know, dear. Put the Golden Egg in the cage. The Giant will want it, the Wolves will have to open the cage to take it out, and . . . (*she is too late.*)

Giant (*calling*)   Goosey Goosey! Ha, ha, ha, ha.

Mother Goose *retreats under the chair.* **Jack** *leaps back on to the table and carefully puts the Golden Egg through the bars of the cage. Then he spots a dining fork – large scale – on the table top, and arms himself with it. Finally he hides at the side of the cage.*

Suddenly the **Wolves** *enter, on the table, leading in the* **Giant**, *who should naturally be as large as possible. It may be an idea to use another actor's voice from a microphone off, so that a huge headmask could be employed.*

SONG: **Fee Fi Fo Fum**

During the song, the **Wolves** *climb down from the table via the chair.* **Mother Goose**, *hiding, looks terrified as the* **Wolves** *pass so near her.*

Giant	Fee fi fo fum
	I am the Giant, here I come
	Fee fi fo fum
	Goosey for dinner, yum yum
	yum.
	Fee
Wolves	Fee
Giant	Fi
Wolves	Fi
Giant	Fo
Wolves	Fo
Giant	Fum
Wolves	Fum
Giant	I am the Giant, here I come.

	Fee
Wolves	Fee
Giant	Fi
Wolves	Fi
Giant	Fo
Wolves	Fo
Giant	Fum
Wolves	Fum
Giant	Goosey, prepare to meet my tum.

Giant (*speaking*)   Wolves!

Wolves   Yes, Boss?

Giant   Light the oven.

Wolves   Yes, Boss.

The **Wolves** *go to the oven and turn the dial, which makes an unpleasant ratchet noise, gleefully through 'HOT', and 'HOTTER' to 'OUCH'.* **Gertie** *is reacting.*

Giant   We'll see if Goosey Goosey tastes better than she works. Ha, ha, ha, ha.

The **Bigger Badder Wolf** *opens the oven door a little – a red glow tells us the oven is on.*

Stubborn bird. All I wanted was one Golden Egg.

The audience may well shout out, 'look in the cage'.

(*Eventually.*) But you wouldn't lay. So now you'll pay. Wolves!

Wolves   Yes, Boss?

Giant   Open the cage.

Wolves   Yes, Boss.

The **Bigger Badder Wolf** *deliberately hands the key to the* **Big Bad Wolf**.

Big Bad Wolf   Oh, no, please, not again . . .

Bigger Badder Wolf   Go on. Hurry up.

Giant (*roaring*)   What are you muttering about?

Bigger Badder Wolf   Nothing, Boss.

Big Bad Wolf   N-n-nothing, B-b-boss.

Reluctantly the **Big Bad Wolf** *climbs up on to the table. A dramatic drum roll as he approaches the cage. He puts the key in the lock, turns it and opens the door.*

Come on, Goosey Goosey.

Leaving the key in the lock, he grabs **Gertie***, who tries to point out the Golden Egg. This proves difficult, and she is pulled out of the cage and a few steps away from it before the* **Big Bad Wolf** *realizes.*

It's no use struggling, I'm too strong . . . (*If the audience are shouting.*) What? (*He suddenly spots the Golden Egg.*) Hey! She's done it! She's done it! B-b-boss, l-look – a Golden Egg. (*He takes it reverently from the cage – it is quite large now, say eighteen inches high – and holds it out.*)

Giant (*roaring*)   What? Aaaaaaah! At last, at last! Gold. Real gold! Ah ha ha ha.

The **Giant** *takes the Golden Egg and, roaring with laughter, does the nearest a* **Giant** *can to hopping about with joy, stroking and kissing the Golden Egg.*

The **Big Bad Wolf** *stands smiling on the table top. The* **Bigger Badder Wolf** *is still by the oven.*

Music. **Little Jack Horner** *creeps round from his hiding place by the cage and prods the* **Big Bad Wolf** *with the outsize fork. The* **Big Bad Wolf** *nearly has heart failure – he could have fallen over the edge! He turns, sees* **Little Jack Horner** *and reacts terrified.* **Little Jack Horner** *stalks him round with the fork. Meanwhile* **Gertie** *hangs back by the cage door and the* **Bigger Badder Wolf** *is too busy watching the ecstatic* **Giant** *to notice. Suddenly the* **Big Bad Wolf** *has an idea. He brings out his tranquillizers and starts throwing them at* **Little Jack Horner***, who has to use the fork as a shield: but the tranquillizers run out, and the* **Big Bad**

Wolf *puts up his hands in submission.* **Little Jack Horner** *forces him at fork point back, round and into the cage, the door of which* **Gertie** *holds open for him. They slam the door shut, turn the key and remove it from the lock. They raise their arms/wings in triumph.*

Mother Goose *manages to peep out occasionally from under the chair, and glean some idea of* **Little Jack Horner**'s *progress. Now, she watches him bring the key of the cage to the edge of the table top. He indicates he is going to throw it down and she stands by to catch it.*

He throws, but she misses, and it hits the floor. The sound is heard by the **Bigger Badder Wolf**, *who turns and sees* **Mother Goose**. *In a rage, he advances on her. She picks up the key and tries to fend him off with it. He grabs the other end and they have a heave-ho tug-of-war with it, ending with the* **Bigger Badder Wolf** *tripping over a tome and falling. But* **Mother Goose** *has let go of the end of the key, and soon the* **Bigger Badder Wolf** *is up again, advancing on her and using the key as a weapon.*

Mother Goose *looks wildly around and spots her dressing-gown, which is a red one. There follows a short, amusing bullfighting sequence to appropriate music, with* **Mother Goose** *using her dressing-gown as a cape, and the* **Bigger Badder Wolf** *charging her. On one of his charges, he overruns, bumping into the still drooling* **Giant**, *who notices, and turns – just in time to see the* **Bigger Badder Wolf** *charge in the other direction, towards* **Mother Goose**, *who has manoeuvred herself to the oven. At the last minute she opens the door and the* **Bigger Badder Wolf** *charges straight into the red glowing oven.* **Mother Goose** *shuts the door, and raises her arms in a bullfighter's triumph.* **Little Jack Horner** *and* **Gertie** *have watched from above. But now the* **Giant** *is ranting and roaring and advancing towards the table, arms flailing with rage, that his henchmen have been disposed of. In his excitement he drops the Golden Egg, which is caught by* **Mother Goose** *below. Just as the* **Giant** *appears to aim a blow towards* **Little Jack Horner** *and* **Gertie**, *the action freezes and the lighting changes to just a follow spot on* **Little Jack Horner**.

SONG: **My Big Moment** (*reprise*)

Little Jack Horner   This must be my big moment
My moment of glory
In the story
This will be my closest shave
This must be my big moment
This is my time to be brave.

The lighting returns to its former state and the action resumes. **Little Jack Horner** *and the* **Giant** *fight their duel – the action climax of the drama! The actual mechanical details of the combat will have to be left to the ingenuity of the individual directors, having regard for the capabilities and limitations of their* **Giant**. *Clearly, a lavish production might have a* **Giant** *capable of more mobility and tricks – like picking up* **Little Jack Horner** *with one hand – than a more modest production: or some directors may feel it better to see the* **Giant** *only in silhouette, thus using back-projection on to a screen. Another idea is that the* **Giant** *could be a huge puppet, even operated from inside. It might be possible for* **Little Jack Horner** *to leap on the* **Giant**'s *shoulders, or to have a sort of sword fight with him; the* **Giant** *could use his dagger and* **Little Jack Horner** *the fork. If the actor playing* **Little Jack Horner** *were athletic or acrobatic, further exciting ideas could develop, using ropes on which to swing to the ground, etc. Certainly* **Gertie** *should help the cause with the odd peck – her come-uppance against her cruel master adds an important element of poetic justice: and* **Mother Goose** *can shout encouragement; but she should not be actively involved in the battle, because this is* **Little Jack Horner**'s *moment of glory. Naturally the contest ends in triumph for* **Little Jack Horner**, *as the* **Giant** *topples from the high window and falls to the moat below. A huge splash is followed by the snapping of jaws and the contented munching of the* **Monster** *of the moat. Victory yells of triumph from all, as* **Little Jack Horner** *climbs down the chair to floor-level, where* **Mother Goose** *hugs him.*

Little Jack Horner   Back to the Book.

Mother Goose   Take the Golden Egg, dear. It's grown again.

Little Jack Horner   What we've come to eggspect! Tara!

Mother Goose *groans. They set off for the exit. Meanwhile,* **Gertie**, *on the table top, tries gingerly to put one foot down towards the chair in an attempt to get down. Now she flaps her wings. The audience may call out to* **Mother Goose** *and* **Little Jack Horner**.

(*Eventually, suddenly remembering.*) Gertie!

They turn back.

(*Seeing Gertie.*) Come on.

Gertie *shakes her head and mimes flight.*

She can't get down, Mother Goose.

Mother Goose   Cooped up in that cage for so long she can't fly any more.

Little Jack Horner   But we can't leave without her. She's the reason we came.

Mother Goose   Crisis time. (*To the audience, indicating the decorations box.*) One, two, three.

All (*including audience*)   Fairy Lethargia.

Pause

Fairy Lethargia (*in the box*)   Co–ming!

Fairy Lethargia *struggles, yawning, out of the decorations box and goes to collect her wand.*

Right. Spell Three. And you'd better look sharp. I'm so drained, my wings are beginning to droop and my wand's wilting. (*Turning and seeing the* **Giant**'s *workshop.*) Oo-er, I'm shrinking too!

Mother Goose   No, you're not. We're in the Giant's workshop.

Fairy Lethargia   Oh. Well, I don't like it. I want to go home.

Mother Goose   So do we. But Gertie's stuck.

Gertie *flaps her wings.*

Fairy Lethargia   Right. No problem. You two – up on the table.

Little Jack Horner *and* **Mother Goose** *climb up.*

Huddle together and hang on tight. Fasten your seat belts for Spell Three. (*She comes forward.*)

SONG: **Fairy Lethargia's Magic Spell** (*reprise*)

It may be practical to bring in tabs behind **Fairy Lethargia** *as she sings the spell, to facilitate the scene change, or the tabs could fly in behind the table, but in front of the rest of the* **Giant***'s workshop. This would mean that* **Gertie***,* **Mother Goose** *and* **Little Jack Horner** *could be visible during the spell.*

Fairy Lethargia   Gertie and Jack and his Mother
                             All want to go home – so do I
                             Abracadabra, hocus pocus
                             Makes us all able to fly.

At the end of the song, there is a flash, leading, as quickly as possible, into the following scene.

Scene Six

In the Sky.

We see **Gertie** *in flight, complete with* **Mother Goose** *and* **Little Jack Horner** *'on board' her. They are joined by* **Fairy Lethargia** *flying under her own steam. This sequence should take only a minute or two, and can be done in several different ways:*

(1) The table could become a platform on which they all stand, and lighting makes it look as though they are suspended in mid-air, flying.

(2) Projection of moving clouds against the sky could give an impression of movement, plus, perhaps, some sort of wind machine off stage.

(3) The whole thing could be done in U.V. lighting in front of black tabs. The sequence could start with small cut-out figures in rods, 'walked across' by stage-hands clad in black, changing over to medium-sized ones, then ending up with the real characters, being pulled across on a black truck, invisible against the black tabs. **Fairy Lethargia** *could be on a separate one.*

(4) Kirby's Flying Ballet.

The scene could be very effective because it represents the traditional picture of **Mother Goose** *of Nursery Rhyme fame – flying on a goose. Also, if it can be made to look magical, it will be a very exciting visual moment.*

Mother Goose   You're flying, Gertie. This is your big moment.

SONG: **Her Big Moment**

Mother Goose	⎫	This must be her big moment
Little Jack Horner	⎬	Her moment of glory
Fairy Lethargia	⎭	In the story
		This must be her closest shave
		This must be her big moment
		This is her time to be brave
		This must be her big moment
		This is her time to be brave.

As the song ends, the lights fade to a black-out.

Scene Seven

Back at the Book.

As quickly as possible, the lights go up on the 'cover' side of the Book. It is dusk: **Little Miss Muffet**, **Little Polly Flinders**, **Little Bo Peep** *and* **Little Tommy Tucker** *are putting the final touches to the Christmas decorations: but they are not happy – because they are worried about* **Mother Goose**, **Little Jack**

Horner *and* **Gertie**. *A table of food lies untouched. During the song even* **Little Tommy Tucker** *refuses to eat anything.*

SONG: **Getting Ready for Christmas** (*reprise*)

A slow, sad version.

Little Miss Muffet	We're getting ready for
Little Bo Peep	Christmas
Little Tommy Tucker	We're getting ready for
Little Polly Flinders	Christmas Day
	Building a snowman
	From cotton-wool snow
	Hanging up the holly
	And the mistletoe . . .

Suddenly they hear the loud beating of wings overhead. Dramatic musical rumble. They look up into the flies and follow **Gertie**'s *'progress' across the stage above their heads.*

Little Miss Muffet   It's them! Look!

The others cheer, and 'watch' **Gertie** *land, off.*

SONG: (*continued*)

The song speeds up.

Little Miss Muffet	We're getting ready
Little Bo Peep	Getting ready for Christmas
Little Tommy Tucker	Ready
Little Polly Flinders	Steady –
	Go, go, go –

Mother Goose *enters, with* **Little Jack Horner** *and* **Gertie**. *The others warmly greet them.*

All, *with*	Christmas
Mother Goose	Hallo.
Little Jack Horner	

At the end of the song, all chatter animatedly – 'What happened?', 'Did you see the Giant?', 'Thank goodness you're safe', etc., etc.

Fairy Lethargia *enters, almost on her knees with tiredness. She stands, looking at the excited 'family group', none of whom see her.*

She coughs to get their attention. No reaction: and again: no reaction. So she puts her fingers in her mouth and does a vibrant, shrill whistle. All shut up and turn to her.

Fairy Lethargia   Is that it, then? Till next year? (*She yawns.*) I can't twinkle much longer.

Mother Goose   But Christmas Day hasn't begun yet!

Fairy Lethargia   No, but the story's finished, isn't it? Must be; you've had your three spells.

Mother Goose   Yes, almost. The children wanted adventure, something out of the ordinary, and we've certainly had that; and they've all been so brave that I for one will never think of them as 'Little' again. But, Fairy Lethargia, you must keep your eyes open a little longer. It's time for our Christmas party. (*She calls.*) Polly!

Little Polly Flinders (*confidently*)   Yes, Mother Goose?

Mother Goose   Put the kettle on!

Laughter.

Little Polly Flinders *goes inside.*

Music, as **Gertie** *comes forward and gently pecks* **Mother Goose**, *who turns.* **Gertie** *embraces her.*

Little Jack Horner   She's saying thank you!

Gertie *bows to all the* **Children**.

Mother Goose   Well, Gertie, the best way you can thank us is to stay with us as long as you like. Right, everyone?

All nod and agree.

Gertie *suddenly runs off, nudging* **Little Jack Horner** *and* **Little Tommy Tucker** *off too.*

What's she up to now?

Gertie *returns with the two boys carrying the Golden Egg – even larger, say thirty inches high – wrapped with ribbon and with a label.* **Gertie** *presents it to* **Mother Goose**.

For me? Oh, thank you, Gertie. It won't grow any more, will it?

Little Jack Horner   It's getting a little eggcessive! Tara!

All groan.

Mother Goose   Oh, look, a label. (*Reading.*)

Happy Christmas to you,
Happy Christmas to you,
Happy Christmas dear Mother Goose,
Happy Christmas to you.

Thank you.

Gertie *mimes singing.*

Little Jack Horner   She says, let's sing it. Come on, then. Everybody.

SONG: **Happy Christmas to You**

The audience is encouraged to join in this, the equivalent of a songsheet.

All, *including audience, except* **Mother Goose**

Happy Christmas to you
Happy Christmas to you
Happy Christmas dear Mother Goose,
Happy Christmas to you.

Little Jack Horner (*speaking*)   Once more. With eggstra voice!

All, *including audience except* **Mother Goose**

Happy Christmas to you
Happy Christmas to you
Happy Christmas dear Mother Goose,

Happy Christmas to you.

At the end of the song, the music continues as the Golden Egg, to everyone's surprise, starts moving. Then it 'grows' arms and legs and a head. It in fact 'hatches'.

Mother Goose   Hallo, dear. Who are you?

Humpty Dumpty   Humpty Dumpty.

Mother Goose   Humpty Dumpty?

SONG: **Humpty Dumpty Sat on a Wall**

Humpty Dumpty *acts out his nursery rhyme.*

Humpty Dumpty   Humpty Dumpty sat on a wall
Humpty Dumpty had a great fall
All the king's horses and all the
king's men
Couldn't put Humpty Dumpty
together again.

At the end of the song, all clap.

Mother Goose   Thank you, Humpty Dumpty. You're a very welcome addition to my Nursery Rhyme family. And we'll all take care to see you don't fall off that wall too often.

Little Polly Flinders *enters with the kettle.*

Little Polly Flinders   Kettle's boiled!

Mother Goose   Then it's time for the party.

Music, as **Fairy Lethargia** *comes forward in her best rhyming couplet fashion.*

Fairy Lethargia
Now Mother Goose's story has been well and truly told'n
For her and for her family, this Christmas will be golden.

If possible, **Fairy Lethargia** *waves her wand two or three times causing magical lighting changes to occur in stages, each accompanied by a musical chord.*

SONG: **Mother Goose's Golden Christmas**

*During the song, if possible, the whole set, and perhaps some of the
costumes, become enriched with gold – streamers, glitter, lights, etc.
There is no reason why, as a gesture of goodwill, the 'Baddies' should
not arrive during the song, to be made welcome by Mother Goose and
her Family. Thus the number could be a curtain call in itself – also,
being the final number, the more singing voices on stage the merrier.*

All

It's Mother Goose's Golden
    Christmas
So come and join us ev'ryone.

So
Come and join us
Come and join us
Come on in
The party has begun
It's Mother Goose's Golden
    Christmas
Come and join us ev'ryone
It's Mother Goose's Golden
    Christmas
Come and join us ev'ryone.

It's a day we shall remember
Throughout the coming year
That golden day in December
When our troubles seem to
    disappear

So
Come and join us
Come and join us
Come on in
The party has begun
It's Mother Goose's Golden
    Christmas
Come and join us ev'ryone
It's Mother Goose's Golden
    Christmas

Come and join us ev'ryone.

Never mind the wintry weather
Forget the rain and snow
With all the fam'ly together
Celebrating in the fireside glow

So
Come and join us
Come and join us
Come on in
The party has begun
It's Mother Goose's Golden
　Christmas
Come and join us ev'ryone
It's Mother Goose's Golden
　Christmas
Come and join us ev'ryone.

So
Come and join us
Come and join us
Come on in
The party has begun
It's Mother Goose's Golden
　Christmas
Come and join us ev'ryone
It's Mother Goose's Golden
　Christmas
Come and join us ev'ryone.

Girls　　　So
　　　　　　　Come and join us
Boys　　　Come and join us
Girls　　　So
　　　　　　　Come and join us
Boys　　　So
　　　　　　　Come and join with Mother
Girls　　　It's Mother
All　　　　Goose's Golden Christmas

Come and join us ev'ryone.

Optional extra scene

At the end of the song, the cast bow, and the audience should think it is the end: but suddenly **Little Bo Peep** *bursts into tears.*

Mother Goose   Oh no, Bo Peep. What's the matter? We're all meant to be happy. It's the end of the story.

Little Bo Peep   How can I be happy? I still haven't found my sheep. (*She sobs.*)

Mother Goose   Oh dear. We can't finish like this. Fairy Lethargia, can't you help?

Fairy Lethargia   Well, I'm so tired, my magic's almost run out, but (*Taking in the audience.*) if everyone could chip in and give me a hand, I dare say . . .

Mother Goose   Oh, we will. (*To the audience.*) Won't we?

All   Yes.

Fairy Lethargia   Right, then. After me. Abracadabra, help Bo Peep.

All   Abracadabra, help Bo Peep.

Fairy Lethargia   Hocus pocus, find her sheep.

All   Hocus pocus, find her sheep.

Fairy Lethargia   Smashing. Now, let's put it together and say it as loud as we can. After three. One, two, three.

All (*as* **Fairy Lethargia** *waves her magic wand*)
  Abracadabra, help Bo Peep
  Hocus pocus, find her sheep.

A flash; and then by magic, **Little Bo Peep**'s *sheep – real – are revealed. Perhaps they could 'enter' from the decorations box or simply be led on stage. All cheer.* **Little Bo Peep** *is happy again.*

SONG: (*continued*)

	So Come and join us Come and join us Come on in The party has begun It's Mother Goose's Golden Christmas Come and join us ev'ryone It's Mother Goose's Golden Christmas Come and join us ev'ryone.
Girls	So Come and join us
Boys	Come and join us
Girls	So Come and join us
Boys	So Come and join with Mother
Girls	It's Mother
All	Goose's Golden Christmas Come and join us ev'ryone.

Curtain.